北大版对外汉语教材·公共选修课系列

汉英对照

学打太极拳
TaiJi Quan (Shadowboxing)

白淑萍　编著
罗　斌　翻译
Ming Tran（陈健明）　校译

北京大学出版社
PEKING UNIVERSITY PRESS

图书在版编目(CIP)数据

学打太极拳 /白淑萍编著. —北京：北京大学出版社，2009.9
（北大版对外汉语教材·公共选修课系列）
ISBN 978-7-301-05391-1
Ⅰ.学… Ⅱ.白… Ⅲ.太极拳—教材 Ⅳ.G852.11
中国版本图书馆 CIP 数据核字(2009)第 166390 号

书　　　　名：	学打太极拳
著作责任者：	白淑萍　编著　罗　斌　翻译　Ming Tran(陈健明)　校译
责 任 编 辑：	沈　岚
封 面 设 计：	宗爱群
标 准 书 号：	ISBN 978-7-301-05391-1/H·0721
出 版 发 行：	北京大学出版社
地　　　　址：	北京市海淀区成府路 205 号　100871
网　　　　址：	http://www.pup.cn
电　　　　话：	邮购部 62752015　发行部 62750672　编辑部 62753374　出版部 62754962
电 子 邮 箱：	zpup@pup.pku.edu.cn
印 刷 者：	北京大学印刷厂
经 销 者：	新华书店
	787 毫米×1092 毫米　16 开本　15.5 印张　380 千字
	2009 年 9 月第 1 版　2015 年 5 月第 4 次印刷
定　　　　价：	52.00 元(含 1 张 DVD)

未经许可，不得以任何方式复制或抄袭本书之部分或全部内容。
版权所有，侵权必究　举报电话：010-62752024
　　　　　　　　　　　电子邮箱：fd@pup.pku.edu.cn

目　录

第一章　简化 24 式太极拳　　1

一、简化 24 式太极拳的由来 / 1

二、简化 24 式太极拳的特点 / 1

三、简化 24 式太极拳基本技术、动作要领 / 4

　（一）技术要领 / 4

　（二）太极拳的动作要领 / 16

四、简化 24 式太极拳基本动作练习 / 20

　（一）太极步（猫行步）/ 20

　（二）野马分鬃 / 25

　（三）搂膝拗步 / 26

　（四）左右倒卷肱 / 29

　（五）云手 / 30

　（六）揽雀尾 / 32

　（七）左右下势独立 / 34

　（八）左右蹬脚 / 35

　（九）摆莲脚、弯弓射虎 / 35

　（十）组合动作练习 / 37

五、简化 24 式太极拳动作说明 / 42

　第一组 / 42

　　（一）起势 / 43

　　（二）左右野马分鬃 / 45

　　（三）白鹤亮翅 / 49

　第二组 / 51

　　（四）左右搂膝拗步 / 51

　　（五）手挥琵琶 / 57

　　（六）左右倒卷肱 / 59

学打太极拳

第三组 / 65
    （七）左揽雀尾 / 65
    （八）右揽雀尾 / 70

第四组 / 75
    （九）单鞭 / 75
    （十）云手 / 77
    （十一）单鞭 / 81

第五组 / 83
    （十二）高探马 / 83
    （十三）右蹬脚 / 85
    （十四）双峰贯耳 / 87
    （十五）转身左蹬脚 / 89

第六组 / 91
    （十六）左下势独立 / 91
    （十七）右下势独立 / 95

第七组 / 98
    （十八）左右穿梭 / 98
    （十九）海底针 / 101
    （二十）闪通臂 / 103

第八组 / 104
    （二十一）转身搬拦捶 / 104
    （二十二）如封似闭 / 107
    （二十三）十字手 / 109
    （二十四）收势 / 111

六、简化24式太极拳之新练法：反正结合之练法 / 112

第二章　太极文化　　114

一、《太极拳论》（王宗岳）/ 114
二、太极拳在京城的发展简史 / 119
三、太极拳（太极文化）的传播和影响 / 126
四、太极拳之阴阳浅识 / 133
五、太极拳与外家拳的不同 / 138

　　六、练习太极拳"十大要领" / 140

　　七、太极拳基本功 / 145

　　　　（一）身体素质之腿功 / 145

　　　　（二）桩功 / 148

第三章　教学随笔　　　　　　　　　　　　　　　　167

　　一、练好太极拳具备的条件 / 167

　　二、关于简化 24 式太极拳的教学方法 / 169

　　　　（一）关于讲解、示范和领做 / 169

　　　　（二）分解教学与完整教学 / 171

　　　　（三）诱导性练习和辅助练习 / 172

　　　　（四）信号刺激 / 172

　　　　（五）矫正错误 / 173

　　　　（六）新旧教材的安排 / 175

　　三、浅谈太极拳技术教学法 / 176

　　　　（一）课型式训练 / 176

　　　　（二）示范式训练 / 177

　　　　（三）启发式教学训练 / 179

　　　　（四）理论联系实际是搞好教学的关键 / 182

　　四、初学太极拳易犯的毛病及纠正办法 / 184

　　五、练习太极拳要防止膝关节损伤 / 199

　　　　（一）练太极拳容易损伤膝关节之原因 / 199

　　　　（二）造成膝关节损伤的主要原因 / 200

　　　　（三）怎样预防膝关节的损伤 / 202

　　六、浅谈太极拳的腰裆功 / 206

　　七、练太极拳动作与呼吸的配合 / 209

　　　　（一）自然呼吸法 / 209

　　　　（二）调解自然深呼吸法 / 212

　　　　（三）逆式呼气法 / 213

　　八、太极拳的眼神——眼功 / 214

学打太极拳

九、太极拳的修炼方向 / 220

十、练太极拳的注意事项 / 221

附录   223

主要参考书目   235

后记   236

Contents

Chapter One Simplified Twenty-Four-Step *Taiji Quan*   1

  I. Origin of the Simplified Twenty-Four-Step *Taiji Quan*/ 1

  II. Characteristics of the Simplified Twenty-Four-Step *Taiji Quan* / 1

  III. Essentials for Basic Skills and Movements / 4

    i. Essentials for Skills / 4

    ii. Essentials for Movements / 16

  IV. Basic Movements of the Simplified Twenty-Four-Step *Taiji Quan* / 20

    i. *Taiji* Stepping (Cat-Style Stepping) /20

    ii. Splitting the Horse's Mane / 25

    iii. Knee Brushing and Twisting Step / 26

    iv. Reversed Brachium Twisting: Left and Right Form / 29

    v. Cloud-Waving Hands / 30

    vi. Grabbing the Bird's Tail / 32

    vii. Left and Right Single-Legged Squatting/ 34

    viii. Left and Right Kicking Step / 35

    ix. Waving-Lotus Step and Tiger Shooting with Bow-and-Arrow / 35

    x. Combined Practice / 37

  V. Specific Instructions to the Simplified Twenty-Four-Step *Taiji Quan* Movements / 42

  Group One: / 42

    i. Beginning Pose / 43

    ii. The Wild Horse Splits Its Mane: Left and Right Form / 45

    iii. White Crane Spreading Its Wings / 49

  Group Two: / 51

    iv. Knee Brushing and Twisting Step: Left and Right Form / 51

    v. Playing the Lute / 57

学打太极拳

  vi. Reversed Brachium Twisting: Left and Right Form / 59
 Group Three: / 65
  vii. Left Form / 65
  viii. Right Form / 70
 Group Four: / 75
  ix. Single Whip / 75
  x. Cloud-Waving Hands / 77
  xi. Single Whip / 81
 Group Five: / 83
  xii. Patting the Horse / 83
  xiii. Right Kicking / 85
  xiv. Striking Ears with Both Hands / 87
  xv. Turning and Kicking with Left Foot / 89
 Group Six: / 91
  xvi. Squatting and Single-Legged Standing: Left Form / 91
  xvii. Squatting and Single-Legged Standing: Right Form / 95
 Group Seven: / 98
  xviii. Shuttle Throwing / 98
  xix. Picking the Needle from the Seabed / 101
  xx. Flashing Arm / 103
 Group Eight: / 104
  xxi. Turning to Carry, Block and Punch / 104
  xxii. Obstructing / 107
  xxiii. Cross Hands / 109
  xxiv. Ending Pose / 111
VI. Combination of the Original and Reversed Directions: A New Practicing Method / 112

Chapter Two   The *Taiji* Culture   114

 I. "On *Taiji Quan*" (by Wang Zongyue) / 114
 II. A Short History of *Taiji Quan* in Beijing / 119
 III. Spread and Influence of *Taiji Quan* (and the *Taiji* Culture) / 126

Contents

- IV. A Simple Introduction to *Yin* and *Yang* in *Taiji Quan* / 133
- V. Differences between *Taiji Quan* and External-Exercising *Kongfu* Boxing / 138
- VI. The "Ten Essentials" for Practicing *Taiji Quan* / 140
- VII. Basic Skills of *Taiji Quan* / 145
  - i. Physical Qualities: Basic Leg Skills / 145
  - ii. "Piling" Skills / 148

Chapter Three Random Sketches on Teaching 167

- I. Conditions for the Mastery of *Taiji Quan* / 167
- II. Teaching Methods for the Simplified Twenty-Four-Step *Taiji Quan* / 169
  - i. Explanation, Demonstration, and Practice Leading / 169
  - ii. Dissembled and Complete Teaching / 171
  - iii. Guided Practice and Assistant Practice / 172
  - iv. Signal Stimulation / 172
  - v. Error Correction / 173
  - vi. Review and Learn / 175
- III. Methods of Teaching *Taiji Quan* Skills / 176
  - i. Training with Class Types / 176
  - ii. Training with Demonstration / 177
  - iii. Heuristic Training / 179
  - iv. Combination of Theory and Practice / 182
- IV. Common Errors among Beginners and the Ways to Correct Them / 184
- V. Preventing Knees from Being Hurt / 199
  - i. Why Knees Are Easily Hurt? / 199
  - ii. Major Causes to the Knee Hurts / 200
  - iii. Ways to Prevent the Knee Joints from Being Hurt / 202
- VI. The Waist and Crotch Skills in *Taiji Quan* / 206
- VII. Cooperation between Movements and Respiration / 209
  - i. Natural Respiration / 209
  - ii. Adjusted Deep Natural Respiration / 212

学打太极拳

iii. Reversed Respiration / 213
VIII. Eye Skills in *Taiji Quan* / 214
IX. Starting Directions for Practicing *Taiji Quan* / 220
X. Cautions / 221

Appendix　　　　　　　　　　　　　　　　　　　　　　　　　223

Bibliography　　　　　　　　　　　　　　　　　　　　　　　235

Postscript　　　　　　　　　　　　　　　　　　　　　　　　236

第一章 简化 24 式太极拳
Chapter One Simplified Twenty-Four-Step *Taiji Quan*

一、简化 24 式太极拳的由来
Origin of the Simplified Twenty-Four-Step *Taiji Quan*

"简化 24 式太极拳"是国家体委在 1956 年为适应群众体育活动的需求,根据民间流传较广的杨式太极拳套路为原型,按照内容简明、先易后难、循序渐进的原则,去掉了原套路中大量的重复动作,整编出简化 24 式太极拳,为全国广大爱好者学习太极拳提供了方便。

In 1956, in order to meet people's needs in sports practice, the National Sports Committee, adhering to the principle of simplicity and gradual advancement, made this set of *Taiji Quan* from the widespread *Yang*-style by removing repeated movements. This project facilitated *Taiji* lovers and helped make *Taiji Quan* practice a national fashion and a beloved sport.

二、简化 24 式太极拳的特点
Characteristics of the Simplified Twenty-Four-Step *Taiji Quan*

简化 24 式太极拳归纳起来有以下特点:

1. 动作轻松柔和:24 式太极拳拳架平稳舒展、大方、不拘不僵,符合人体的生理习惯;动作没有明显高低起伏的变化和激烈的跳跃动作;一般练习两三遍约 16 分钟左右,即感到全身微微出汗,呼吸平稳,没有或很少发生气喘现象,给人

学打太极拳

以练拳之后的一种非常轻松、愉快、舒服的感觉。由于太极拳这一特点,适合于不同年龄、性别、体质的人,尤其对体质较弱、多病和患有某些疾病的人,如患有高血压、高血脂、高尿糖、失眠、便秘、腰腿痛的人,更是一种较好的体疗手段。

  This set of *Taiji Quan* is renowned for the following characteristics:

  1. Relaxed and gentle: The gestures of the Simplified Twenty-Four-Step *Taiji Quan* are balanced and natural in relation with human physiology. Its movements do not include drastic changes and violent jumps. Two to three rounds of practice would take 16 minutes or so, causing slight sweating and would rarely require rough breaths, which gives the student a feeling of relaxation, pleasure, and comfort. This characteristic entitles the set of *Taiji Quan* to people of different ages, gender, and physical conditions. It is also very helpful to those that are physically weak and that are suffering from certain diseases such as hypertension, diabetes, insomnia, constipation, and sour waist or legs.

  2. 动作连贯均匀:24式太极拳的"起势"到"收势",不论动作的虚实变化和姿势的过渡转换,都是紧密衔接、连贯一气的,套路演练起来,速度均匀,前后贯穿,如行云流水,绵绵不断。

  2. Continuous and even: From the "Beginning Pose" to the "Ending Pose", each movement or gesture is closely connected to another, forming smooth transitions. When practicing, one may feel the even speed and strong continuity as that of moving clouds and flowing water.

  3. 动作圆活自然:太极拳是圆的运动,它不同于其他拳术,动作要求处处走弧线,避免直来直去,符合人体骨关节自然弯曲状态,通过弧形运动进行锻炼,有利于动作的圆活自然,体现出柔和的特点,也使身体各部分得到均匀的发展。

  3. Rounded and natural: Unlike other styles of *Kongfu*, *Taiji Quan* is composed of rounded movements that demand each movement to follow an arc-line instead of straight lines. This is in accordance with the natural bending state of human joints. Practicing with arc-lined movements helps make actions flexible, natural, gentle, and promotes an even development of body parts.

第一章　简化 24 式太极拳

4. 动作协调完整：在演练太极拳的动作过程中，无论是整个套路还是单个动作姿势，都要求上下相随，做到两手的开合、两脚的虚实，手与足的上下协调、腰与四肢之间都要做到密切配合。演练一套 24 式太极拳都要做到以腰为轴带动四肢，使整套动作协调完整。

4. Coordinated and complete: In the process of practice, both the whole procedure and a single pose demand precise coordination of body parts, such as in the opening and closing of hands, transition of the standing force between the two feet, cooperation of hands and feet, waist and limbs, etc. To finish a coordinated and complete procedure, one should manage to make his/her waist the axis around which the limbs follow.

5. 易于开展：24 式太极拳适应不同年龄、性别、体质的人练习，动作先易后难，易于掌握，为练习较复杂的高难度动作打下了良好的基础。

5. Easy to practice: The 24-step *Taiji Quan* is suitable to people of different ages, gender, and physical conditions. The movements evolve from the simple to the complex and are easy to master, thus laying a solid foundation for the practice of more complex boxing movements.

总之，其运动特点可以用以下 6 点作为概括：
（1）中正安定、舒展自然（姿势）
（2）轻灵沉稳、圆活连贯（动作）
（3）基于腰腿、周身相合（协调）
（4）虚实刚柔、松整合顺（劲力）
（5）动中寓静、意领身随（意念、精神）
（6）心静体松、呼吸平顺（风格、节奏）
其风格特点为：舒展中正；柔中有刚；圆活饱满；沉稳浑厚。

In summary, its characteristics are generalized to the following six aspects:
(1) Balanced and natural (gestures)
(2) Light, steady, rounded and continuous (movements)
(3) Waist-and-leg based accompanied by other body parts (coordination)

(4) Combination of firmness and gentleness, along with void and solid forces (force)
(5) Serenity implied in movements, with the body led by will (will, spirit)
(6) Heart relaxation, with the body relaxed, and breaths smooth (style, rhythm)

In conclusion, its styles could be concluded as: natural, decent, gentle as well as firm, rounded, flexible, and poised.

三、简化24式太极拳基本技术、动作要领
Essentials for Basic Skills and Movements

（一）技术要领 Essentials for Skills

1. 手型 Hand-Shapes

（1）掌：五指微屈分开，掌心微含，虎口成弧形。
（2）拳：五指卷屈，自然握拢，拇指压于食指、中指第二关节上。
（3）勾：五指第一指节自然捏拢，屈腕，勾尖向下。

各种手型都要求用力自然、舒展，不可僵硬。握拳不要过紧或松空。掌指不要僵直，也不要松软过屈，腕部要保持松活。

(1) **Palm**: Fingers are slightly bent and separated from each other; the center of the palm withdraws a bit; the "tiger's mouth" (the part between thumb and forefinger) forms an arc.

(2) **Fist**: Fingers hold together naturally, with the thumb pressing the second knuckles of the forefinger and middle finger.

(3) **Hook-shaped hand**: The first knuckles bend naturally, with the wrist is bent and the "hook" facing down.

All hand-shapes are required to be natural and flexible.

2. 手法 Hand Movements

（1）掤(bīng)：手臂半屈成弧形，前臂由下向前掤架，横于体前，掌心向内，与膻中穴相对，高与肩平。肘稍低于腕，着力点在前臂外侧。

第一章 简化 24 式太极拳

Bing: Arms form arcs; forearms rise from below to the front till they are on the horizontal level with the shoulders; palms face inward opposite of the nipples; elbows are in a slightly lower level than the wrists; place force on the outside of forearms.

（2）捋：两臂微屈，掌心斜相对，两掌随腰的转动，由前向后划弧捋至体侧或体后侧。无论动作大小，都必须臂呈弧形，不可直着回抽。

Stroking: Arms are slightly bent; facing each other slantingly and relative to the shape of the waist, palms stroke from the front to the body's side or backside. Remember to keep the arms follow arc-lines at all times.

（3）挤：一臂屈于胸前，另一手贴附于屈臂手的前臂内侧，两臂同时向前挤出，挤出后两臂撑圆，高不过肩，低不过胸，着力点在后手掌和前小臂。

Squeezing: One arm is bent in front of the chest; the hand of the other arm should be attached to the inside of its forearm. Both arms squeeze forward simultaneously, forming a circle lower than the shoulder and higher than the chest. Force is placed on the bent forearm and the attaching hand.

（4）按：前按的两掌同时向后向前弧形推按，按出后手腕高不过肩，低不过胸，掌心向前，指尖朝上，臂稍屈，肘部松沉，按时与弓步、松腰协调一致，力至掌根。下按：单掌或双掌由上向下或侧下方按出。力达掌根。

Pressing: In forward pressing, the two hands push and press back and forth at the same time, with the wrists no higher than the shoulders nor lower than the chest while the hands push out; palms face forward and fingers point skyward; arms are slightly bent, and elbows are relaxed and steady. Remember to keep the forward pressing in accordance with the bow-shape step and relax the waist. Force should be placed on the end of the palm. Downward pressing refers to one hand, or both hands, to press downward, with the force being placed on the end of the palm.

学打太极拳

(5) 采：掌由上向下或斜向下塌，腕下捋带，虎口自然张开，掌心朝下并内含。

Picking: Palms fall down straightly or slantingly in the stroking way, with the "tiger's mouth" being naturally open; the center of the palm, then is drawn in, and faces downward.

(6) 打拳(冲拳)：拳从腰间旋转向前打出，打出后拳眼向上成立拳，高不过肩，低不过胸，臂微屈，肘部放松下垂不可僵直，着力点在拳面。

Punching: The fist spins and punches forward from the waist to a position between the shoulders and the chest, posing finally to stand with the "fist's eye" faced upward; arms are slightly bent, and elbows should be relaxed and drooped a little; force is on the fists' front facet.

(7) 贯拳：两拳从侧下方向斜上方弧形圈打；高与头平，前双臂内旋，两拳眼斜向下，肘微屈，沉肘沉肩，着力点在食指根关节上，如双峰贯耳。

Piercing Fists: Fists hit slantingly upward to the level of the head from the lower sides of the body, following arc-lines; the forearms spin inward; the "fists' eyes" face slantingly downward; elbows bend slightly; elbows and shoulders droop down; the force is on the last knuckles of forefingers.

(8) 抱掌：两掌心上下相对或微微错开，在体前或体侧成抱球状，上手腕高与肩平，下手与腰平，两臂屈肘呈弧形，两掌撑圆，松肩垂肘。

Opposing Palms: The two palms form a shape as if holding a ball at the front or flank of the body, the center of the palms face either directly or indirectly each other; the upper wrist is on the same level with the shoulders, and the lower with the waist; the arms form arc-shapes and the palms are concave; shoulders and elbows droop naturally.

(9) 分掌：两掌由胸前交叉合掤向斜前方与斜后方分开，腕与肩平，两掌心朝前，两臂微屈成弧形。

Splitting Palms: The two crossing palms split (one backward and the other forward slantingly) in front of the chest; the wrists maintain the same level with the shoulders; the centers of the palms face forward; and the arms form arc-shapes.

（10）搂掌：右掌或左掌经膝前弧形横搂，停于胯旁，掌心朝下。

Brushing Palm: The left or right hand brushes across the knees and stops at the side of the hip; the palm faces down.

（11）推掌：掌从肩上或胸前向前推出，掌心向前，指尖向上，指高不过肩，低不过胸或肩，臂微屈呈弧形，肘部松垂不可僵直。力达掌根。

Pushing Palms: Palms push forward from the shoulders or chest with the center of the palms facing forward, the fingers point skyward and are between the shoulders and the chest, the arms are slightly bent, and elbows should be kept relaxed. Force is exerted on the end of the palm.

（12）云手：两掌弧形在体前交叉向两侧划立圆，指高不过头，低不过裆，两掌内外旋臂（如在云中拨转），不可僵直。

Cloud-Waving Hands: Wave the hands in arc-lines to form vertical circles which cross in front of the body; keep the fingers between the head and crotch in height; the forearms should be kept turning inward and outward during the process, without being stiff.

（13）架掌：屈臂内旋成弧形上举，掌自下向上或向侧上方架于额头上方，掌心斜向外，掌略高于头或与头同高。力达小臂。

Fending Palm: Bend the inward-turning arm into an arc, and move the hand from below to a position higher than the forehead (higher or on the same level with the head), with the center of the palm facing slantingly outward. Force is on the forearm.

学打太极拳

(14) **拦掌**：即拦截。掌由体侧向体前划弧拦截,高不过头。

Blocking Palm: Move the hand in an arc-line from the side of the body to the front (no higher than the head) for the purpose of blocking.

(15) **挑掌**：侧掌向下向前上方划弧挑起,高不过头,力达拇指、食指一侧。

Digging Palm: Move the slanting palm downward and then upward to the front (not exceeding the head). Exert force onto the side of thumb and forefinger.

(16) **穿掌**：前穿掌。臂由屈而伸,掌沿大腿内侧向前穿出,指尖向前。

Piercing Palm (Forward-piercing Palm): The bent arm stretches, and the hand pierces forward along the inner side of the thigh, with the fingers pointing forward.

(17) **插掌**：臂由屈而伸,掌自上向前下方插出,掌与腕自然伸直,指尖向插出方向,力达指尖。

Poking Palm: The bent arm stretches and its hand pokes downward to the front (fingers pointing to the poking direction); keep the palm and the wrist naturally straight. Exert force onto the tip of the fingers.

(18) **搬拳**：屈臂握拳,前臂翻转,拳自体侧搬至胸前或另一侧,拳心向上,臂呈弧形,力达拳面。

Moving Fist: Bend the arm and close the hand into a fist; turn the forearm; move the fist from one side of the body to the front or another side; keep the center of the fist upward and the arm bent; exert force onto the front facet of the fist.

各种手法均要求走弧形线路。不可直来直往,生硬转折,并注意与身法、步法、眼法的协调配合。臂伸出后,肩肘要松沉,腕要松活,掌指要舒展,掌心微含,皆不可僵硬或浮软。关于上述所讲着力点,主要是说明其攻防含义,在练习中应重意不重力地去体现,不可故意僵劲或拙劲。

All of the above hand movements are required to follow arc-lines, thus straight movements and stiff turns should be avoided. Also make sure you pay attention to the coordination of your hands, body, steps, and eyes. When arms are stretched, shoulders and elbows should be kept relaxed and steady, wrists flexible, palms and fingers to be stretched and natural, and the center of palms withdrawn. No stiffness or softness is allowed. The placement of force mentioned above is for attacking or defending. In practicing, it is more of perceptional ideas than actual doings; therefore, to be used in any actual situation, so intentional exertion of force in practicing is not proposed.

3. 步型 Types of Steps

(1) 平行步(开立步):两脚平行开立,左右脚的距离同肩宽,两脚尖向前,两腿自然直立或屈膝半蹲,体重平均置于两腿,如起势。

Parallel Step: (Standing with feet separated) Stand with the feet separated on parallel lines with a distance equal to that between the shoulders; point the feet forward; keep the legs naturally straight or in a half-squatting way; place weight equally on both legs. E.g. The Opening Pose.

(2) 弓步:前腿屈膝前弓,脚尖向前,膝关节不得超过脚尖,与脚尖垂直,后腿自然伸直或微屈,脚尖斜向前约45到60度角;两脚横向距离10—30厘米。两脚全脚着地,如野马分鬃、搂膝拗步。

Bow-Shape Step: Put one leg forward and bend it to form a bow shape with the foot pointing forward, along with the knee and the tip of the toes in a vertical line; keep the other leg naturally straight or slightly bent, the feet pointing to a direction about 45 to 60 degrees from the central line, so that the parallel distance between the two feet is about 10 to 30cm; both feet stand solidly. E.g. "Splitting the Horse's Mane," "Knee Brushing and Twisting Steps."

学打太极拳

（3）**虚步**：后腿屈膝半蹲,全脚掌着地,脚尖斜向前约 45 到 60 度角,前腿屈膝不可挺直。前脚掌或脚跟着地,落于体前,如手挥琵琶、海底针。

Void Step: Bend one leg in a half-squatting way, with the foot standing solidly on the ground and pointing to the direction about 45 to 60 degrees from the central line; the other leg is put forward and bent, with the sole or heel touching the ground, as in "Playing the Lute" and "Picking the Needle from the Seabed."

（4）**仆步**：一腿全蹲,全脚掌着地,脚尖朝外展成 45 度角,膝与脚尖同向,另一腿侧伸,自然伸直,脚尖朝前距另一脚跟约 10 厘米宽,如下势穿掌。

Crouching Step: One leg fully squats; the foot stands solidly on the ground and forms 45 degrees angle along the front-pointing axis; with the knee pointing in the same direction with the foot. Another leg stretches naturally straight to the side with the foot pointing forward (about 10cm wide from the other heel), as in the "downward piercing palm."

（5）**独立步**：一腿自然直立支撑全身体重,另一腿屈膝提起,大腿高于水平,小腿及脚自然下垂,如金鸡独立、左右蹬脚。

Single-Legged Standing: One leg stands naturally straight to support the whole body, and another one is bent and lifted to the position where the knee is above the hip, with the foreleg and foot drooping naturally, as in "The Golden Rooster Standing Single-Legged" and "Left and Right Kicking."

（6）**侧弓步**：两腿平行或斜向前,腿屈膝半蹲,膝与脚尖同向,另一腿侧伸屈膝。

Sideways Bow-Shape Step: Bend one leg in a half-squatting way, the knee in the same direction with the foot, and put the other leg to the side of the body with the knee bent.

第一章 简化24式太极拳

4. 步法 Foot Movements

（1）**上步**：后脚向前进一步或前脚前移半步,脚跟先着地。

Forward Step: The back foot goes one-step forward or the front foot goes half a step forward, with the heel touching the ground first.

（2）**退步**：前脚后退一步或后脚后移半步,脚前掌先着地。

Backward Step: The front foot moves one-step backward or the back foot moves half a step backward, with the front sole touching the ground first.

（3）**跟步**：后脚向前脚收拢半步,脚前掌先着地,如手挥琵琶。

Following Step: The back foot draws half a step closer to the front foot, with the front sole on the ground first, as in "Playing the Lute."

（4）**侧行步**：一脚向外侧横开,脚前掌或脚跟先着地,随之重心侧移,全脚落实,重心移于此腿,另一脚变虚向内收并；落实,成小开步,依次侧行,如云手。

Side-Walking Step: One foot steps sideways, with the heel or front sole on the ground first; the center of gravity is put on this leg thereafter; another foot draws close to the former one, touches the ground firmly and forms the minor parted feet. Then repeat the procedure, as in the "Cloud-Waving Hands."

（5）**小开步**：两脚距离不超过20厘米,两腿屈膝,两脚尖平行向前,如云手。

Minor Parted Feet: The feet keep a distance no more than 20cm; the legs are bent and the feet point forward in parallel lines, as in the "Cloud-Waving Hands."

（6）**扣步**：上步脚脚尖内扣着地或脚跟着地、脚尖内扣,然后全脚踏实。如十字手之脚、揽雀尾转单鞭,左揽雀尾转右揽雀尾。

Buckling Step: The forward-stepping foot touches the ground with the tiptoe turned inward, or the heel touches the ground while the tiptoe is turned inward, and then the whole foot stands on the ground, as that in "Crossing Hands,"

"Grabbing the Bird's Tail" transiting to "Single Whip," and "The Left Style of Grabbing the Bird's Tail" transiting to "The Right Style of Grabbing the Bird's Tail."

(7) 蹍脚：以脚跟为轴，脚尖外展或内扣；以脚前掌为轴，脚跟外展或扭顺脚掌。

Grinding Foot: The tiptoe turns outward or inward with the heel as the axis; or the heel turns outward and back with the front sole as the axis.

各种步法均需转换轻灵，重心平稳，虚实清楚，屈伸自然，距离适当，蹍转适度。前进时脚跟先着地，后退时前脚掌先着地，迈步如猫行，不可忽起忽落，沉重笨滞。每式要做到重心平稳、姿势和顺，腿要自然直伸，膝部不可挺直。

All these foot movements require gentle and deft transition, steady gravity, clear void and solidity, natural bending or stretching, appropriate distance, and proper turning. The heel touches the ground first during moving forward movement and the front sole in backward moving. The steps should be like that of cats; straight, clumsy, and heavy steps must be avoided. Each movement should be done with steadiness, balance, gentleness and smoothness. When the legs are stretched, they are supposed to be natural; the knees cannot be stiffly straight.

5. 腿法 Leg Movements

（1）**左右蹬脚**：支撑腿微屈站稳，另一腿屈膝提起，小腿上摆，脚尖上勾，脚跟向前蹬出，高过腰部，如右左蹬脚；(2)分脚；(3)拍脚；(4)摆莲脚；(5)侧踹；(6)十字腿；(7)震脚；(8)扫腿；(9)里合腿；(10)跳跃等腿法在24式太极拳中没有出现，略。

Left or Right Kicking: Set the supporting leg (slightly bent) steadily on the ground; lift the other one with its knee bent; wave the foreleg up to a position higher than the waist with the tip of the toe bent upward and the heel popped forward.

The following movements are not included in the 24-step *Taiji Quan*: (2) Separating the Feet, (3) Patting the Feet, (4) Lotus-Waving Feet, (5) Sideway Kicking, (6) Cross Legs, (7) Quaking Feet, (8) Sweeping Leg, (9) Inward-Closing Leg, and (10) Jumping.

各种腿法均要求支撑稳定,膝关节不可僵直,胯关节松活,上体要立身中正,不可低头弯腰,前俯后仰,左右歪斜。

All leg movements require steady support, along with loose and flexible knee and hip joints, and an upright upper body.

6. 身型 Essentials for Body Parts

(1) 头：虚领顶劲,不可歪斜摇摆。

Head: naturally upright, with force seemingly pushing up; no slanting or shaking.

(2) 颈：自然竖直,肌肉不可紧张或松弛。

Neck: naturally straight; with the muscles neither tight nor loose.

(3) 肩：保持松沉,不可上耸,也不可后张或前扣。

Shoulders: relaxed and drooping; no raising, stretching back or bending forward.

(4) 肘：自然松坠,不可外翻、上扬和僵挺。

Elbows: naturally relaxed and drooped; no turning outward or upward, or stretching stiffly straight.

(5) 胸：舒松微含,不可挺胸,也不可故意内缩。

Chest: relaxed and slightly withdrawn; no projecting or withdrawing.

(6) 背：舒展伸拔，不可驼背。

Back: extended upright; no crooked back.

(7) 腰：松活自然，不可后弓或前挺。

Waist: relaxed, agile and natural; with no thrusting back or forth.

(8) 脊：中正竖直，不可左右歪扭。

Spine: central and upright; no bending to either side.

(9) 臀：向内收敛下垂，不可后突或前挺。

Buttocks: held in and reclined; no thrusting back or forth.

(10) 胯：保持松正，不可左右外突或前挺。

Crotch: relaxed and central; no moving to either side or to the front.

(11) 膝：屈伸自然松活，不可僵直。

Knees: bending or stretching naturally; no stiffness.

总之，身型要求：虚领顶劲，含胸拔背，沉肩坠肘，松腰敛臀，气沉丹田。

In short, the requirements for the body are: natural uprightness, with the chest withdrawn and back straight, along with the shoulders and elbows drooped, and the waist relaxed and buttocks held in, with the air held in the pubic region.

7. 身法 Essentials for Body Movements

身法要求保持中正安舒，自然平稳，以腰为轴带动四肢，旋转松活，不偏不倚，上下相随，不可僵滞浮软，俯仰歪斜，忽起忽落，要与步型步法、腿法密切配合，和顺适度。

The body should be kept upright, natural, balanced, and steady, with the waist taken as the axis that leads the limbs, making all movements rounded, relaxed, agile, appropriate, and coordinated. The following should be avoided: stiffness, sluggishness, unstableness, feebleness, and sudden movements. Every movement of the body should be in accordance with the steps and legs, following the criteria of harmony, coherence, and moderation.

8. 眼法 Essentials for Eye Movements

总的要求是思想集中,意念引导,全神贯注。定势时,须注视前方、前手或意念、技法指引的方向。转换中,须与手法、身法、腿法协调配合,势动神随,神态自然。一是随视法,二是注视法。

The general requirements are concentration and mind-direction. Two movements are essential for the eyes: gazing and following. In still gestures, the eyes gaze at the front, with the hand (or hands) at the front, or in the direction indicated by the mind or the procedure. In transitions, the eyes are supposed to be in coordination with hands, body, and legs, following their movements in a natural way. One is following, the other is gazing.

俗话说,"神聚于眼","眼为心之苗"。过去太极拳讲究技击打法,在眼法上要求"目光如电"、"目光四射",这有利于在技击时识清对方的动向,用眼光慑服对方,做到先发制人。

There is a traditional Chinese saying that goes, "concentrate the spirit into the eyes," or "eyes are the outpost of the mind." In the past, *Taiji Quan* focused on attacking, requiring that the "eyes should stare as the lightening flashes," or "the eyes should flare about." This is helpful in fighting for catching the opponent's moving directions and taking control by staring the opponent into fear.

现在太极拳多用于健身,自然眼神也就"神宜内敛"。练拳时眼神应看手的动作向前平视,动作变化,眼神也转向前去的方向,然后身法、手法、步法跟上去。这是"始而意动,继而内动,然后形动"的细致锻炼方法。这样细心体会地去练,可以逐渐做到:意到、眼到、身到、手到、步到。说动一起动,说到一起到,"形神合一"。

学打太极拳

总之,练拳时眼必须看到手,但不是死盯着手,眼要随手转,看到手后,眼神要从主动手的方向平视出去,切忌板滞和四下野顾。打哪看哪,没有看这打那和看那打这的。做到眼观六路(前、后、左、右、上、下)耳听八方(四正方、四斜角),这就是眼神在打拳中的重要作用。

In modern day, *Taiji Quan* is mostly practiced for the sake of health; consequently, it is appropriate to keep your in a safe spot. In practice, the eyes should lead the hands while still looking horizontally forward. When the movement changes, the eyes should first look at the direction where the hands go, then the body, followed by the steps. The reasoning behind the practicing of this method: "The mind moves first, then the inside force, and finally the body." Practicing in this way helps achieve gradually the complete readiness of the mind, eyes, body, hands, and legs and feet. During this practice, they would be moving simultaneously, reaching the level where "the mind and the body become one." In short, the eyes must be able to see the hands, but should not stare at them; they should turn according to their respective hand movements; then after seeing the hands, the eyes should look forward from the direction with their full attention to the major moving hand. The eyes should keep in sync with the attacking direction, while being able to look in every direction. (the eye sees six ways: front, back, left, right, up, and down, while the ear hears eight directions-four straight directions and four slanting ones, meaning being observant and alert).

(二) 太极拳的动作要领 Essentials for Movements

(1) 心静体松、呼吸自然。身体各部要求自然舒松,不用拙力。思想要静集中,专心引导动作。呼吸自然平稳,深长细匀,并与动作和运动协调配合。一般规律是"虚吸实呼"、"开吸合呼"、"起吸落呼",不可勉强憋气。

Keep the heart peaceful, body relaxed, and breathe normal. All parts of the body are supposed to be in their natural state, without exerting any force. The mind should be kept peaceful and solely concentrated on directing movements, and the breaths should be normal: unexcited, deep, even, and in accordance with

第一章 简化24式太极拳

movements and actions. The general rules are: "breathe in when executing void actions and breathe out when executing solid actions"; "breathe in when body parts are apart and out when they are together"; "breathe in when body parts are raised and out when they are put down"; furthermore, do not hold your breath during this practice.

(2) 动作弧形,虚实分清。动作变换要走弧形,不可直来直去,生硬转换。重心移动要沉稳,虚实分清,不可呆滞双重。太极拳的动作每一式都有虚有实,有阴有阳,实者为阳,虚者为阴[①]。阴阳虚实交替变化,贯穿到太极拳的练习中来。

Keep movements rounded; distinguish between void and solid movements. Arched lines are to be followed by every movement, while straight and unnatural transitions should be avoided. The center of gravity should be transferred steadily, with void and solid movements distinguished clearly; being sluggish with one's movements will cause an unbalanced transference. Each movement of *Taiji Quan* contains void and solidity, or *Yin* and *Yang*, void being *Yin* and solidity being *Yang*. These two form constant transitions throughout the practice.

(3) 上下相随,圆活完整。动作要以腰为轴,带动四肢,上下配合,完整一体,不可手脚脱节,腰身分离,割裂断劲。

Keep the upper and lower body in great harmony. The waist acts like an axis that leads the limbs to cooperate with each other, as if they were in complete unity. Any other supplementary movement is failure of this section.

(4) 均匀连贯,和顺自然。动作要连贯柔和,绵绵不断。速度要保持均匀,不可忽快忽慢,保持前后动作衔接自然和顺,气势完整不散。

Keep movements smooth, continuous, even-speeded, gentle, natural, and at a steady pace throughout this process. The transition of movements should be natural and smooth, thus keeping the atmosphere undisturbed.

---

① 太极拳中的阴、阳见本书134—135页,The *Yin* ang *Yang* in *Taiji Quan* can be seen in page 134—135 in this book.

（5）轻灵沉稳，刚柔相济。运动要轻灵不浮，沉稳不僵，外柔内实，刚柔相济。

One must keep movements agile and unhurried, with strong and weak forces mutually assisting each other. The movements should be agile but steady, unhurried but not dull, and weak on the appearance but strong inside (the two assist each other mutually).

（6）以腰为轴带动四肢。练太极拳要由腰带动四肢和身体其他部位弧形慢慢转动，动作的完成靠腰左右转动带动胳膊、手上下弧形转动，带动腿的抬、收、伸；在腰的主宰下，全身各部位都在做弧形运动。有些人练习太极拳多年，都不知道用腰，更不懂得腰裆结合的妙用，所以在练起动作来，只是一味地比手画脚，或者用腰过度，形成扭腰晃肩，身法不稳。身体各处不是丢就是顶；如与人交手更是处处受制，难以取胜。正如拳论所云："有不得机不得势处，身便散乱，心致偏倚，其病必于腰腿求之。"在太极拳的训练中，腰的转动是有规律的，只有掌握了这一规律，练习太极拳的腰劲就不难了。

Use the waist like an axis to lead the limbs. In *Taiji Quan*, the waist leads the limbs and other body parts to turn slowly in curved lines. To complete these sets of movements, as the arms and hands are curved, turning up and down, along with the raising, withdrawing, or stretching of legs, are all led by the left or right twisting of the waist. Under its command, all other body parts move in curved lines. Some people may have practiced *Taiji Quan* for many years without knowing how to fully utilize the waist, not to mention understanding the importance of the combination of the waist and the crotch. Therefore, they imitate the gestures only, or overuse the waist, making the body unbalanced (the body parts either fall short of or go beyond the position required). This is evident when they are fighting against others, as they would be defeated because of their inefficient use of the waist. Wang Zongyue points out in his on *Taiji Quan*: "When chances and advantages are lost, the body becomes clumsy, and the mind gets disturbed. The reason lies in the misuse of the waist and legs." In *Taiji Quan*, the waist turns in a certain way, which, when understood, makes it easy to build up the waist force.

第一章 简化24式太极拳

(7) 动作要做到无过不及、适中。练太极拳的每一招式,过与不及都不对。要求练者在做每一式练习中,做到不要做不到位的动作,也不要做过了头的动作。

The movements should be done exactly. Neither falling short nor exceeding is appropriate for any movement. It is requested that one does not make movements that either go beyond or fall short of the required position.

(8) 圆裆开胯:裆要撑开撑圆,会阴部分肌肉要微微收紧,不可用力,要与头的虚领顶劲相呼应。做动作时要求裆部圆虚松活(裆下是座桥),裆部虚圆则下盘有力,支撑八面;两胯放松则裆可松活,虚实转换也就轻灵快捷。在练拳过程中要避免出现尖裆、塌裆和死裆的毛病。尖裆、人字裆,是动作虚实不分,两膝不开;塌裆是臀部低于膝关节。膝关节有了死弯,犯了转换不灵的毛病;死裆是不结合腰劲,不松胯,使上下之劲不能相随。

The crotch should be opened into a round arc-shape; and the muscles at the perineum are slightly tightened (without force), which is supposed to be in response to the head's force being gathered indigenously at the top. The crotch is requested to be arc-shaped, void, relaxed, and flexible, which enables the lower body to be forceful and supportable. Relaxing the hips makes the crotch flexible and the transition between void and solidity more nimble. One should avoid the peak-arched, the flat, or the rigid crotch. The peak-arched crotch, or the inverted "V" shape crotch, is usually a common mistake because void and solidity are undistinguished and the knees are not opened wide enough. The flat crotch is formed by getting the buttocks lower than the knees, hence causing stiff bends at the knee joints which make transitions unsmooth. The rigid crotch is the result of the rigid hips and the separation from the waist force, which makes the forces in the upper and lower body uncoordinated.

学打太极拳

四、简化24式太极拳基本动作练习
Basic Movements of the Simplified Twenty-Four-Step *Taiji Quan*

(一) 太极步(猫行步) *Taiji* **Stepping (Cat-Style Stepping)**

如何迈好太极步,即如何做到"迈步如猫行"需注意以下几点。以24式太极左弓步之后迈右步为例。

The following points should be paid special attention to for making the correct *Taiji* stepping (stepping as the cat walks). Take the stepping with the right foot after the "left bow-shape step" for example.

(1) 左弓步后,重心移至左脚跟,腰胯左移,向左撇脚,逐渐坐实左腿重心百分之百在左脚,左膝与左脚尖上下相应,臀部与脚跟齐平。

After the left leg bows, the center of gravity moves to the left heel; the waist and hips move to the left; the left foot turns outward; the whole weight of the body is gradually put on the left foot; the knee and tiptoe are on the same vertical line, and so are the hips and heel.

(2) 当以左脚跟为轴外撇时,右脚跟应随之离地外展,以便身法、步法相随和,动作顺达。

If one foot moves, the other one moves too. When the left tiptoe turns outward with the heel as an axis, the right heel should turn outward at the same time, so that the body and steps are in harmony and the movements are smooth.

(3) 肩胯相合。腰左转时,肩与胯也要同时左转,如腰、肩转,胯不转,则成了扭腰,因此说腰、胯同时转。

Keep the shoulders, waist, and hips coordinated. When the waist turns left, the shoulders and hips turn to the same direction. If the waist and shoulders turned and the hips did not, a twisted waist would be formed.

（4）内劲潜转。腰胯左转时产生的内劲，经腿、膝至脚跟，像钻头似地左旋入地，左腿稳固了，迈右脚方能做得轻灵、稳健。

The internal force is swirled downward. When the waist and hips turn left, they produce an internal force that drills into the ground through the left leg, knee, and heel. This fixes the left leg, so that the right foot movement can be agile and steady.

（5）两肩齐平。腰胯左转时，不能出现左肩低、右肩高的现象，以免破坏立身中正。

Shoulders are kept balanced. When the waist and hips turn, the left shoulder should not be on a lower level than the right one; otherwise, the balance of the body would be broken.

（6）点起点落。提右脚不要蹬地而起，也不要擦地拖起，更不能全脚掌同时离地，而是脚跟外侧先离地，然后脚掌内侧离地，犹如从泥浆中轻轻地将腿拔起，点起点落是迈太极步的规律之一。

Rise and fall by bits. The right foot is not lifted by kicking the ground, being dragged rubbing the ground, or taking the whole foot away at the same time. The correct way: the right side of the heel leaves the ground first, and the left side of the sole leaves last, as if lifting the leg lightly from mud. Rising and falling by bits is one of the essential rules of the *Taiji* stepping.

（7）旋踝转腿。提右脚时，右腿应内旋，右脚前伸时，右腿要外旋，其旋转的幅度要比旋腕转臂小得多，不要做得太明显。

Twist the ankle and leg. When the right foot is lifted, the leg should be twisted inward; and when it is put forward, the leg should be twisted outward. The degree of twisting is much smaller than that of twisting the arm; therefore, it should not be done too obviously.

(8) 提脚不能过高。右脚不要提得过高,离地宜超过一拳,脚尖自然下垂。

Remember not to lift the foot too high. The right foot cannot be lifted too high; a fist's width would be appropriate for the distance between the foot and the ground. Keep the tiptoe naturally drooped.

(9) 关节放松。提脚伸腿均以大腿带小腿,右踝关节和膝关节放松自然。

Keep the joints relaxed. Let the thigh lead the foreleg in either lifting the foot or stretching the leg. The right ankle and knee should be kept naturally relaxed.

(10) 脚走弧形。右脚提起后不要直向前迈,应略靠近左踝旁弧形前伸。

The foot should move in an arc-line. After the right foot is lifted, do not move it straightly forward. Make it move in an arc-line with the top of the arc close to the left ankle.

(11) 轻轻出步。左膝微屈,以最小的力送右脚前伸,轻起轻落,又是迈太极步的法则之一。

Step lightly. Bend the left leg slightly and put the right foot forward with the least force. Rising and falling lightly is another rule of the *Taiji* stepping.

(12) 敛臀。右脚前伸时要敛臀,不可突臀或扭臀,影响立身中正。

Keep the buttocks withdrawn. When the right foot moves forward, the buttocks should be retracted. Do not make them protruded or twisted since it will affect the balance of the body.

(13) 松胯。右脚前伸应与腰胯左转同时开始,右胯松开,使胯关节周围较紧的韧带松弛,腿膝则灵活,迈步会轻灵;另外,松胯后又不可使迈步开阔,以保持右弓步两脚的横向距离。

Keep the hips relaxed. The forward stepping of the right foot should happen at the same time with the left turning of the waist and hips. Relax the right hip (make the ligaments around the hip joint relaxed) so that the leg can be

第一章 简化24式太极拳

nimble and the step can be light and agile. Meanwhile, in order to keep the distance between the feet, the step should not be made too large after the relaxation of the hip.

(14) 边伸边落。右脚前迈时,应边伸边落,当右腿伸直(非挺直)时,脚跟正好着地,切莫在空中伸直后再慢慢着地。

Put the foot downward while stretching the leg. When the right foot steps forward, it should be put down gradually as the leg is being stretched. The heel should touch the ground at the exact time that the leg is stretched naturally straight. Do not put the foot down after the leg is stretched straight.

(15) 自然伸直。右腿伸直时,不可呈笔直状态,膝关节略弯曲,以免大腿肌肉紧张,影响腰胯转换。

Keep the leg naturally straight. When the right leg is stretched, it should not be completely straight. Keep the knee slightly bent, in order not to cause tension to the thigh muscles.

(16) 分清虚实。右脚跟着地要轻,如履薄冰,不要全脚掌同着地,也不要同打夯一样落地有声,右脚落地一刹那,重心仍在左脚。

Distinguish void and solid forces. The right foot touches the ground lightly as stepping on thin ice. Do not stand with the whole foot, or step heavily with loud noises. The moment the right foot touches the ground, the center of gravity should still be on the left foot.

(17) 方向准确。右脚前伸后的方向要正,不要外撇,脚尖朝前,以免影响右弓步的步型。

Keep the direction correct. The right tiptoe should be kept pointing to the front when the foot is put forward. Do not attempt to turn it outward in order to correct the form of the bow-shape.

学打太极拳

（18）平实踏地。右脚跟先着地，依次为脚掌、脚尖着地，待全脚踏平后，再蹬左腿，这样容易扎地生根。

Step on the ground steadily. The right heel touches the ground first, followed by the sole, then the tiptoe. Extend the left leg after the right foot is firmly set on the ground, this helps make the whole body balanced.

（19）步幅自然。迈步的幅度以右脚跟着地的距离为准。拳架高，步幅即小，易分清虚实，但运动量小；拳架低，运动量大，易患换步不灵、起伏和断劲等毛病。总之，步幅大小，要根据个人体质和技术而定。

Keep a natural stepping pace, which is decided by how far the right heel steps on the ground. Small paces make it easy to distinguish between void and solid movements, but decrease the amount of exercise. Large paces use more energy, but unsmooth transition of steps, movements, and forces are more likely to happen. Nevertheless, the degree of pace is decided by one's physical condition and his mastery of the essentials.

（20）速度均匀。在迈步过程中，提脚和前伸速度要均匀，不可忽快忽慢，更不可在左踝旁停留。

Maintain a constant speed. In the process of stepping forward, the lifting and stretching should be in the same speed. Do not make suddenly fast or slow movements and remember not to stop by the left ankle.

（21）身体保持水平，不可起伏。在提脚前伸的整个迈步过程中，拳架要始终如一，不可忽高忽低上下起伏。以避免运动量和步幅忽大忽小。

Keep the body balanced. During the whole stepping process, the height of the pose should be kept uniform, without rising or falling abruptly, to avoid the changes of energy cost and paces.

(22) 随遇平衡。右脚踏平后，重心才徐徐前移，其过程如同太极阴阳图慢慢地、均匀地转变，即从无到有，从小到大，由30%、60%到坐实右腿，随遇平衡是正确调整重心的方法。

Balance is preserved in the whole process. Only after the right foot sets steadily on the ground that the center of gravity moves gradually forward. The transition is slow and smooth, like the *Taiji* symbol, from zero percent to completely setting the weight on the right leg. Preserving balance is the right way to adjust the center of gravity.

接下来迈左腿也是如此，即右脚百分之百的重心又渐渐变为零，这样往复转换，一步一太极，故前人把太极拳的迈步称之太极步。

The left leg moves in the same way, i.e., the weight on the right leg is transferred gradually to the left one. This process is repeated, each step being a completion of the *Taiji*-style transition of force or weight; hence, the stepping in *Taiji Quan* was named the *Taiji* stepping.

（二）野马分鬃 Splitting the Horse's Mane

（1）左野马分鬃　先做太极起势。重心移到右腿上，右手收至胸前平屈，手心向下，左手经体前向右下划弧翻掌停于腹前，手心向上，与右手相对成抱球状；左脚回收在右脚内侧点地成丁步。

The left form of "Splitting the Horse's Mane"

Start by making the beginning pose. Put weight on the right leg. Move the right hand to the front of the chest with the palm bent and facing down. The left hand moves in an arc-line, in a downward movement to the right in front of the body and stops before the belly with the palm facing up, forming a ball-holding gesture with the right hand. The left foot draws back to the side of the right foot and points to the ground with the tiptoe. The feet then form a rough "T" shape.

上体左转，左脚向左前方迈步，脚跟着地，同时左臂向左上，右臂向右下分开，右脚蹬地成左弓步。左手高与眼平，肘微屈，掌心斜向上，右手落于右胯旁，手

学打太极拳

心向下,虎口向前,眼看左手。

Turn the upper body left. The left leg steps forward to the left with the heel touching the ground; and at the same time in which you separate the ball-holding hands, the left one should be moving up to the left while the right one down to the right, while the right leg extends to form the left bow-shaped step. The left hand is kept as high as the eyes, with the elbow slightly bent, and the palm facing slantingly upward. The right hand stops at the side of the hip, with the palm facing down and the "tiger's mouth" facing forward. Keep your eyes on the left hand.

(2) 右野马分鬃　重心后移,左脚尖翘起外展45度,然后重心前移,左脚踏实,上体左转45度左右;左臂屈肘翻掌手心向下,体前平屈,与胸同高;右手划弧前摆翻掌,臂成弧形,手心向上,与左掌相对,两臂成抱球状。以下动作同左野马分鬃,唯方向相反。

The right form of "Splitting the Horse's Mane"

Move the center of gravity backward. Raise the left tiptoe and turn it 45 degrees outward. Then move the center of gravity forward, and set the left foot completely on the ground and move the upper body turns 45 degrees to the left. Bend the left arm to the front of the chest and turn the palm to face down. Then wave the right hand forward in an arc-line, turning the palm face up, forming the ball-holding gesture with the left palm. The movements followed are the same to the left form of "Splitting the Horse's Mane", except for the direction.

(三) 搂膝拗步 Knee Brushing and Twisting Step

(1) 太极起势　两脚并立,两臂下垂,眼看正前方。两脚开立同肩宽,两脚平行脚尖向前;两臂内旋,慢慢向前平举,高与肩平,手心向下,手指向前。眼看前方。

The Beginning Pose

Stand with the feet close to each other, the arms drooping down, and the eyes looking at the front. Then move the feet so they are separated by parallel

第一章 简化24式太极拳

lines as wide as that of the distance between one's shoulders, with the toes pointing forward. The arms twist inward and rise slowly to the horizontal level with the shoulders; the palms face down, and the fingers point forward. Eyes should remain focusing at the front.

(2) 左搂膝 两臂同时向右、向前、向左再向体前划一小圆,再向前方划弧,右手心斜向右前方,掌指斜向上,高与肩平,左手体前平屈,手心向下。同时收左脚,左脚尖在右脚内侧点地,眼看右手方向。

身体左转,左脚向左前方出步,屈膝前弓,右脚蹬地伸直成左弓步;同时左掌向下向左弧形搂至左膝外侧,掌心向下,掌指向前,右掌由右耳侧向前推出,掌心向前,掌指向上,眼看前方。

Left Knee Brushing

The arms move to make a small half circle simultaneously following the course of right, front, left, front, then right again. Then move them to the front in arc-lines. The right palm, on the same level with the shoulders, faces the right front; the fingers point slantingly upward. Then place the left hand horizontally in front of the chest with the palm facing down. At the same time, the left foot draws back to the side of the right foot and points the ground with the tiptoe. The eyes follow the direction of the right hand.

The body turns to the left. The left foot steps forward to the left with the knee bent to make a bow shape, while the right leg stretches to form the left bow-shape step. Meanwhile, the left hand goes down and forms an arc, passing the knee to the outside, with the palm facing down and the fingers pointing forward; the right hand pushes slantingly forward from the position of the right ear, with the palm facing forward and the fingers pointing upward. Eyes should remain looking at the front.

(3) 右搂膝 身体左转,重心前移,左脚尖外撇45到60度角;右脚跟提起,向左脚靠拢;左掌心翻转向上,由下向后上划弧,掌心斜向上,右掌随身体左转,由前向左后划弧至左胸前,掌心向下。以下动作同左搂膝,唯方向相反。

27

学打太极拳

Right Knee Brushing

The body turns to the left and the center of gravity moves forward; the left toes turn 45 to 60 degrees outside. The right heel is lifted and drawn close to the left foot. The left palm turns to face up, and moves up to the back from below in an arc-line while the palm faces slantingly upward. Following the body turning left, the right hand moves in a left-and-back arc-line to the left side of the chest, the palm facing down. The consequent movements reversed for the left form of knee brushing.

左右搂膝动作反复前进练习，根据场地大小，可以再向后转继续练习。以左搂膝为例，重心后移，左脚尖内扣135度左右，上体从右向后体转；右臂回收胸前平屈，手心向下，左手斜后侧举，坐腕舒指成立掌，拇指一侧在里，身体后转180度；然后再出右脚继续做右搂膝拗步。也可从右搂膝开始，从左边向后转，再往回做左搂膝。这个练习要求速度要慢、匀，重心不能忽高忽低。可按数量要求练习者，做一百个左右搂膝，或者八十个左右搂膝。也可按时间要求，练15分钟搂膝或练20分钟搂膝。这两种练习都可以。

These movements should be repeated without stopping a lot. One should go to a different spot if the practicing ground is not large enough. For example: suppose one has finished the left knee brushing and needs to turn back, they will need to move the center of gravity backward. The left tiptoe turns inward for about 135 degrees, and the upper body turns backward from the right. The right arm draws back to lay horizontally before the chest with the palm facing down. The left hand is raised slantingly to the back with the palm standing vertically. The body turns 180 degrees back, and then the right foot moves forward for another round of right knee brushing. This could also begin from the right knee brushing: turn around from the left and start a new round of left knee brushing. The practice needs to be done slowly and smoothly, and the center of gravity should not rise or fall abruptly. One may practice by the number of rounds (80 or 100 a time) or by time (15 minutes or 20 minutes once); both methods are advisable.

第一章 简化 24 式太极拳

（四）左右倒卷肱 Reversed Brachium Twisting: Left and Right Form

（1）**左倒卷肱**　做太极起势，两脚开立同肩宽，上体左转 90 度，右脚尖内扣 45 到 60 度角，重心移至右脚，左脚跟提起脚尖点地；左臂从下向前，翻掌平举，手心向上，右手向后划弧至侧后举 45 度角，手心向上。两手高均与肩平，两臂夹角大约 135 度。左脚提起，向斜后方退一步，前脚掌先着地；右臂折回，经耳侧向前推掌，左臂从右臂下回抽，同时身体左转 45 度；右手体前高不过肩，左掌置于腰间，手心向上，眼看右手方向。

Left Reversed Brachium Twisting

Start by making the beginning pose first. Stand with the feet parted as wide as the shoulders. Turn the upper body 90 degrees to the left and the right tiptoe 45 to 60 degrees to inside. Transfer the center of gravity to the right foot, while the left heel is lifted up with the tiptoe touching the ground. The left arm is raised forward from below with the palm face up; and the right hand moves in an arc-line up to the back with the palm facing skyward; the forearm forms 45 degrees angle with the ground. The hands and shoulders are then kept at the same height, and the arms form roughly 135 degrees. The left leg is lifted up and takes one step slantingly backward, the front sole on the ground first. The right arm draws back, pushing forward across the ear; the left arm withdraws from under the right one, and meanwhile the body make 45 degrees turn to the left. The right hand is no higher than the shoulders in front of the body, and the left hand is placed beside the waist with the palm facing up. The eyes should follow the right hand's direction.

（2）**右倒卷肱**　同左倒卷肱，动作方向相反。

Right Reversed Brachium Twisting

Reverse the direction of the above movements to do Right Reversed Brachium Twisting.

左右倒卷肱，可以同左右搂膝结合在一起练习。左右搂膝练习进到折回点时，作一个琵琶式，然后作左右倒卷肱练习，行进到折回点时，再进行搂膝练习。

学打太极拳

This set of movements could be combined with that of "Knee-Brushing" for practice. When the left and right "Knee-Brushing" reaches the returning point, one may make the "lute-playing" pose, and go on to practice "Reversed Brachium Twisting," which in turn can be transferred to the "Knee-Brushing" at the returning point.

(五) 云手 Cloud-Waving Hands

太极起势。重心移于右脚,左脚提起收至右脚内侧,右掌向左前变勾手举于右侧(约45度角)方,左掌向左往下向右划弧至右手内侧;身体左转,左脚向左前迈步,右脚蹬地重心前移,成左弓步,同时左掌向左侧方推出,掌心向左,掌指向上。眼看左前方成左单鞭。

Start by making the beginning pose first. Then move the center of gravity to the right foot, so the inner side of the left foot is lifted and drawn back. The right palm transforms into a hook and moves forward to the left, and then rises to the right side (about 45 degrees from the central front line); the left palm, following the left-down-right arc course, reaches the inner side of the right hand. Then turn the body left. The left foot should then step in the left-front direction, and the right foot stretches to transfer the weight onto the other leg, forming the left bow-shape step. Meanwhile, the left hand should push to the left side, with the palm facing left and the fingers pointing skyward. Focus the eyes to the front left direction. These movements make a "Left Single Whip" pose.

左云手:重心右移,左脚尖内扣90度,左掌随转体向下弧形摆至左肩前;然后重心左移,身体稍左转,右勾手变掌由下向左上划弧,置左肩内侧,掌心斜向上,同时左掌再向左弧形摆至左侧约45度角(东南方)①;左手翻掌手心向下,同时收右脚距左脚25厘米处落地,与左脚平行。眼看左掌。

Left Cloud-Waving Hand: Move the center of gravity to the right, and move the left tiptoe turns 90 degrees inward (i.e., to the right), while the left palm,

---

① 书中所指的方位都是以习练者面向南为准。The practicer is supposed to face the south in this book.

following the body turn, goes downward in an arc-line to the position in front of the left shoulder. Then move the center of gravity left, and turn the body left a bit; the right hand, changing from hook to palm, goes from below the upward position to the left (the inner side of the left shoulder) in an arc with the palm facing slantingly up. Meanwhile, the left hand waves in an arc-shape to the left about 45 degrees from the central line. The left palm is turned face down, and the right foot is drawn back to a parallel position 25cm from the left foot. The eyes are set on the left hand.

重心右移,身体稍右转,右掌由左向上经面前向右运至右侧,约45度角(西南方),掌心斜向下;左掌由左向下经腹前向右运至右肘内侧,掌心斜向右上,同时重心移至右腿,左脚提起向左横开步,脚掌着地,眼看右手方向。

Move the center of gravity to the right, and turn the body right slightly; raise the right hand up from the left to the right (passing the face) about 45 degrees from the central line with the palm facing slantingly down; the left hand goes down from the left to the inner side of the right elbow (passing the stomach), with the palm facing up to the right. Meanwhile the center of gravity is transferred to the right leg, and the left foot is lifted to step to the left side only with its sole on the ground. The eyes are set on the direction of the right hand.

以下动作同前,反复向左,作左云手练习。

The movements that follow are the same. Repeat these movements for practice, moving constantly leftward.

做到一定数量要折回时,左掌运至左侧变勾手举于左侧;上体右转,左脚尖内扣45度,右脚向右侧迈步,前弓成右弓步,右手翻掌向右前推出,成右单鞭。眼看右手方向。以同样方式向右方作右云手练习。

When it is time to turn back after certain rounds, the left palm should wave in a curved way to the left and transform into a hook; while the upper body turns right; the left tiptoe turns inward for 45 degrees, and the right foot steps to the right with the leg bent to form the right bow-shaped step; the right palm swirls and pushes in the right-front direction, forming the "Right Single Whip." Set the eyes on the direction of the right hand. Then do the "Right Cloud-Waving Hand" to practice the right side.

如单练两臂的动作,也可原地作云手练习,也可直立练习,也可蹲马步练习,但身体重心一定要随转体移动。

For the sole practice of arm movements, one may stay at the same standing point, stand straight, or practice in a half-squatting way; but the center of gravity must follow when the body turns.

(六) 揽雀尾 Grabbing the Bird's Tail
(1) 左揽雀尾　太极起势。重心右移,然后收左脚于右脚内侧,脚尖点地成丁步;左手向左向下划弧至小腹前,臂成弧形,手心向上,右小臂折回收至胸前,手心向下。成抱球状,目视前方。

Left Form of Grabbing the Bird's Tail

Start by making the beginning pose. Move the center of gravity rightward, and then draw the left foot back to the inner side of the right one with the tiptoe touching the ground. Wave the left hand left and then down in an arc to the front of the belly with the arm in an arc-shape, and the palm facing up. The right forearm returns to the front of the chest with the palm facing down, forming the ball-holding gesture with the left palm. Eyes look remain looking forward.

"掤(bīng)":左脚向左斜前方出步,身体左转,重心前移,右腿后蹬成左弓步;同时左臂向前掤出,手心斜向上,右臂随左臂前送,右手向下置右胯侧,手心向下,指尖向前。目视前方。

"*Bing*": The left foot steps to the front left; the body turns to the left; move the center of gravity forward; stretch the right leg to make the left bow-shape step. In the meantime, the left arm sheds forward with the palm facing slantingly up; the right arm follows forward and down with the right hand placed at the right hip side, with the palm facing down and the fingers pointing to the front.

第一章　简化 24 式太极拳

"捋"：弓步不变，两臂同时经前送翻掌，左手在前高与肩平，手心斜向下，右手手心斜向上；然后身体重心后移到右脚，两臂往右后捋至右腰侧；左手翻掌手心向里，对应坛中穴；右手翻掌手心向上，搭在左小臂内侧靠腕处。

"Stroking": The bow-shape step does not change. Arms simultaneously push forward and twist the palms; the left hand (palm facing slantingly down) should be at the front on the same level with shoulders and the right palm facing slantingly up. Then transfer the center of gravity to the right foot, while arms stroke back to the right side of the waist, the left hand faces inward in opposition to the medial forearm, and the right hand faces up, attaching to the inner side (close to the wrist) of the left forearm.

"挤"：身体重心前移，成左弓步，同时，两臂向前挤出；右手从左手背上向前伸出，两掌心向下，两手分开与肩同宽。

"Squeezing": Move the center of gravity forward, forming the left bow-shape step; meanwhile, the arms squeeze forward; the right hand extends to the front from above the left hand's back; with the palms face down, parted as wide as the shoulders.

"按"：重心后移，两臂随身体后移垂肘至胸前，手心斜相对，掌指斜向上，右脚蹬地，左腿前弓，两臂向前弧形按出，高与肩平。眼看前方。

"Pressing": Move the center of gravity back, followed by the arms drawing back and bending in front of the chest; the palms slantingly face each other and the fingers point slantingly up; the right leg extends and the left one bends, while the arms press forward in arc-shapes. The eyes are set on the front.

重心右移，左脚里扣 135 度，两臂同时向右划弧，右臂往右往下翻掌掌心向上，左手心向下成抱球状，同时收右脚至左脚内侧成丁步。

Move the center of gravity right, and the left foot turns 135 degrees inward; arms simultaneously wave to the right in arc-shapes, the right one going right and then down with the palm which is turned face up, and the left palm facing down to form the ball-holding gesture; meanwhile the right foot is drawn back the inner side of the left foot to make a T-shaped step.

(2) 右揽雀尾 同左揽雀尾,唯动作方向、路线相反。

Right form of Grabbing the Bird's Tail
The movements are the same to that of the left form, except for the reversed directions and moving courses.

(七) 左右下势独立 Left and Right Single-Legged Squatting
(1) 左下势独立 太极起势。然后两掌向右向前再向左划弧,然后再向右上,右掌变勾稍高于肩,左掌心斜向外,对右肘内侧,同时左腿收回成丁步。眼看右手。

The Left Form of Single-Legged Squatting
Start by making the beginning pose. The hands move in arcs following the right-central-left course, and then goes up to the right. The right palm then forms a hook which is a little higher than the shoulder, and the left palm facing slantingly out toward the inner side of the right elbow; meanwhile the left leg is drawn back to make the T-shaped step. Set the eyes on the right hand.

右腿下蹲,左腿直腿向左伸出,脚尖向内扣,右脚尖稍外展全蹲,上体正直,成坐仆步。

The right leg fully squats with the tiptoe slightly turned out, while the left one stretches to the left with the tiptoe turned inside; keep the upper body upright. This makes the squatting step.

左掌沿左腿内侧向前穿出,手指向前,拇指一侧在上;重心前移成左弓腿,左掌继续向前上穿,右臂在体后,臂内旋,勾尖向上;右腿向前上提起,小腿自然下垂,右掌随重心前移向上挑起,掌指向上,拇指一侧在里,对准鼻尖,肘与膝关节垂直,手心向左,左掌由前收回,往下采,落至左胯外侧约20公分处,手心向下,虎口向前。眼看前方。

The left palm moves along the inner side of the left leg with the fingers pointing forward and the thumb-side on the top; move the center of gravity forward to make the left leg bow-shaped, while the left palm keeps piercing forward and upward; the right arm, turned inward, is at the back of the body with the hook pointing up; the right leg is then lifted up, with the foreleg drooping naturally; and following the forward-moving gravity, the right palm (facing the left) is raised, the fingers pointing up, the thumb in front of the nose, and the elbow on the same vertical line with the knee; the left hand withdraws from the front and goes down to the left hip-side (about 20cm from the left hip), the palm facing down and the "tiger's mouth" facing forward. Set eyes on the front.

(2) 右下势独立 右腿下落,前脚掌脚尖点地,身体左转,左臂左上提成勾手,右掌经面前往左划弧,手指斜向上,掌心对左肘关节。重心落于左脚。然后作右下势独立,要领同左下势独立,唯方向相反。

The Right Form of Single-Legged Squatting

The right leg falls down with the toes touching the ground; the body turns left, and the left arm is raised to the left with the palm transformed into a hook; the right palm makes an arc to the left across the face, the fingers pointing slantingly up and the palm in opposite to the left elbow. The center of gravity is set on the left foot at this time. Then do the right form of single-legged squatting, which, of course, has the same movements with the left form except for the reversed direction.

(八) 左右蹬脚 Left and Right Kicking Step

左右蹬脚:支撑腿微屈站稳,另一腿屈膝提起,小腿上摆,脚尖上勾,脚跟向前蹬出,高过腰部,如右左蹬脚。

Set the supporting leg (slightly bent) steadily on the ground; lift the other one with the knee bent; wave the foreleg up to the position higher than the waist; bend the toes upward and pop the heels forward.

(九) 摆莲脚、弯弓射虎 Waving-Lotus Step and Tiger Shooting with Bow-and-Arrow

太极起势。两臂体前划弧,右脚尖里扣45度左右,向右转体,重心移于右腿;

学打太极拳

左掌向右向上经面前划弧至胸前右侧,同时右掌心斜向外,向右侧划弧,高与耳平,拇指一侧在上。同时左脚向左前方迈步,脚跟着地;然后向左转体,重心前移左脚,右脚向前一步,脚尖点地;右臂向前摆出,高与肩平,左掌随身体转动至右肘里侧,手心向下。右脚提起从左侧向上向右摆腿,两掌从右向左摆动,掌心向外,依次击拍右脚背外侧;击拍后,右腿屈膝提起,两臂至左上方,手心向左下。左掌高与眼平,右掌在左臂肘关节内侧,眼看左手。

  Start by making the beginning pose. Wave the arms in arcs in front of the body; turn the right tiptoe 45 degrees inward, turn the body right, and transfer the center of gravity to the right leg. Move the left palm in a right-upward arc until it reaches the right side of the chest so it passes the face; in the meantime, the right palm, facing slantingly outward and with the thumb-side on the top, moves in an arc-line to the right side of the body as high as the ear. Simultaneously the left foot steps to the left front with the heel touching the ground. Then turn the body left and transfer the center of gravity to the left foot; the right foot then makes one-step forward with the tiptoe touching the ground. The right arm waves forward so it is on the same level as the shoulders; the left hand, following the body turn, reaches the inner side of the right elbow with the palm facing down. The right foot is lifted and waved right and upward from the left, and the hands, waving from left to right, pat the outside of the instep during the turn. After that, the right leg is bent and lifted, and the arms go up on the left with the palm facing down to the left. The left palm is as high as the eyes and the right one at the inner side of the left elbow. Set eyes on the left hand.

上体右转,右脚向右侧前方落地,重心前移,两臂由左向下划弧经体前握拳,往右后划弧,眼看右拳。

  Turn the upper body right, the right foot falls to the front right direction, then move the center of gravity forward; the arms wave down in arc-lines from the left and, when passing in front of the body, the hands form fists; then they wave in arcs to the back on the right, with the eyes set on the right fist.

第一章　简化 24 式太极拳

上体左转，两拳同时向左前方击出，右拳在上，左拳在下，右腿前弓成右弓步。眼看左前方。

Turn the upper body left, and the two fists strike forward to the left at simultaneously, the right one at the top and another below; the right leg bends forward to make the right bow-shaped step. Set eyes in the front left direction.

左脚向前一步，重心前移至左腿，右脚进一步成右虚步；左拳变掌，向里向前划弧至右肩前，右拳变掌，向里向前划弧至左掌前，掌心向前下方，稍高于左掌，然后再作摆莲脚动作。

The left foot takes one step forward, transfer the center of gravity to the left leg, and the right foot should take one step forward to form the "right void step." The left fist changes back to the palm and reaches the front of the right shoulder following an inward-forward arc-line; and the right fist changes back to the palm, too, and moves in an inward-forward arc line to reach the front of the left palm; the palm faces down and is slightly higher than the left one. Do the "Waving-Lotus Step" again.

（十）组合动作练习 Combined Practice

(1) 搂膝蹬脚　　太极起势。两臂体前划平圆，右掌向右向前向左再向右前方划弧至西南方，翻掌手心向上，左掌向左向前向右划弧，至右肩前，掌心向下，身体稍左转，眼看右手方向；左脚收回右脚内侧点地。

Knee Brushing and Kicking Step

Start by making the beginning pose. Wave the hands in a horizontal circle in front of the body; move the right hand in the arc course of right, front, left, and right in the front, with the palm turned to face skyward; the left palm follows the left-front-right arc course until it reaches the front of the right shoulder, with the palm facing down; the body turns slightly left and the eyes follow the direction of the right hand. The left foot draws back to the inner side of the right foot with its tiptoe touching the ground.

学打太极拳

1) <u>左搂膝</u>　左脚向左前方迈步,脚跟先着地,重心前移,身体左转;左掌经腹前向前下搂过膝关节,在左大腿外侧按掌,掌心向下,手指向前,右掌屈肘回收,通过耳旁成立掌向前推出,掌指向上,小指一侧在前。眼看右手。

The Left Form of Knee Brushing

The left foot goes to the front left side, with the heel touching the ground first; then move the center of gravity forward and turn the body left. The left hand should move down to the front, passing the belly along the way, and brushes across the knee, and presses down at the outside of the left thigh; the palm faces down and the fingers point forward. The right hand is drawn back by bending the elbow, and pushes forward by the ear with the fingers pointing upward and the little finger at the front. Set eyes on the right hand.

2) <u>右蹬脚</u>　左脚尖外撇约45度,身体稍左转,重心左移,两掌由左右两侧向上向里合,两臂交叉,左手在里,掌心均向里;同时右脚提起,往前提膝,左腿自然站起,同时两臂上举向左右弧形分开,合抱于胸前,左臂在内,右臂在外,两掌心均向内,右腿放松上提。

The Right Kicking

Turn the left tiptoe about 45 degrees outward, followed by a slight left turn of the body and the left moving of one's weight; the hands move from two sides up to the central front till the arms cross, the left hand on the inside and the two palms both facing inward. Meanwhile lift the right foot forward and have the left leg stand straight naturally, while the arms are raised, parted in arc-lines to the sides, and then crossed in front of the chest with the left one on the inside and the palms facing inward. The right leg is kept lifted.

两臂上举额前,再分手向左右两边撑掌,手指向上手心向前;右脚上提脚尖勾起,向右前方蹬出(右手方向),力在脚跟,高过胯。眼看右脚方向。做到手与足、肩与胯、肘与膝相合。

Then raise the arms to the front of the forehead, then split and extend them to their respective side, fingers pointing up and palms facing forward. The right foot rises with the tiptoe bent back and kicks with force on the heel to the right-front (the direction of the right hand) higher than the hips. Focus your eyes on the direction of the right foot. Then only can the coordination between hands and feet, shoulders and hips, and elbows and knees should be achieved.

右脚收回向正前方迈步,脚跟着地;右手向左划弧,至左肩前,掌心向下,左掌放松下沉。接着练右搂膝加左蹬脚。反复练习。

Then the right foot draws back to step to the central front with the heel touching the ground. The right hand waves leftward in an arc to the front of the left shoulder with the palm facing down then have the left hand drop down. Next, practice the right knee brushing plus the left kicking step. Repeat the procedure.

(2) 野马分鬃蹬脚 Splitting the Horse's Mane and the Kicking Step

1) 左野马分鬃　太极起势。左掌向左斜下划弧里收,翻掌手心向上,右掌向里划弧,手心向下,两臂体前成抱球状。

身体左转,左脚向左前方出步,脚跟着地,左掌心向上,向前划弧至左肩前,左肘左膝上下相对,右掌向右下划弧至右胯旁,掌心向下,虎口向前。同时右腿蹬地,成左弓步,左膝不超过左脚尖,两脚横向距离同胯宽。

Left Form of Splitting the Horse's Mane

Start by making the beginning pose. The left palm goes slantingly down to the left and draws inward in an arc-line; turn the palm face up; and the right hand moves inward in an arc-line with the palm facing down, forming the ball-holding gesture with the left hand.

Turn the body left; the left foot steps to the left-front with the heel touching the ground; wave the left hand (palm facing up) in an arc-line to the front of the left shoulder, with the elbow in opposition to the left knee; then wave the right hand down to the left in an arc-line reaching the right hip-side, with the palm facing downward and the "tiger's mouth" forward. Meanwhile, the right leg extends to make the left bow-shaped step. The left knee does not go beyond the left tiptoe, and the distance between the feet is the same as that of the hips.

2）右蹬脚　重心前移,上体稍左转,两臂向两侧分掌,同时右脚跟提起;两臂从两侧合抱交叉翻掌,掌心均向内,右掌在外;右脚继续上提,脚尖勾起,向右侧蹬击;两臂左右撑开,掌心向前,掌指向上。眼看右脚方向。

右脚下落收回,两手从两侧向下向里划弧成抱球状,右脚支撑体重,左脚尖在右脚内侧点地,身体稍左转。眼看左前方。

The Right Kicking

Move the center of gravity forward and turn the upper body slightly left; split the arms to their respective side, and at the same time lift the right foot. Move the arms to cross in front the chest, the palms facing inward and the right arm on the outside. Keep lifting the right foot; bend up the tiptoe and then kick to the right. Part and extend the arms to the sides, with the palm facing forward and the fingers pointing up. Keep the eyes on the direction of the right foot.

Drop the right foot down to its original position. The hands should make the ball-holding gesture. Put the weight on the right foot; then have the left tiptoe touch the ground at the inner side of the right foot; then turn the body slightly left. Set eyes on the left-front side.

再做右野马分鬃、左蹬脚,继续循环前进练习。

Then do the right form of "Splitting the Horse's Mane" and the left kicking step. Keep practicing them together.

3）左蹬脚　两臂交叉上提,左腿提起,作左蹬脚。要领同前面右蹬脚。

Left Kicking Step

Cross and lift the arms, lift the left leg and make the left kicking step. Consult the right kicking above for instructions on how to do it.

4）**右蹬脚** 左脚前进一步，重心前移，身体左转，两臂从两侧向下划弧合抱，右腿向前提起，作右蹬脚。动作要领同前面右蹬脚。

Right Kicking Step

The left foot makes a step forward, which moves the center of gravity moves forward, too; then turn the body left. Wave the arms down in arc-lines from the sides to cross, and lift the right leg forward to make the right kicking. Consult the right kicking above for instructions.

5）**右下势独立** 左掌变勾，勾尖向下，稍高于肩，身体左转，右掌收至左臂内侧，手心对左肘，掌指斜向上，右腿收回成丁步。

左腿下蹲，右脚沿地面向右出步，成右仆步，右掌收至腹前，掌指向右脚方向，掌心向外，拇指一侧在上。目视右脚方向。

Right Single-Legged Squatting

Transform the left palm into a hook a bit higher than the shoulder with the points facing downward; turn the body left, and draw the right hand back to the inner side of the left arm, with its palm facing the left elbow and fingers pointing slantingly upward; then withdraw the right leg to make the T-shape step.

Squat on the left leg, while the right one steps to the right side to form the right squatting step; the right hand should draw back to the front of the belly, with fingers pointing in the right foot's direction, palm facing outward and the thumb on the top. Set eyes on the right foot's direction.

重心前移，右掌顺右腿内侧前穿；右腿蹬起自然直立，左腿向前上提，小腿自然下垂，脚尖向下，膝高过胯；右掌向前向上再向下按掌，掌心向下，虎口向前，左手由勾变掌，向前向上挑起，指尖向上，掌心向右，高与鼻平。眼看前方。

Move the center of gravity forward, while the right palm pierces forward along the inner side of the right leg, which should stand naturally straight; and then lift the left leg forward, and have the foreleg naturally drooping, tiptoe pointing down and with the knee higher than the hip. The right hand goes forward and upward, and then presses down, with the palm facing downward and the "tiger's mouth" forward. The left hand then transforms back into palm, goes forward and then upward to a position as high as the nose, fingers pointing up and the palm facing right. Eyes set on the front.

6) 左下势独立　接上式。左脚在右脚前以脚尖点地,身体右转,右手变勾手,左手划弧至右臂内侧,左掌心对右肘内侧,然后作左下势独立。动作要领同右下势独立,唯方向相反。

Left Single-Legged Squatting

Start from the above pose. Point the left tiptoe at the ground before the right foot; turn the body right; have the right hand transforms into the hook and the left hand make an arc to the inner side of the right arm with the palm facing the inner right elbow. Notice that the left form of "Single-Legged Squatting" begins with the same movement essentials to the right form except for the reversed directions.

要练好太极拳要在有经验的老师指导下练习,这就会少走弯路。

Practicing under the instruction of an experienced *Taiji* master helps make smooth progress.

五、简化24式太极拳动作说明
Specific Instructions to the Simplified Twenty-Four-Step *Taiji Quan* Movements

第一组:起势　左右野马分鬃　白鹤亮翅

Group One: Beginning Pose, the Wild Horse Splits Its Mane & the White Crane Spreads Its Wings

第一章　简化24式太极拳

（一）起势 Beginning Pose

1. 面向南身体自然直立，两脚并拢脚尖朝前。头：虚领顶劲微收下额，竖颈，眼平视前方，肩松沉，两臂自然下垂，两手放在大腿外侧。含胸拔背，收腹敛臀，两膝微松，气沉丹田。（图1）

Facing the south (lower part of your body), the body stands naturally straight with feet in juxtaposition and pointing forward. Head: force exerted indigenously on the top, with jaw withdrawn slightly and the neck kept straight. Eyes should be set on the front. Shoulders droop in a relaxed way. Arms droop naturally with hands on the outside of the thighs. Keep the chest, belly, and buttocks withdrawn and the back straight. Knees are slightly relaxed. The air force is exerted to the pubic region.

2. 提起左脚向左开步，同肩宽成开立步。（图2）

The left foot moves left, forming the parted step with feet that is parted as wide as that of the shoulders.

3. 两臂慢慢向前平举，两手与肩同高、同宽，手心向下。（图3、4）

Arms rise forward slowly, with the hands as high and wide as the shoulders and palm facing down.

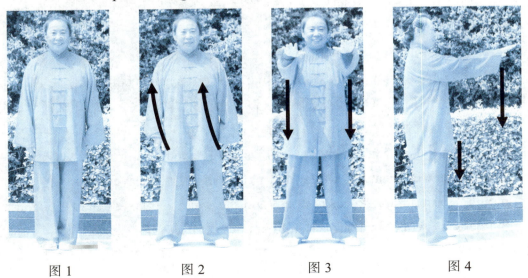

图1　　　　　图2　　　　　图3　　　　　图4

学打太极拳

4. 上体保持正直,两腿屈膝下蹲,同时两臂垂肘,两掌坐腕慢慢下按至腹高。肘与膝相合,眼平视前方。(图5、6、7)

Keep the upper body straight and balanced, while the legs squat halfway, while the elbows fall downward and the palms press slowly to a position as high as the belly. Elbows are in opposition to the knees and eyes are set on the front.

图5　　　　　　　图6　　　　　　　图7

口诀:① 两脚开立同肩宽;② 两臂前平举肩高肩宽;③ 屈蹲按掌按在腹前。

Mnemonic lines: ① Part the feet as wide as shoulders; ② Arms rise as high and wide as shoulders; ③ Squat half and press hands before the belly.

要点:两肩松沉,两肘松垂,手指自然微屈,掌心微含,虎口成弧形,屈膝松腰,收腹敛臀,臂部不可后凸。

Essentials: Shoulders and elbows are relaxed and drooped, fingers slightly bent in a natural way, and palms slightly concave; the "tiger's mouth" form an arc; knees are bent and the waist is relaxed; the belly and buttocks are withdrawn; arms should not project backward.

第一章　简化24式太极拳

（二）左右野马分鬃 The Wild Horse Splits Its Mane: Left and Right Form

1. 左野马分鬃 Left Form

（1）上体微向右转（约30—40度），身体重心移至右腿上，同时右臂成弧形上掤至胸平，手心向下，左手外旋手心向上，两手心相对（劳宫穴相对），成抱球状，左脚随即收至右脚内侧（内踝骨），脚尖点地，眼看右手。（图8、9）

图8

Turn the upper body right (about 30 to 40 degrees), and transfer the body weight to the right leg at the same time the right arm, with the palm facing down, reaches to the front of the chest. The left hand twists to form the ball-holding gesture; the left leg then draws to the inner side of the right foot (the inner ankle) tiptoeing the ground. Eyes are set on the right hand.

图9

（2）上体微向左转，左脚向左前进方向迈出，脚跟先着地，脚脖放松全脚掌着地，右脚跟后蹬，右腿自然伸直成左弓步，同时上体继续向左转，左右手随转体慢慢分别向左上右下分开，左手腕高于肩平，手心斜向上，肘微屈成弧形，右手落在右膀旁，掌心向下指尖朝前，眼看左手方向，胸向正东偏南。（图10、11）

图10

图11

学打太极拳

> **口诀：**①转体划弧；②收脚抱球；③转体开胯上步；④弓步分掌。
> **Mnemonic lines:** ① Turn the body and move in arcs; ② Draw the foot back and make the ball-holding gesture; ③ Turn the body and step forward; ④ Make the bow-shaped step and part the palms.

Turn the upper body slight to the left, and put the left foot forward to the left, with the heel touching the ground first and then followed by the whole foot; the right heel pushes backward and the leg stretches naturally straight to form the left bow-shaped step; meanwhile the upper body keeps turning left, and the hands part as the body turns, with the left one up to the left (wrist as high as the shoulders, with its palm facing slantingly upward and elbow slightly bent), and the right one down to the right (palm facing down and fingers pointing forward). The eyes are set on the left hand's direction, and the chest faces southeast.

图 12

2. 右野马分鬃 Right Form

（1）屈右腿后坐膝关节找右脚尖，身体重心移至右腿，左脚尖翘起，上体微向左转，左脚外撇（大约45到60度角），随后脚掌慢慢踏实，重心移至左腿，左腿慢慢前弓，此时右脚成虚步随即收到左脚内测，脚尖点地，同时左手内旋掌心向下，左臂屈肘弧形收在胸前，右手外旋掌心向上下挪至腹前，两手心相对成抱球状，眼看左手。（图12、13）

Sit on the right leg with the knee in a vertical line with the tiptoe; lift the left tiptoe up; turn the upper body slightly left; then turn the left foot outward (about 45 to 60 degrees) to step on the ground gradually. Transfer the center of gravity to the left leg, which bends forward slowly, and the right foot is made void-forced and lifted to the inner side of the left foot with the tiptoe touching the

图 13

ground. Meanwhile, the left hand twists inward to make the palm face down and the arm bends to lay in front the chest; the right hand, going down to the front of the belly, turns to face upward (in opposition to the left palm), forming the ball-holding gesture. Set eyes on the left hand.

(2) 右脚向前右方迈出一步，脚跟着地然后全脚着地，重心前移成右弓步，同时上体右转，左腿自然伸直左右手随转体分别向左下右上分开，右手腕高与肩平，肘微屈下垂，左手落在左跨旁，屈肘手心向下，指尖朝前，眼看右手，胸向东北。(图 14)

图 14

Put the right foot a step to the right-front with the heel touching the ground first before putting the whole foot down, and move the weight forward to form the right bow-shaped step; at the same time, turn the upper body rightward, while the left leg stretches naturally straight, and the hands split to opposite directions: the right one goes up to the right, with the wrist on the same level with the shoulders and the elbow slightly bent and drooping, while the left one falls to the left hip-side with the elbow bent, and its palm facing down with its fingers pointing forward. Eyes are set on the right hand and the chest faces northeast.

3. 左野马分鬃 Left Form

(1) 屈左腿后坐，左膝关节与脚尖同向，身体重心移至左腿，右脚尖翘起，上体微向右转，右脚外撇45到60度角，随后脚掌踏实，重心移至右腿，右腿慢慢成右弓步，此时左脚跟提起收至右脚跟内侧，脚尖着地，同时右手内旋掌心向下，右臂屈肘弧形收在胸前，左手外旋掌心向上下掤至腹前，两手心相对成抱球状，眼看右手。(图 15、16)

Sit on your bent left leg with the knee and toes facing the same direction. Transfer the weight to the left leg; lift the right toes up; turn the upper body

学打太极拳

slightly rightward; turn the right foot outward about 45 to 60 degrees and keep it completely on the ground; move the center of gravity to the right leg, which should transform slowly into a bow-shape. At this time, the left foot is lifted and drawn to the inner side of the right foot with its tiptoe touching the ground. Meanwhile, the right hand twists inward to make the palm face down and the arm bends to lay before the chest, while the left hand moves to the front of the belly with the palm facing upward (in opposition to the right palm), forming the ball-holding gesture. Eyes should be set on the right hand.

图 15　　　　图 16

(2) 左脚向前正东偏北迈出一步,脚跟着地,然后全脚掌着地,重心前移成左弓步,同时上体左转,右腿自然伸直,左右手随转体分别向右下左上分开,左手腕高于肩平掌心向上,肘微屈下垂,右手落在右胯旁,屈肘手心向下,指尖朝前,眼看左手方向,胸向东南。(图17)

图 17

口诀:① 后坐翘脚;② 撇脚转身;③ 抱球上步;④ 弓步分掌。

Mnemonic lines: ① Sit back and lift the tiptoe; ② Twist the foot outward and turn the upper body; ③ Make the ball-holding gesture and step forward; ④ Form the bow-shaped step and split hands.

要点:上体不可前俯后仰,胸部必须宽松舒展,两臂分开时要保持弧形。身体转动时要以腰为轴。弓步与分手动作速度要均匀,迈步的脚尖向前,弓步

第一章 简化 24 式太极拳

时膝关节不可超出脚尖。前后脚的横向距离约 10—30 厘米，不可走迭步，要在中轴线两侧。

Essentials: The upper body does not bend back or forth. The chest should be relaxed. Arms are kept in arc-shapes when they are parted. The waist should be taken as the axis for the body turn. The bow-shaped steps and hand splitting should be done with the same speed; the tiptoe of the forward-stepping foot should point to the front; the knee of the bow-shaped leg does not go beyond the tiptoe. The parallel distance between the feet is about 10 to 30cm, and the feet should be kept on their respective side of the central line.

Take one step left with the left foot with the heel on the ground first and then the whole foot, and move the center of gravity forward to form the left bow-shaped step; at the same time the upper body turns leftward, while the right leg should stretch naturally straight, and the hands split to opposite directions as the upper body turns: the left one goes up to the left, with the wrist on the same level with the shoulders, palm facing up and elbow slightly bent and drooping, and the right one falls to the side of the right hip, with the elbow bent, palm facing down and fingers pointing forward. Eyes follow the direction of the left hand. The chest faces southeast.

（三）白鹤亮翅 White Crane Spreading Its Wings

1. 上体微向左转，左手内旋掌心向下屈臂胸前，右手外旋掌心向上至腹高，两臂成弧形手心相对成抱球状，眼看左手。（图 18、19）

Turn the upper body slightly to the left. The left arm bends to lie

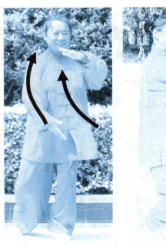

图 18　　　　图 19

学打太极拳

before the chest and twists inward to make the palm face down, and the right hand moves up to the front of the belly with the palm facing upward. The arms are in arc-shapes and the palms form the ball-holding gesture. Eyes are set on the left hand.

2. 右脚跟进半步,脚掌着地,脚跟里落脚尖朝东南角,上体后坐,身体重心移至右腿向右微转体,然后左脚稍向前移半步,前脚掌着地成左虚步,同时上体再微向左转面向前方,两手随转体慢慢向右上左下分开,右手分至右额前,手心向左后方,左手落于左胯旁,手心向下指尖朝前,胸向正东眼平视前方。(图20)

图 20

The right foot takes half a step forward, with the sole on the ground; then the foot sets completely on the ground with the tiptoe turned outward. The upper body just sits back and turns slightly to the right when the center of gravity transfers to the right leg. The left leg goes half a step forward with the sole on the ground to make the left void step; in the meantime the upper body turns back to the front, and the hands, following the body turn, split slowly to different

口诀:① 跟半步抱球;② 后坐转体搭手;③ 分手下落;④ 虚步点脚。

Mnemonic lines: ① Put the foot behind half a step forward and make the ball-holding gesture; ② Sit back, turn the body, and put the hands together; ③ Split the hands and droop down; ④ Make the void step with the front sole touching the ground.

要领:完成姿势胸部不可前挺,两臂上下要保持弧形,左膝要微屈不可僵直。重心后移和右手上提,左手下按,要协调一致。

Essentials: In the ending pose, the chest should project out. Arms are kept in arc-shapes. The left knee is slightly bent without being stiff. The backward moving of the center of gravity is in accordance with the uplifting of the right hand and the downward pressing of the left.

第一章 简化24式太极拳

directions: the right hand up to the right-front of the forehead, palm facing inward to the left, and the left one down to the left hip side, palm facing downward and fingers pointing forward. Eyes are set on the horizontal front.

第二组：左右搂膝拗步　手挥琵琶　左右倒卷肱

Group Two: Knee Brushing and Twisting Step, Playing the Lute, and Reversed Brachium Twisting

（四）左右搂膝拗步 Knee Brushing and Twisting Step: Left and Right Form

1. 左搂膝拗步 Left Form

（1）向左转体右手从体前下落，由下向右后扬起45度角西南角，手腕同肩平，手心斜向上，左手由左下向上向右划弧至右胸前，手心斜向下，同时上体微向左再向右转，左脚收至右脚内侧，脚尖点地，眼看右手，胸向东南。（图21、22）

Turn the body leftward. The right hand falls before the body and then rises backward and rightward about 45 degrees to the southwest (the right side of the back), the wrist should be on the same level with shoulders and the palm slanting up. The left hand goes up and rightward in an arc-line to the right chest, palm facing slanting down. Meanwhile, the upper body turns left and then right, and

图21　　　　　　　图22

51

the left foot draws to the inner side of the right foot, with the tiptoe touching the ground. Eyes are set on the right hand, and the chest faces southeast.

（2）上体微左转，提起左脚向正东偏北方向迈出，脚跟着地，右手拇指尖与鼻尖同高。掌心斜向前方，左手向下落至腹前护裆，掌心向下，左臂呈弧形。（图23）

The upper body turns leftward. The left foot steps to the northeast with the heel on the ground. The tip of the right thumb is on the same level with the nose and the palm faces slantingly forward. The left hand falls to the front of the belly to protect the crotch, palm facing down and the arm in an arc-shape.

（3）左脚掌放平，右腿自然伸直，左腿成弓步，膝关节垂直于脚尖不可超出，同时左手由腹前向前经左膝弧形搂出，左手搂到左胯旁，掌心向下，指尖朝前，同时右手屈肘右手由耳侧向前推出（正东），眼看右手方向。（图24、25）

Set the left foot completely on the ground and stretch the right leg naturally straight to make the bow-shaped left leg (the knee on the vertical line with the tiptoe). Meanwhile the left hand moves forward from the belly, crosses the left knee in an arc-line, and comes back to the left hip side with the palm facing down and fingers pointing forward; at the same time the right arm bends and

图23　　　　　　图24　　　　　　图25

pushes the hand forward (east) by the ear. Eyes look at the direction of the right hand.

> 口诀：① 转体划弧；② 收脚扬掌；③ 迈步屈臂；④ 搂膝弓步推掌。
> **Mnemonic lines:** ① Turn the body and move arms in arc-lines; ② Raise hands and withdraw feet; ③ Step forward and bend arms; ④ Brush the knee (hand crosses knee), and make the bow-shaped step, then push the right hand forward.

2. 右搂膝拗步 Right Form

（1）右腿屈膝后坐，右膝与脚尖同向，重心移于右腿，左膝放松左脚尖翘起，身向左转左脚外撇 45 到 60 度角，随后脚掌落地，左腿屈膝前弓，左膝与脚尖同向，身体重心移至左腿。

Sit back on your bent right leg (with its knee pointing in the same direction with the toes) to which the center of gravity is transferred. The left knee is relaxed while the left tiptoe is bent up. Turn the body leftward; twist the left foot outward about 45 to 60 degrees and then completely step on the ground. When the left leg bends forward with the knee and tiptoe pointing at the same direction then move the body weight to the left leg.

（2）右脚收至左脚内侧，脚尖点地，同时左手外旋掌心朝上，由左向上划弧至左肩外侧 45 度（西北角），肘微屈，手腕与肩平，手心向上，右手随左转体向上，经面前向左下划弧落于左胸前，手心向下，眼看左手方向，胸向东北。（图 26、27）

The right foot draws to the inner side of the left one, with the tiptoe touching the

图 26   图 27

ground. In the meantime, the left hand twists to face up and waves up from the left in an arc-line to the outside of the left shoulder (45 degrees from the shoulder), with the elbow slightly bent and wrist as high as the shoulder; and the right hand goes up following the body's left turn, by passing the face and falls to the front of the left chest in an arc-line with the palm facing down. Eyes should follow the direction of the left hand, and the chest faces northeast.

（3）上体微右转，提起右脚向正东偏南方向迈出，脚跟着地，同时左臂屈肘左手至左耳侧。掌心斜向前，右手向下落至腹前护裆，掌心向下右臂呈弧形。(图28)

Turn the upper body slightly rightward, and step the right foot toward the east (slightly straying to the south) with the heel on the ground. Meanwhile bend the left arm and move the hand to the side of the left ear. Palm facing slantingly forward, the right hand falls to the front of the belly to protect the crotch, and then the palm turns to face down while the arm is in an arc-shape.

（4）右脚掌踏实成右弓步，右膝不得超过脚尖，左腿自然伸直，同时右手向前经右膝弧形向右后搂出至右胯旁，左手向前推出（正东），左手指尖同鼻高，掌心斜向前。(图29、30)

Set the right foot firmly on the ground to make the right bow-shaped step (with the knee not going beyond the tiptoe), and stretch the left leg naturally

图28　　　　　　　　　图29　　　　　　　　　图30

第一章 简化 24 式太极拳

straight. At the same time move the right hand forward, cross the right knee in an arc-line and draw back to the right hip side; the left hand pushes forward (the east) with the fingers as high as the nose and the palm facing the front.

3. 左搂膝拗步 Left Form

（1）左腿屈膝后坐，左膝与脚尖同向，重心移于左腿，右膝放松右脚尖翘起，身向右转，右脚外撇 45 到 60 度角，随后脚掌落地，右腿屈膝前弓，右膝与脚尖同向，身体重心移至右腿。（图 31）

Sit back on the bent left leg (with the knee and tiptoe pointing at the same direction) to which the center of gravity is transferred. Relax the right knee and bend up the right tiptoe. Turn the body to the right. Turn the right foot outward for 45 to 60 degrees; then set the whole foot on the ground, and bend the right leg forward (with the knee and tiptoe still pointing at the same direction); move the center of gravity to the right leg.

图 31

（2）左脚收至右脚内测，脚尖点地，同时右手外旋掌心朝上，由右后向上划弧至右肩外侧 45 度（西南角），肘微屈，手腕与肩平，手心向上，左手随右转体向上，经面前向右下划弧，落于右胸前，手心向下，眼看右手方向，胸向西南。（图 32）

The left foot draws to the inner side of the right one with the tiptoe touching the ground. Meanwhile the right hand turns to face up and moves from the right-back upward in an arc to the outside (45 degrees) of the right shoulder, the elbow slightly bent and the wrist as high as the shoulder; then the left hand, following the body's right turn, goes up, passes the

图 32

55

face and falls in a curved way to the front of the right chest with the palm facing down. Eyes should follow the direction of the right hand, and the chest faces southwest.

（3）上体微左转，提起左脚向正东偏北方向迈出，脚跟着地，同时右臂屈肘右手至右耳侧。掌心斜向前，左手向下落至腹前护裆，掌心向下左臂呈弧形。(图33)

Turn the upper body left slightly. Move the left foot to the east (straying a bit to the north) with the heel on the ground; at the same time bend the right arm so that the hand reaches the side of the right ear. With the palm facing slantingly forward, the left hand should fall down to the front of the belly to protect the crotch, with the palm turned facing down and the arm in an arc-shape.

（4）左脚掌踏实成左弓步，左膝不得超过脚尖，右腿自然伸直，同时左手向前，经左膝弧形向左后搂出至左胯旁，右手向前推出（正东），右手指尖同鼻高，掌心斜向前，眼看右手方向。(图34、35)

The left foot steps firmly on the ground to make the left bow-shaped step (the knee not over passing the tiptoe); stretch the right leg naturally straight; meanwhile move the left hand forward, cross it with the left knee in an arc-line and draw back to the left hip side, while the right hand pushes forward (to the east) with its finger point as high as the nose and palm facing slanting forward. Eyes should follow the direction of the right hand.

图33　　　　　图34　　　　　图35

第一章 简化24式太极拳

口诀：①后坐翘脚；②转体收脚扬掌；③迈步屈臂；④搂膝弓步推掌。

Mnemonic lines: ① Sit back and bend up the tiptoe; ② Turn the body, draw the foot back and raise hands; ③ Step forward and bend arms; ④ Brush the knee, make the bow-shaped step, and push the hand.

要求：前推掌时，身体不可前俯后仰，要松腰松胯，推掌时要沉肩垂肘，坐腕舒掌，推掌与弓步上下要协调一致，即上下相随，左右转身应以腰为轴带动四肢。

Demands: When the hand pushes forward, the body should be kept upright, the waist and hips relaxed, and the hand stretched. Pushing the hand forward is in sync with bending the leg. In turning the body, the waist should be made the axis to lead the limbs.

（五）手挥琵琶 Playing the Lute

1. 腰微左转，右脚跟进半步，脚掌着地，随后上体后坐于右腿，同时腰右转，左脚跟略提起，向前移出半步，脚跟着地，脚尖翘起成左屈步，左膝微屈不可挺。（图36）

Turn the waist slightly left, and the right foot follows half a step forward with the sole touching the ground. Then move the upper body back to rest on the right leg; meanwhile the waist turns to the right, and the left foot goes half a step forward with the heel on the ground and the tiptoe bent up. The left knee should be kept slightly bent.

2. 左右手随身体后坐，弧形右转，左手由左下向上平举与肩平，掌心朝下，右手也随右转体，下落至胸高，两臂成弧形。（图37）

图36

学打太极拳

Following the back squatting of the upper body, the hands turn to the right in arc-lines, with the left one rising up from the left to the right (on the same level with the shoulder) with the palm facing down, and the right one falling to the height of the chest. The arms are in arc-shapes.

3. 两臂外旋右手合至左肘内侧,掌心向左,左手掌心向右,拇指对准鼻尖,眼看左手食指。(图38、39)

The arms twist outward, and the right hand moves to the inner side of the left elbow; then right palm faces left and left palm right (thumb pointing at the nose). Eyes are set on the left forefinger.

口诀:①跟半步松手;②后坐划弧;③虚步合臂。

Mnemonic lines: ① Take half a step forward and release hands; ② Sit backward and wave hands in arcs; ③ Make the left step void of force and draw the arms together.

要求:跟步时身体不可前倾,立身中正,沉肩垂肘,重心后移和左手上起,右手下落,虚步合臂要协调一致。

Demands: When the foot from behind follows up, the body does not bend forward and should be kept upright; with the shoulders and elbows are drooped. Coordination should be kept among the backward moving of the center of gravity, along with the rising of the left hand and falling of the right, the void step, and the drawing together of arms.

图37　　　　　　　图38　　　　　　　图39

第一章 简化24式太极拳

(六) 左右倒卷肱 (Reversed Brachium Twisting: Left and Right Form)

1. 左倒卷肱 Left Form

(1) 向右转体，右手外旋掌心向上，由腹前向后上方划弧至45度角，手举至西南方，臂微屈，左手随即外旋掌心向上(正东)。(图40、41)

Turn the body right; twist the right hand outward to face up, and make an arc from before the belly up to the back (southwest; forming 45 degrees angle with the left-right line) with the arm slightly bent. The left hand turns outward to face up (pointing at the east), too.

(2) 左腿提起向后约30度角退一步(正西偏北)脚掌先着地，然后全脚踏实，脚跟里落，使左脚尖朝东北方，身体重心移至左腿上，成右虚步，右脚掌为轴，随重心后移，由45度角蹍正脚尖朝前。(图42)

Take one step backward with the left leg (about 30 degrees to the northwest) with the sole on the ground first; before the whole foot then steps on the ground with the heel moved inward to make the tiptoe point northeast. Then transfer weight to the left leg to make the right foot void-forced, which then turns (the sole as axis) to point forward.

(3) 随左脚后撤、脚掌着地的同时，右臂屈肘向前，折手至右耳侧，掌心斜向前。(图43)

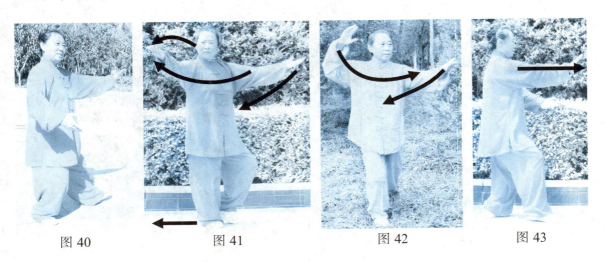

图40　　　　　图41　　　　　图42　　　　　图43

学打太极拳

During the time in which the left foot steps back, one should bend the right arm forward to make the hand reach the side of the right ear with the palm facing slantingly forward.

（4）随身体重心后移，右手经耳侧向前方推出，手心向前，左臂屈肘收至左肋内侧，眼的视线随着向右转体，先看右手，再转向前方看左手。（图44）

After the backward transfer of weight, push the right hand forward from the right ear, with the palm facing forward; bend the left arm to the inner side of the left costal region. Eyes should follow the right hand first when the body turns right, and then turn to look at the left hand at the front.

图 44

口诀：①转体撤手；②提膝翻掌；③撤步卷臂；④后坐蹍脚锉掌。

Mnemonic lines: ① Turn the body and draw the hand back; ② Lift the leg and twist the hand; ③ Draw one-step back and twist the arm; ④ Move the weight backward, turn the right foot to point forward, and push the right hand forward.

2. 右倒卷肱 Right Form

（1）上体微向左转，同时左手随转体向左后上方划弧平举（西北角），手心向上。右手随即掌心翻向上，眼随左转体，先看左手再转向前方看右手。（图45、46、47）

图 45　　　　　图 46　　　　　图 47

60

第一章　简化 24 式太极拳

Turn the upper body slightly left; and at the same time, raise the left hand in an arc-line up to the back (northwest) with palm facing upward. The right hand thereafter twists to face up, too. Eyes first look at the left hand when the body turns, and then move to concentrate on the right hand at the front afterwards.

（2）右腿提起，向右后约 30 度退一步（正西偏南），脚掌先着地，然后全脚踏实，脚跟里落，使右脚尖朝东南方向，身体重心后移坐在右腿上，成左虚步，左脚掌为轴，随重心后坐，跐正脚尖朝前。（图 48）

Take one step backward with the right foot to the southwest (about 30 degrees from the west); the sole touches the ground first, followed then the whole foot, while the heel is turned inward to make the tiptoe face southeast. Move weight to the right leg to make the left foot void-forced, which then turns (the sole as axis) to point at the front.

（3）随右脚后撤、脚掌着地的同时，左臂屈肘向前折，手至左耳侧，掌心斜向前。（图 49）

When the right foot moves backward and the sole touches the ground, bend the left arm to make the hand reach the side of the left ear with its palm facing slantingly forward.

图 48　　　　　　图 49

(4)随身体重心后移,左手经耳侧向前方推出,手心向前,右臂屈肘,收至左肋内侧。(图50)

When the body weight transfers backward, push one's left hand forward from the ear with the palm facing forward, and bend the right arm back to the inner side of the left costal region.

3. 左倒卷肱 Left Form

(1)向右转体,右手随转体向右后上方划弧平举至西南方向,掌心向上,臂成弧形;左手随掌心翻向上(正东),眼随右转体先看右手,再转向前方看左手。(图51、52、53)

图 50

Turn the body right; raise the right hand in an arc-line up to the back (southwest) with palm facing up and arm in arc-shape. The left arm hereafter turns to face up (pointing east). Eyes should follow the right hand first when the body turns right, and then move to focus on the left hand at the front.

(2)左腿提起向左后方约30度角(正西偏北)退一步,脚掌先着地,然后全脚踏实,脚跟里落,使左脚尖朝东北方,身体重心移至左腿上,成右虚步,以左脚

图 51　　　　　图 52　　　　　图 53

掌为轴,随重心后移,蹍正脚尖朝前(东),脚跟离地成左虚步。

Put the left foot one-step back to the northwest (about 30 degrees from the west); have the sole touch the ground first, then followed by the whole foot, Move weight to the left leg to make the right foot void-forced. Then turn the left leg (the sole as axis) to point at the front (east), and lift the heel to make the foot void-forced.

(3)随左脚后撤、脚掌着地的同时,右臂屈肘向前折,手至右耳侧,掌心斜向前。(图54)

When the left foot steps back and the heel touches the ground, bend the right arm to send the hand to the side of the right ear with palm facing slantingly forward while the heel is turned inward to make the tiptoe face northeast.

(4)随身体重心后移,右手经耳侧向前方推出,手心向前,左臂屈肘,收至左肋内侧。(图55)

图 54

图 55

学打太极拳

After the backward transfer of weight, push the right hand forward from the ear with palm facing forward, and bend the left arm back to the inner side of the left costal region.

口诀：① 转体撤手；② 提膝翻掌；③ 撤步卷臂；④ 后坐蹍脚锉掌。

Mnemonic lines: ① Turn the body and draw the hand back; ② Lift the leg and twist the hand; ③ Draw one-step back and twist the arm; ④ Move the weight backward, turn the right foot so it points forward, and push the right hand forward.

4. 右倒卷肱(同第二右倒卷肱)，解说略。 **Right Form**

The movements are the same with that in step 2.

口诀：① 转体撤手；② 提膝翻掌；③ 撤步卷臂；④ 后坐蹍脚锉掌。

Mnemonic lines: ① Turn the body and draw the hand back; ② Lift the leg and twist the hand; ③ Draw one-step back and twist the arm; ④ Move the weight backward, turn the left foot so it points forward, and push the left hand forward.

要求：前推之手不可推直，后撤之手也不可僵直，随转体仍走弧线。无论是撤手还是前推时，两手的速度要一致，要以腰为轴带动四肢，卷臂和撤步，后坐与推掌要上下相随。撤步避免使两脚落在一条直线上。

Demands: Both the forward pushing hand and the backward drawing hand should move in arc-lines following the body turn, and their speeds should be kept the same. The waist acts as the axis to lead the limbs to do the twisting of arms, backward stepping, backward squatting, and pushing hand are in coordination. In backward stepping, the feet should avoid being on the same line.

第三组：左揽雀尾　右揽雀尾

Group Three: Grabbing the Bird's Tail: Left and Right Form

（七）左揽雀尾 Left Form

1. 上体微右转,同时左右手逆时针划弧。（图 56）

Turn the upper body slightly right, and at the same time, the hands move counterclockwise in arc-lines.

2. 收左脚至右脚内侧,同时两手相对成抱球状,右手在上掌心向下,腕与肩平,左手在下掌心向上,眼视右臂前方。左手在下,掌心向上,手与腰平,眼看右手。（图 57）

Draw the left foot to the inner side of the right one; and use the hands to form the ball-holding gesture; the right palm faces down and the wrist should be as high as the shoulders, while the left palm, on the same level with the waist, faces up. Eyes are set on the right hand.

3. 上体微向左转,提起左脚向左前方迈出（正东偏北）,脚跟先着地,然后脚掌放平全脚着地。（图 58）

图 56　　　　　　　图 57　　　　　　　图 58

Turn the upper body slightly left. Put the left foot forward to the left (to the east, slightly straying to the north) with the heel on the ground first and followed then by the whole foot.

4. 左腿屈膝成左弓步,右腿自然伸直,同时上体继续左转,左臂向左前上方掤出,臂呈弧形,掌心向里,掤在胸前,胸向正东。同时右手向右,下落至右胯旁,手心向下,指尖向前,眼视左臂前方。(图59)

Bend the left leg to make a bow-shape, while the right leg stretches naturally straight; meanwhile the upper body keeps turning left, and the left arm (in arc-shape; palm facing inward) moves up to the left-front and stops before the east side of the chest. In the meantime, the right hand falls down to the side of the right hip with palm facing down and fingers pointing forward. Eyes are set on the front of the left arm.

5. 上体微向左转,左臂内旋向前伸出掌心向下,右手外旋掌心向上,经腹前向上、向前伸至左前臂下方。(图60)

Turn the upper body slightly left. The left arm twists inward to make the palm face down while it is stretched forward; and the right hand twists outward to make the palm face up while stretching upward and forward across the belly to the position beneath the left forearm.

图59

图60

第一章 简化24式太极拳

6. 右腿屈膝与脚尖同向,身体重心后移坐于右腿,随即向右转体,两手下捋。(图61)

Bend the right leg (the knee and tiptoe pointing at the same direction); transfer the center of gravity back to the right leg; and at the same time the body turns rightward and the hands should stroke down.

7. 上体向右转,左臂掤至胸前掌心向里,右手向右后上举扬掌,掌心斜向上。(图62、63)

Turn the upper body rightward. Shed the left arm before the chest with the palm facing inward, and raise the right hand to the right-back with the palm facing slantingly upward.

8. 上体向左转正(东),右手屈肘折回,附于左手腕内侧,掌心向前。(图64)

Turn the upper body leftward to the front (east). Bend the right arm to make the hand (palm facing forward) reach the inner side of the left wrist.

图61

图62

图63

图64

学打太极拳

9. 左腿屈膝前弓成左弓步,右腿自然伸直,同时两臂向前挤出,眼向前看。(图65、66)

   Bend the left leg to form a bow-shape, and stretch the right leg naturally straight. Meanwhile squeeze the arms forward. Set eyes on the front.

10. 两手由挤式变掌内旋,左右分开同肩宽,掌心向下。(图67)

    Part the hands as wide as the shoulders with palms turned facing down.

11. 右腿屈膝后坐,左腿自然伸直,膝关节放松,左脚尖上翘,两臂垂肘,两手收至腹前,掌心均向前下方。(图68、69)

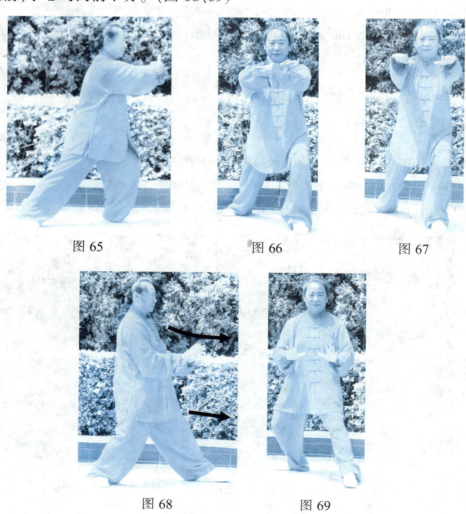

图65　　　　　图66　　　　　图67

图68　　　　　图69

第一章 简化24式太极拳

First, squat on the bent right leg. Then stretch the left leg naturally straight and bend the left toes up. Droop the elbows and draw the hands back to the front of the belly with palms facing down.

12. 脚尖放平,左腿屈膝前弓,右腿自然伸直,同时两手向前,弧形按出同胸高,两手心均向前下方,眼平视前方。(图70、71)

Set the bent left tiptoe back on the ground, and bend the left leg forward into a bow-shape; stretch the right leg naturally straight. At the same time, press the hands forward in arc-lines to a position as high as the chest, with both palms facing downward to the front. Eyes look horizontally forward.

口诀：① 转体划弧;② 收脚抱球;③ 转体上步;④ 弓步掤臂;⑤ 转体旋臂;⑥ 后坐下捋;⑦ 转体扬掌;⑧ 转正搭手;⑨ 弓步前挤;⑩ 抹掌分手;⑪ 后坐垂肘;⑫ 弓步按掌。

Mnemonic lines: ① Turn the body and wave hands in arcs; ② Draw the foot back and make a ball-holding gesture; ③ Turn the body and step forward; ④ Make the bow-shape step and *bing* arm; ⑤ Turn the body and twist the arm; ⑥ Squat backward and stroke hands down; ⑦ Turn the body and wave the hands; ⑧ Turn the body back to face the front and have your hands together; ⑨ Make the bow-shape step and squeeze the hands forward; ⑩ Separate your hands; ⑪ Squat back and droop the elbows; ⑫ Bend the leg into a bow-shape and press the hands.

图70　　　　　　图71

（八）右揽雀尾 Right Form

1. 屈右膝重心后移右腿，上体右转，两手放松，随上体右转，左脚尖内扣45到60度角（西南）。（图72）

Bend the right knee and transfer the center of gravity to the right leg; turn the upper body right with the hands relaxed. After the upper body's rightward turn, turn the left tiptoe about 45 to 60 degrees inward (to the southwest).

2. 右手向右，平行划弧至右侧，掌心向下，屈左膝重心移于左腿，随即收右脚至左脚内侧，同时左臂呈弧形，掌心向下，上掤于胸前，右手由右向下，掤于腹前，掌心向上，两手相对成抱球状，胸向西南。（图73）

Move the right hand in a horizontal arc-line to the right with the palm facing down. Bend the left knee and transfer the center of gravity to the left leg, while the right leg is drawn to the inner side of the left one; and at the same time, shed the left arm (in arc-shape) before the chest with palm facing down, and move the right hand downward to the front of the belly with palm facing up; the hands then form the ball-holding gesture. The chest faces southwest.

3. 上体微向右转，提起右脚向右前方迈出（正西偏北），脚跟着地，然后脚掌放平全脚落地。（图74）

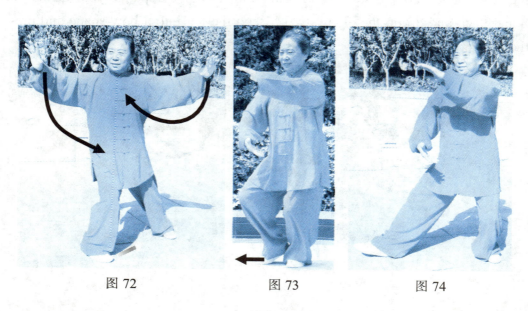

图72　　　　　　　图73　　　　　　　图74

第一章 简化24式太极拳

Turn the upper body slightly right. Put the right foot forward to the right (west, slightly straying to the north) with the heel on the ground first and then the whole foot.

4. 右腿屈膝成右弓步，左腿自然伸直，同时上体继续右转，右臂向右前上方掤出，臂呈弧形，掌心向里，掤在胸前，胸向正西。同时左手向左下落至左胯旁，手心向下，指尖向前，眼视右臂前方。（图75）

图 75

Bend the right leg into a bow-shape and stretch the left leg naturally straight. Meanwhile, keep the upper body turning rightward; the right arm (in arc-shape, palm facing inward) should move up to the right-front and stops before the west-facing chest; and at the same time the left hand falls down to the side of the left hip with palm facing down and fingers pointing forward. Set eyes on the front of the right arm.

5. 上体微向右转，右臂内旋掌心向下，向前伸出，左手外旋掌心向上，经腹前向上向前，伸至右前臂下方。（图76）

图 76

Turn the upper body slightly rightward. Twist the the right arm inward to make the palm face down while stretching forward; and twist the left arm outward to make the palm face up while stretching upward and forward across the belly to the position beneath the left forearm.

71

6. 左腿屈膝与脚尖同向，身体重心后移坐于左腿，随即向左转体，两手下捋。（图 77）

Bend the left leg (with the knee and tiptoe pointing at the same direction); transfer the center of gravity back to the left leg; at the same time the body turns leftward and the hands stroke down.

7. 上体向左转，右臂掤至胸前掌心向里，左手向左后上举扬掌 45 度角（东南），掌心斜向上。（图 78）

Turn the upper body leftward. Shed the right arm before the chest with the palm facing inward, and raise the left hand to the left-back with the palm facing slantingly upward.

8. 上体向右转正（西），左手屈肘折回，附于右手腕内侧，掌心向前。（图 79）

Turn the upper body rightward to the front (west). Bend the left arm to make the hand (with the palm facing forward) to reach the inner side of the right wrist.

图 77　　　　　　　　　图 78　　　　　　　　　图 79

第一章 简化24式太极拳

9. 右腿屈膝前弓成右弓步,左腿自然伸直,同时两臂向前挤出,眼向前看。(图80)

Bend the right leg to form a bow-shape, and stretch the left leg naturally straight. At the same time, squeeze the arms forward. Set eyes on the front.

10. 两手由挤式变掌内旋,左右分开同肩宽,掌心均向下。(图81)

Separate the hands as wide as the shoulders with palms turned facing down.

11. 左腿屈膝后坐,右腿自然伸直膝关节放松,右脚尖上翘,两臂垂肘,两手心均向前方收至腹前。(图82、83)

Squat on the bent left leg while the right leg stretches naturally straight and bend the right tiptoe up. Droop the elbows and draw the hands back to the front of the belly with palms facing forward.

图 80

图 81

图 82

图 83

学打太极拳

12. 右脚尖放平，右腿屈膝前弓，左腿自然伸直，同时两手向前弧形按出，两手心均向前下方，眼平视前方。（图84、85）

Set the bent right tiptoe back on the ground, and bend the right leg forward into a bow-shape: stretch the left leg naturally straight. At the same time, press the hands forward in arc-lines to the position as high as the chest, with both palms facing downward to the front. Eyes look horizontally forward.

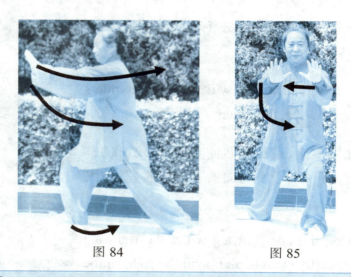

图84　　　　　图85

口诀：① 后坐转体扣脚；② 后坐收脚抱球；③ 转体上步；④ 弓步掤臂；⑤ 转体旋臂；⑥ 后坐下捋；⑦ 转体扬掌；⑧ 转正搭手；⑨ 弓步前挤；⑩ 抹掌分手；⑪ 后坐垂肘；⑫ 弓步按掌。

Mnemonic lines: ① Turn the body and wave hands in arcs; ② Draw the foot back and make a ball-holding gesture; ③ Turn the body and step forward; ④ Make the bow-shape step and *bing* arm; ⑤ Turn the body and twist the arm; ⑥ Squat backward and stroke your hands down; ⑦ Turn the body and wave the hands; ⑧ Turn the body back to face the front and put the hands together; ⑨ Make the bow-shape step and squeeze the hands forward; ⑩ Separate the hands; ⑪ Squat back and droop the elbows; ⑫ Bend the leg into a bow-shape and press the hands.

要求：向前按掌时两手要弧形前按，两肘下垂，松肩、转体、以腰带臂，后坐时松腰胯，眼随主动手走。弓步时膝关节不得超出脚尖，上体保持正直。

第一章 简化 24 式太极拳

Demands: When pressing forward, hands should follow arc-lines; while elbows and shoulders are drooped; turn the body and have the waist leads the arms. When squatting backward, keep the waist and hips relaxed, and eyes follow the major moving hand. In bow-shape step, the knee does not go beyond the tiptoe and the upper body is kept upright.

第四组：单鞭　云手　单鞭

Group Four: Single Whip, Cloud-Waving Hands, and Single Whip

（九）单鞭 Single Whip

1. 屈左膝重心后坐于左腿，右脚尖内扣，45度角（东南方），同时上体左转，左手内旋，掌心向外呈弧形，臂同肩平；右手外旋向下，向左弧形下掤至腹前，掌心斜向里。（图86）

图 86

Bend the left leg, to which the center of gravity is transferred. Turn the right tiptoe 45 degrees inward (southeast); and at the same time, turn the upper body leftward, and twist the left hand inward to make the palm face out, the arm (in arc-shape) on the same level with the shoulder; the right hand twists outward and goes down to the left to shed before the belly, with the palm facing slantingly inward.

2. 重心后移于右腿，同时右手由腹前向左、向上、向右划弧，左手由左上、向下、向右下划弧。

Transfer the center of gravity to the right leg. Meanwhile the right hand makes an arc following the left-up-right course from before the belly, and the left hand goes down to the right in an arc-line.

75

学打太极拳

3. 右手划至右后45度角至西南方，五指捏拢，勾手，指尖朝下突腕，左手划至右手腕内侧，掌心向里，同时提起左脚，收至右脚内侧。（图87）

The right hand goes to the right-back (45 degrees to the southwest) with fingers held together to make a hook which points downward and the wrist projecting up. Stretch the left hand to the inner side of the right wrist with palm facing in. Meanwhile the left foot is drawn to the inner side of the right foot.

4. 上体微左转，提起左脚向前，正东偏西，开胯上步，脚跟着地，脚掌放平踏实，左腿屈膝前弓，成左弓步，右腿自然伸直，同时左臂随上体左转，掤于胸前，随左弓步掌心内旋，掌心朝前推出，腕与肩平。肘松垂，眼视左手。（图88、89）

Turn the upper body slightly left. The left foot steps forward with the heel on the ground first and then the whole foot; bend the left leg to make a bow-shape, while the right leg stretches naturally straight. Meanwhile the left arm sheds before the chest when the upper body turns left and twists inward and pushes forward with palm facing the front; the wrist is then as high as the shoulder and the elbow is drooped. Eyes are set on the left hand.

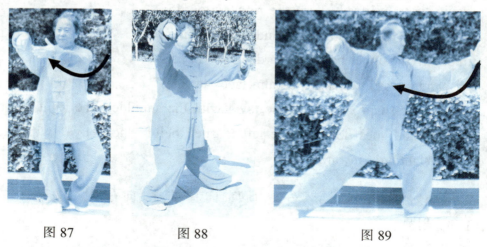

图87　　　　　　图88　　　　　　图89

口诀：①后坐转体划弧；②划弧收脚勾手；③转体上步；④弓步推掌。

Mnemonic lines: ① Squat back, turn the body and wave hands in arcs; ② Move the hand in an arc-line, draw the foot back, and transform the hand into

第一章 简化24式太极拳

a hook; ③ Turn the body and step forward; ④ Make the bow-shape step and push the hand.

要求：保持上身正直，左肘与左膝相对，右勾手与右脚尖相对，弓步时做到肩胯相合，力达掌根。

Demands: Keep the upper body upright. The left elbow should responds to the left knee and the right hook to the right tiptoe. When making the bow-shape step, keep the shoulders and hips in coordination. Exert force on the end of the palm.

（十）云手 Cloud-Waving Hands

1. 云手 1 Cloud-Waving Hands 1

（1）右腿屈膝重心移至右腿，上体右转，左脚尖内扣90度角（正南），同时左手随上体右转，向下向右外旋划弧，掌心斜朝里至腹前，继续向右上方划弧，掌心斜向上，掤于右胸前，同时松开右勾手，变掌心向下。（图90）

图90

Transfer the center of gravity to the bent right leg. Turn the upper body rightward with the left tiptoe 90 degrees inward (south). At the same time, the left hand, which is twisting outward, should wave in an arc-line down to the right when the upper body turns right, and reach the front of the belly with palm facing slantingly inward. Then it should keep moving up to in front of the right chest in an arc-line with palm facing slanting up, while the right hook transforms back into the palm which faces downward.

（2）左腿屈膝重心移至左腿，上体左转，左手经面前向左侧运转至左侧（东南方），左臂内旋，掌心斜朝下，右手由右向下经腹前，向左上划弧至左臂肘内侧，手心斜向里，同时右脚提起，靠近左脚约20公分落脚，成小开步，眼视左手方向。（图91）

图91

Bend the left leg, to which the center of gravity is then transferred. Turn the upper body leftward. The left hand then passes the face, moves to the left side (southeast), and the arm turns inward to make the palm face slantingly down. The right hand goes (in an arc-line) down from the right, which passes the belly, and waves up and leftward, to the inner side of the left elbow, with the palm facing slantingly inward. Meanwhile the right hand draws back to the position about 20cm from the left foot to form the minor parted step. Eyes are set on the direction of the left hand.

2. 云手 2 Cloud-Waving Hands 2

（1）上体再向右转，重心移于右腿，右手上掤，随右转体，内旋掌心，斜向下至西南方。同时左手经腹前，向右上划弧至右肩内侧，手心斜向上，随之左腿向左横跨一步，脚掌着地。（图92）

图92

Turn the upper body rightward again, and transfer the center of gravity to the right leg. The right hand, following the rightward turn of the upper body, goes up to the southwest with the palm twisted to face slantingly down. Meanwhile the left hand, passing the belly, goes in a curved line up and rightward to the inner side of the right shoulder, with the palm facing slantingly up. Shortly after, the left foot goes one-step to the left side with the sole touching the ground.

（2）向左转体，落实左脚跟，脚尖朝前（南方），随之左腿屈膝，重心移于左腿。

Turn the body leftward, and put the left foot completely on the ground, with the tiptoe pointing forward (south), while bending the left leg and the center of gravity is transferred to it.

第一章 简化24式太极拳

(3) 上体继续左转,右手由右向下,经腹前向左上划弧至左肩内侧,左手上掤,随左转体,内旋掌心斜向下至东南方。(图93)

The upper body keeps turning leftward. The right hand (from the right side) goes down, passes the belly, and waves up and leftward to the inner side of the left shoulder in an arc-line; while the left hand, following the left turn of the upper body, goes up to the southeast with the palm twisted to face slantingly down.

图 93

(4) 提起右脚,靠近左脚约20公分落脚,成小开步。眼视左手方向。(图94)

Lift the right foot up and put it to the position 20cm from the left one to form the minor parted step. Set eyes on the direction of the left hand.

3. 云手3 Cloud-Waving Hands 3

(1) 上体再向右转,重心移于右腿,同时左手向下经腹前,向右上划弧至右肩内侧,手心斜向上,右手上掤随右转体,内旋掌心,斜向下至西南方。随之腿向左横跨一步,脚掌着地。(图95)

图 94

Turn the upper body right, while the center of gravity is transferred to the right leg. Meanwhile the left hand falls down and passes the belly, then moves up and rightward in an arc-line to the inner side of the right shoulder with the palm facing slantingly up; while the right hand, following the rightward turn of the upper body, goes up to the southwest, with the

图 95

palm twisted to face slantingly down. Whereat, the left leg goes one-step to the left side with the sole on the ground.

(2) 向左转体,落实左脚跟,脚尖朝前(南方),随之左腿屈膝,重心移于左腿;

Turn the body left and put the left foot completely on the ground with the tiptoe pointing forward (south). Then bend the left leg so the center of gravity is transferred to it.

(3) 上体继续左转,右手由右向下,经腹前向左上划弧至左肩内侧,左手上掤,随左转体,内旋掌心,斜向下至东南方。(图96)

The upper body keeps turning leftward. The right hand (from the right side) goes down, passes the belly, and waves up and leftward in an arc-line to the inner side of the left shoulder; while the left hand, following the left turn of the upper body, goes up to the southeast with the palm twisted to face slantingly down.

图 96

(4) 提起右脚,靠近左脚约20公分落脚,成小开步。眼视左手方向。(图97)

Lift the right foot up and put it to the position 20cm from the left one to form the minor parted step. Set eyes on the direction of the left hand.

口诀:①后坐扣脚转体划弧;②转体划弧收脚称掌;③转体划弧出步称掌;④转体划弧收脚称掌。

Mnemonic lines: ① Squat back, turn the tiptoe inward, turn the body, and wave the hand in arc-line; ② Turn the body, wave the hand in arc-line, draw back

图 97

the foot, and exchange the hand movements; ③ Turn the body, wave the hand in arc-line, step to the side, and exchange the hand movements; ④ Turn the body, wave the hand in arc-line, draw back the foot, and exchange the hand movements.

要求：身体左右转动要以腰脊为轴，松腰、松胯。两脚平行运动，身体保持水平高，不可忽高忽低。下肢运动时重心要平稳，做到上下相随。

Demands: When the body turns, the waist and spine should be taken as the axis, while the waist and hips are relaxed. Feet should move in parallel lines, and the body is kept at a constant level (no sudden rising or lowering). The body should be kept balanced when the legs move, so coordination between the upper and lower body should be achieved.

（十一）单鞭 Single Whip

1. 向右转体，右手随之向右运转至西南方，掌内旋成右勾手，突腕。左手向下经腹前，向右上划弧至右腕内侧，手心斜向里，身体重心移于右腿，左脚收至右脚内侧，脚尖着地，成左虚步，眼看右手。（图98、99）

Turn the body rightward, and the right hand follows to reach southwest (right side) while twisting inward to form the hook with the wrist projected up.

图98

图99

学打太极拳

The left hand goes down, passes before the belly, and waves up, rightward to the inner side of the right wrist, with the palm facing slantingly inward. Transfer the weight to the right leg, and draw the left foot to the inner side of the right one, the tiptoe touching the ground (left void step). Set eyes on the right hand.

2. 上体微向左转,左脚向左前方,正东偏北迈出一步,脚跟着地,左手随左转体,掤在胸前,落实左脚,重心移于左腿成左弓步,右腿自然伸直,右脚蹬地,脚尖朝东南方,同时左掌内旋向前推出(正东)。力达掌根,眼视左手方向。(图100)

图 100

Turn the upper body slightly left. Put the left foot one-step forward to the left with the heel touching the ground, while the left hand, as the upper body turns, sheds before the chest. Set the whole left foot on the ground; bend the left leg into a bow and transfer the weight on it; stretch the right leg naturally straight, with the whole right foot on the ground and the tiptoe pointing southeast (left-front). At the same time, the left hand twists inward and pushes forward (east) with force exerted on the end of the palm. Set eyes on the direction of the left hand.

口诀:① 转体划弧虚脚勾手;② 转体上步弓步推掌。

Mnemonic lines: ① Turn the body, wave the hand in arc-line, make the foot void-forced, and transform palm into hook; ② Turn the body, make a step, bend the leg into a bow, and push the hand.

要求:与前边单鞭式要求相同。

Demands: Consult that of the Single Whip above (ix).

第一章　简化24式太极拳

第五组：高探马　右蹬脚　双峰贯耳　转身左蹬脚

Group Five: Patting the Horse, Right Kicking, Striking Ears with Both Hands, and Turning Kicking with Left Foot

（十二）高探马 Patting the Horse

1. 重心前移左腿，右脚向前跟进半步，同时右勾手变成掌，掌心向上，身体重心逐渐后移，坐至右腿上，左脚抬起脚掌着地成左虚步。左手同时外旋掌心向上，两肘微屈呈弧形。（图101）

图 101

Move the center of gravity forward to the left leg, and take a half a step forward with the right foot. Meanwhile the right hand changes from hook into palm (facing up). The weight moves slowly back to the right leg, and the left foot is lifted with only the sole touching the ground (left void-step). Simultaneously the left hand twists outward to make the palm face up and the elbows are slightly bent and the arms in arc-shape.

2. 重心后移时身体微向右转，然后身体再向左转，胸向正东，右臂屈肘，右掌经耳侧向前推出，手心向前，指尖高不过口，左手屈臂，收至左侧腰前，手心向上。（图102、103）

图 102　　　　　　图 103

学打太极拳

Turn the body slightly rightward when the weight moves back. Then turn the body leftward, with the chest facing east; while bending the right arm and pushing the hand forward from the side of the right ear, with the palm facing forward and fingers not higher than the mouth; the left hand draws back to the front of the left waist side, palm facing upward.

3. 同时左脚向前移动，脚前掌着地成左虚步，眼看右手方向。（图104）

At the same time, move the left foot forward with the front sole touching the ground. Set eyes on the direction of the right hand.

图104

口诀：①跟半步松勾；②后坐翻掌；③虚步锉掌点脚。

Mnemonic lines: ① Follow half a step forward and transform hook into palm; ② Squat backward and twist the palm; ③ Make the void step, move the hands (passing each other) to opposite directions, and point at the ground with the tiptoe.

要求：上体自然正直，沉肩垂肘，跟步重心前移时身体不可起伏，虚步锉掌时上下要协调配合，两掌相锉后右掌心斜向下，左掌心朝上。

Demands: Keep the upper body upright, and the shoulders and elbows drooped. The body should not move up and down when the center of gravity moves forward. The passing by of hands and the void step should be coordinated. After the hands pass by each other, the right palm should face slantingly down and the left one up.

第一章 简化24式太极拳

（十三）右蹬脚 Right Kicking

1. 重心于右腿，左脚收至右脚内侧，身体微向右转，同时左掌心向上，向前伸，穿至右手腕背面，两手交叉。（图105）

Transfer the center of gravity to the right leg and draw the left foot to the inner side of the right one. Turn the body slightly rightward;   have the left hand (palm facing up) pierce forward to the back of the right hand (to make the hands cross).

2. 身体微左转，提起左脚向左前方上步（正东偏北），脚跟着地，落实左脚掌，同时左手内旋，掌心朝外，两手微分，掌心均斜朝前。（图106）

Turn the body slightly left. Step the left foot to the left-front (northeast) with the heel on the ground first and then followed by the whole foot. Meanwhile the left hand twists inward to make the palm face outward. Separate the hands slightly with both palms facing slantingly forward.

3. 重心前移左腿，右腿自然伸直，成左弓步；同时两掌分别向左右弧形分开，与肩平。（图107）

Move your weight forward to the left leg and stretch the right leg naturally straight to form the left bow-shape step. At the same time, separate the hands to their respective sides (on the same level with shoulders).

图105　　　　　图106　　　　　图107

学打太极拳

4. 重心全部移于左腿，两手继续弧形，向下、向上划弧，运转交叉，合抱于胸前，右手在外，掌心均向里，同时提起右腿，同腰平，膝关节与右肘上下相合，左腿直立，膝关节放松，成左独立步。（图108、109）

First put weight completely on the left leg. Hands keep going downward and upward in arc-lines to cross before the chest, the right one on the outside with both palms facing inward. Meanwhile, the right leg is lifted up to the level of the waist; and the knee responds to the right elbow. The left leg then stands straight with the knee relaxed.

5. 两臂分别向左右划弧，分开平举，肘部微屈，手心均向外，同时右脚向右前方慢慢蹬出（东南方），眼视蹬脚方向。右手与右蹬脚方向一致，左手分至左后方（西北角）。两臂微屈。（图110、111）

Arms part to their respective side with elbows slightly bent and palms facing forward. Meanwhile the right foot kicks slowly to the right-front (southeast). Eyes should be set on the kicking direction. Put the

图110

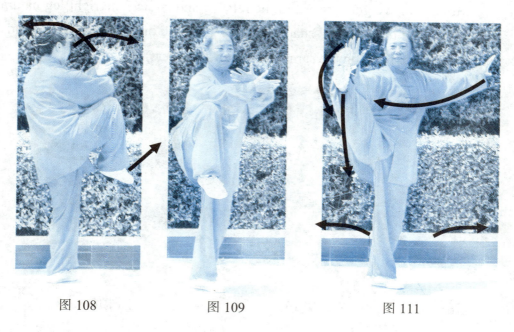

图108　　　　　图109　　　　　图111

right hand in the same direction with the kicking, and move the left one to the left-back (northwest). Keep elbows slightly bent.

口诀：①收脚穿掌；②上步翻掌；③弓步分掌；④提膝合抱；⑤蹬脚分掌。

Mnemonic lines: ① Draw the foot and put the hand through; ② Step forward and twist the hand; ③ Make a bow-shape step and part hands; ④ Lift up the leg and cross hands; ⑤ Kick with the right foot and part hands.

要求：独立步要平稳定，不可前俯后仰，两手分开时腕部与肩平，提膝合抱掌时，右膝与右肘相合。分掌蹬脚之右肘与右膝，右手与右脚，右肩与右胯要相合，做到外三合。

Demands: The single-legged standing should be steady (the upper body does not swing back and forth). Wrists should be on the same level with shoulders when hands are separated. When the right leg is lifted and hands cross, the right knee should be in opposition to the right elbow. At the time of kicking and parting hands, coordination should be achieved between the right elbow and knee, the right hand and foot, and the right shoulder and hip.

（十四）双峰贯耳 Striking Ears with Both Hands

1. 右小腿屈膝收回，小腿自然下垂，脚脖自然放松，膝关节同腰平。同时向右转体，左手由后向上、向前下落至体前，两手心均外旋，掌心向上，并同时向下划弧，分别落于右膝关节两侧，眼看前方。（图112）

The right foreleg draws back to droop down naturally; the ankle is relaxed; and the knee is on the same level with the waist. Meanwhile turn the upper body rightward; the left hand goes up and forward from the left-back to the front of the body; both palms twist outward to face up and fall down in arc-lines to each side of the right knee. Eyes are fixed at the front.

图 112

2. 左腿屈膝下沉, 右脚向右前方落下, 脚跟先着地, (正东偏南), 两掌同时向下分至腰间。(图113)

The left leg bends down and the right foot drops (to the right-front) with the heel touching the ground first. Both hands go downward to the waist side.

3. 右脚踏实, 身体重心移于右腿, 逐成右弓步, 后腿自然伸直, 同时两手握拳, 分别从两侧向上、向前圈打, 与头同高同宽, 两拳相对, 拳眼斜向下。(图114)

Set the right foot solidly on the ground and move weight to the right leg to make the right leg bow-shaped; then stretch the left leg straight. Meanwhile the hands form fists, and strike from the sides up and forward in a circled way, reaching the position as high and wide as the head, the fists in opposition and the thumb-sides facing slanting downward.

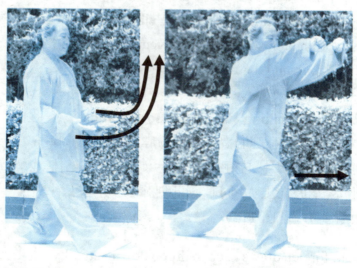

图113　　　　　　　图114

口诀：① 转体收脚落掌；② 上步分掌握拳；③ 弓步贯拳。

Mnemonic lines: ① Turn the body, draw back the foot, and drop hands; ② Step to the right-front, part hands, and form fists; ③ Make a bow-shape step and strike with fists.

第一章　简化24式太极拳

> **要求**：头颈正直,两拳松握,双峰贯耳方向同蹬脚方向一致,两臂保持弧形,沉肩坠肘,松腰胯。
>
> **Demands:** Keep the head and neck upright. Close hands in a loose way. The direction of ear striking is the same as that of the kicking. Keep both arms in arc-shapes. Keep shoulders and elbows drooped, and keep waist and hips relaxed.

（十五）转身左蹬脚 Turning and Kicking with Left Foot

1. 左腿屈膝后坐,身体重心移于左腿,上体左转,右脚内扣,脚尖扣至约东北角。同时两拳变掌。（图115）

Bend the left leg to squat on it, while the weight is transferred to it. Turn the upper body leftward. The right tiptoe turns inward (approximately northeast). Meanwhile the fists change back into palms.

2. 上体继续左转,身体重心再移至右腿,两掌由上向左右划弧,分开平举,两肘微屈,手心向前,眼看左手。（图116）

The upper body keeps turning leftward while the weight is transferred back to the right leg. Hands part in arc-lines to opposite directions (left and right) with elbows slightly bent and palms facing forward. Set eyes on the left hand.

图 115

图 116

学打太极拳

3. 左腿屈膝提起同腰平，两手向下、向上划弧交叉合抱于胸前，左手在外。（图117、118、119）

Lift the left leg up to make the knee on the same level with the waist. Move the hands downward and then upward in arc-lines to cross before the chest (the left one on the outside).

4. 左脚向左前方慢慢蹬出（西北方），两手同时左右弧形分开，眼看左手蹬脚方向，左手与左蹬脚方向一致，右手分至右后方（东南角）。两臂微屈。（图120）

Kick the left foot slowly to the left-front (northwest); at the same time the hands part to their respective sides in arc-lines. Eyes are set on the direction of the kicking, and the left hand points to the same direction; while the right hand moves to the right-back (southeast). Keep the arms slightly bent.

口诀：①后坐转体扣脚松掌；②转体后坐分掌；③提膝合抱；④蹬脚分掌。

Mnemonic lines: ① Squat back, turn the body, turn the tiptoe inward, and change fists into palms; ② Turn the body, squat backward, and separate the hands; ③ Lift the left leg and cross the hands; ④ Kick with the left foot and part hands.

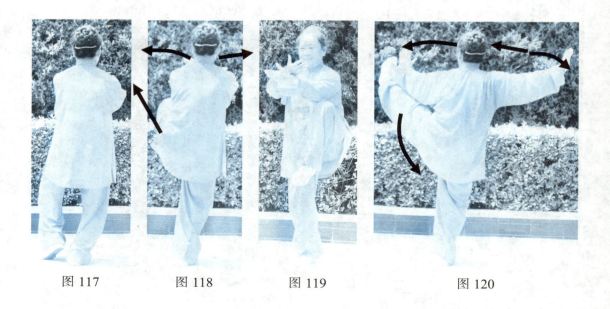

图117　　　　图118　　　　图119　　　　图120

第一章 简化24式太极拳

要求：与右蹬脚式相同，只是左右相反，左蹬脚方向与右蹬脚方向成180度。独立步要平稳，做到外三合。

Demands: Same as the right form of kicking except for the direction. Keep the legs balanced and steady. Coordination should be achieved between the left elbow and knee, the left hand and foot, and the left shoulder and hip.

第六组：左下势独立　右下势独立

Group Six: Squatting and Single-Legged Standing: Left and Right Form

（十六）左下势独立 Squatting and Single-Legged Standing: Left Form

1. 左腿屈膝收回与腰平，上体右转，左掌随转体向上、向右划弧，下落立于右肩前，掌心斜向外，右掌抓勾成勾手，略高于肩，勾尖向下，突腕（东北角）。（图121、122）

Draw the left leg back by bending the knee as high as the waist. Turn the body rightward. The left hand, as the body turns, moves up and rightward in an arc-line, and falls down to before the right shoulder, palm facing slantingly forward; the right hand (northeast) transforms into a hook a little higher than the shoulder and pointing down. The wrist projects up.

图121　　　　　　图122

2. 右腿屈膝身体下沉，右腿全蹲，右膝关节与右脚尖同向。左腿向左侧偏后伸出，脚掌落地，脚跟外蹬，使左脚尖直朝前（北）成左仆步。（图123、124）

Bend the right leg until it completely squats with the knee and tiptoe pointing at the same direction. Stretch the left leg to the left side (straying slightly to the back) with the sole touching the ground and the heel thrusting outward to make the tiptoe point forward (north), which should form the left form of crouching step.

3. 左手下落经右膝裆前，顺左腿内侧向前穿出，至左脚脖内侧，右勾手不变。（图125、126）

The left hand falls and pierces along the right knee with the crotch and the inner side of the left leg to the ankle, while the right hook does not move.

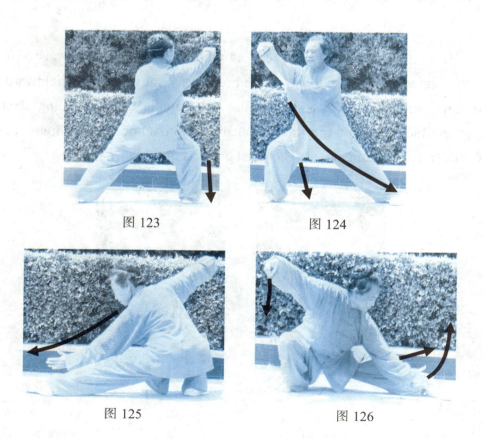

图123　　　　　　　图124

图125　　　　　　　图126

第一章 简化24式太极拳

4. 以左脚跟为轴,脚尖外撇至正西偏南,左腿屈膝前弓,重心前移成左弓步,右腿随左弓步自然蹬直,右脚内扣西北方,随重心前移。同时上体向左转身并向前起身,左掌继续向前、向上立掌穿出,拇指对鼻尖,掌心向右,右勾手下落至右胯后,勾尖翻向上,眼看左手。(图127、128、129)

Make the left heel axis and turn the tiptoe outward to the west (straying slightly to the south); bend the left leg and move the center of gravity forward to make the left bow-shaped step while the right leg stretches naturally straight and the tiptoe turns to the northwest. Meanwhile the upper body turns left and rises forward; and the left hand keeps piercing forward and upward (fingers pointing up) with the thumb pointing at the nose and the palm facing right. Then the right hook falls to the back of the right hip with fingers turned to point up. Set eyes on the left hand.

图 127

图 128

图 129

学打太极拳

5. 重心全部移至左腿，右腿慢慢提起平屈，膝关节同腰平，小腿自然下垂。左腿直立膝微屈，同时右勾手变掌，由后下方顺右腿外侧向前弧形挑出，掌心向左（拇指同鼻高），屈肘立于右膝上方（肘与膝相合），左手下落于左胯旁，掌心向下，指尖朝前，眼看右手方向。（图130、131、132、133）

图 130

Transfer weight completely to the left leg. Lift up the right leg slowly until the knee is on the same level with the waist, and then have the foreleg drooping naturally. Stand on the left leg with the knee slightly bent. At the same time, the right hook changes into a palm, rises up along the outside of the right leg (palm facing left) and stops above the right knee (thumb as high as the nose) with the elbow bent (responding to the knee). The left hand falls to the side of the left hip with palm facing down and the fingers pointing forward. Eyes follow the direction of the right hand.

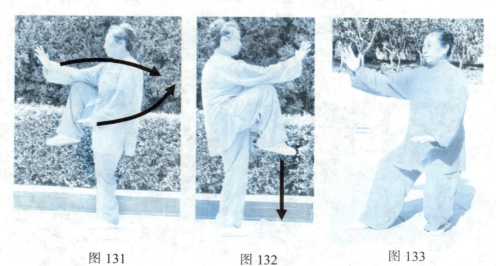

图 131　　　　图 132　　　　图 133

口诀：①收脚勾手；②蹲身仆步；③下势穿掌；④弓步起身；⑤独立挑掌。
Mnemonic lines: ① Draw back the foot and form the hook; ② Squat down

and make the crouching step; ③ Droop down and pierce with the hand; ④ Make the leg bow-shaped and rise; ⑤ Stand single-legged and raise the right hand in a digging way.

要求： 仆步时左脚尖与右脚跟踏在中轴线上。弓步起身时臀部不可左右摇摆。独立步要稳定。支撑腿膝关节微屈。

Demands: In the crouching step, the left tiptoe and right heel should be on the central line. When the left leg bends and the body rises, the hips do not swing to either side. Keep the single-legged standing steady and balanced and the supporting leg slightly bent.

（十七）右下势独立 Squatting and Single-Legged Standing: Right Form

1. 左腿屈膝下沉，右脚下落于左脚前，脚掌着地。

The left leg bends to droop down and the right foot drops down before the left foot with its sole touching the ground.

2. 以左脚前掌为轴脚跟转动，身体随之向左转至东南方，右脚收至左脚内侧，同时左手随转体向下向后划弧提腕成勾手至东南方略高于肩。右手也同时随转体向左划弧至左勾手内侧前掌心斜向勾手，眼看左勾手。（图134）

图 134

The left heel turns around the sole (the axis); the body turns left to the southeast and the right foot draws back to the inner side of the left foot. Meanwhile the left hand, as the body turns, moves down, backwards, and up to the southeast (a little higher than the shoulder) while the palm is changed into a hook. The right hand, in the meantime, moves leftward in an arc-line to the inner side of the left hook, with the palm facing the hook slantingly. Set eyes on the left hook.

学打太极拳

3. 左腿屈膝下沉提起右腿向右侧偏后伸出,脚掌落地,脚跟外蹬,使右脚尖朝前(南)成右仆步,右手下落经左膝、裆前顺右腿内侧向前穿出,至左脚脖内侧,掌心朝外,左勾手不变。(图135、136)

Bend the left leg to squat, and stretch the right leg to the right side (straying slightly backward) with the sole on the ground and the heel thrusting outward to make the right form of crouching step (tiptoe pointing forward to the south). The right hand falls down and pierces along the left knee, the crotch, and the inner side of the right leg to the ankle, with the palm facing outward, while the left hook does not change its gesture.

4. 以右脚跟为轴,脚尖外撇至正西偏北,右腿屈膝前弓,重心前移成右弓步,左腿随右弓步自然蹬直,脚尖内扣(西南方),随之重心前移,同时身体向右转身并向前起身,右掌继续向前、向上,立掌穿出,拇指同鼻高,掌心向左,左勾手下至左胯后,勾尖翻向上,眼看右手。(图137)

Turn the right tiptoe outward to the west (straying a bit to the north) by taking the heel as the axis. Then bend the right leg and move the center of gravity forward to make the right bow-shaped step, while the right leg stretches naturally straight

图 135

图 136

图 137

第一章 简化 24 式太极拳

and the tiptoe turns inward to the southwest. Meanwhile the upper body turns right and rises forward; and the right hand keeps piercing forward and upward (fingers pointing up) with the thumb pointing at the nose and the palm facing left; the left hook then falls to the back of the left hip with fingers turned to point up. Set eyes on the right hand.

5. 重心全部移至右腿，左腿慢慢提起平屈，膝关节同腰平。右腿直立膝微屈，同时左勾手变掌，由后下方顺左腿外侧向前弧形挑出，掌心向右，屈肘立于左膝上方（肘与膝相对），拇指对鼻尖，右手下落至右胯旁，掌心向下，指尖朝前。眼看左手方向。（图138）

图 138

Transfer weight completely to the right leg. Lift up the right leg slowly until the knee is on the same level with the waist with the foreleg drooping naturally. Stand on the right leg with the knee slightly bent. At the same time, change the left hook into a palm, and rise up along the outside of the left leg (palm facing right) and stops above the left knee (thumb as high as the nose) with the elbow bent (responding to the knee). The right hand falls to the side of the right hip with the palm facing down and fingers pointing forward. Eyes follow the direction of the left hand.

口诀：① 转体收脚搭手；② 蹲身仆步；③ 下势穿掌；④ 弓步起身；⑤ 独立挑掌。

Mnemonic lines: ① Turn the body, draw back the foot, and form the hook; ② Squat down and make the crouching step; ③ Droop down and pierce with the hand; ④ Make the leg bow-shaped and rise; ⑤ Stand single-legged and raise the left hand in a digging way.

要求：同左下势独立（略）。

The essentials are the same as that of the left form.

学打太极拳

第七组：左右穿梭　海底针　闪通臂

Group Seven: Shuttle Throwing (Left and Right Forms), Picking the Needle from the Seabed, and Flashing Arm

（十八）左右穿梭 Shuttle Throwing

1. 左穿梭 Shuttle Throwing: Left Form

（1）右腿屈膝下沉，身体微向左转，左脚向前迈出一步（西偏南方），脚跟落地，脚脖放松，使脚尖平放至正西偏南。重心前移同时右脚跟离地，两腿屈膝成半坐盘式，左手内旋掌心向下，右手外旋掌心向上，左手在上、右手在下。（图139）

图 139

Bend the right leg and turn the body slightly left. Put the left foot one-step forward (west, straying slightly to the south) with the heel on the ground first; relax the ankle, and let the tiptoe point at the west (straying slightly to the south). Move the center of gravity forward, and at the same time that the right heel is lifted up; bend both legs to form the half-hunkering pose. The left hand twists inward to face down, while the right one twists outward to face up (the left one above the right one).

图 140

（2）随转体在胸前成抱球状，右脚同时收至左脚内侧，眼看左前臂。（图140）

Following the body turn, hands form a ball-holding gesture, and at the same time, the right foot withdraws to the inner side of the left foot. Set eyes on the left forearm.

（3）身体右转，提起右脚向右前方迈出（正西偏北），脚跟先着地，脚掌放平。（图141）

图 141

第一章 简化24式太极拳

Turn the body rightward. Lift the right foot and put it to the right-front (west, straying slightly to the north) with the heel on the ground first and then the whole foot.

(4) 屈膝成右弓步，同时右手由脸前向上使小臂内旋，掤架在右额前上方，掌心斜向上；左手由上向左下，经左腰前，向前推出（西南方），掌心朝前。眼看左手。（图142）

图142

Bend the right leg to make it bow-shaped. Meanwhile, the right hand goes up, passes the face, and stops before (a little higher) the right side of forehead, with the forearm twisted inward and the palm facing slantingly up. The left hand goes down to the left and pushes forward (southwest) from the left-front of the waist with palm facing forward. Eyes are set on the left hand.

> **口诀：**① 沉身落脚；② 收脚抱球；③ 上步滚球；④ 弓步推架。
>
> **Mnemonic lines:** ① Move the center of gravity down and set the foot on the ground; ② Draw the foot back and make a ball-holding gesture; ③ Step forward and roll the "ball"; ④ Make the bow-shape step, raise the right hand in the shedding way, and push the left hand forward.

2. 右穿梭（Shuttle Throwing: Right Form）

(1) 身体微向左转，左腿屈膝，重心后移至左腿，右脚尖翘起，外撇至西北角，身体重心即再移至右腿，然后收左脚至右脚内侧，同时两手成抱球状（左手在下、右手在上），眼看右前臂。（图143）

Turn the body slightly leftward. Bend the left leg and move weight to it. Bend the right tiptoe up, and turn it outward to the northwest, while the body weight is transferred back to

图143

the right leg. The left foot then is drawn back to the inner side of the right one; and at the same time the hands make the ball-holding gesture (left hand above right hand). Eyes are set on the right forearm.

（2）身体左转，左脚向左前迈出（正西偏南），脚跟着地，脚掌放平。（图144）

Turn the body leftward, and put the left foot forward to the left-front (west, straying a bit to the south) with the heel on the ground first and then followed by the whole foot.

图144

（3）屈膝成左弓步，同时左手由脸前向上，使小臂内旋掤架在左额前上方，掌心斜向上；右手由上向左下经右腰前向前推出，掌心朝前。眼看右手。（图145）

Bend the left leg to make it bow-shaped. Meanwhile the left hand goes up, passes the face, and stops in the shedding way before (a little higher) the left side of forehead with the forearm twisted inward and the palm facing slantingly up. The right hand goes down to the left and pushes forward from the right-front of the waist with palm facing forward. Eyes are set on the right hand.

图145

口诀：①后坐转体划弧；②移重心收脚抱球；③转体上步滚球；④弓步推架。

Mnemonic lines: ① Squat back, turn the body, and wave hands in arcs; ② Move the center of gravity back and forth, draw the foot back and make a ball-holding gesture; ③ Turn the body, step forward and roll the "ball"; ④ Make the bow-shape step, raise the left arm in the shedding way, and push the right hand forward.

第一章 简化 24 式太极拳

> **要求**：弓步推掌后，上体不可前倾，滚球上步时，上步与掤臂要协调一致，上下相随，要与上掤臂协调一致。
>
> **Demands:** The upper body does not lean forth after the leg bends and the hand being pushed forward. The forward stepping and the upward should be in coordination.

（十九）海底针 Picking the Needle from the Seabed

1. 身体微向左转，右手放松，同时右脚跟进半步，脚前掌着地。（图 146）

   Turn the body slightly leftward; make the right hand relaxed. The right foot follows half a step forward with the front sole touching the ground.

2. 放平右脚跟，身体右转，重心移于右腿上，右手随右转体，向下经腹前向右划弧至腹前，掌心向里；左手外旋，随右转体，立掌至右肩内侧，掌心向右。（图 147、148）

   Set the right heel on the ground, turn the body rightward, and transfer the center of gravity to the right leg. The right hand, as the body turns, goes down, passes the belly and moves rightward in arc-line to the front of the belly (palm facing in). The left hand twists outward and, as the body turns right, reaches the inner side of the right shoulder with fingers pointing up and the palm facing right.

图 146　　　　　图 147　　　　　图 148

学打太极拳

3. 右手向上提抽至右肩上方,掌心向内,指尖斜向前下方,左手同时下落至腹前,掌心向下。(图149、150)

Lift the right hand up to above the right shoulder with palm facing in and fingers pointing slantingly down to the front. At the same time the left hand falls to the front of the belly with palm facing down.

4. 提起左脚微向前移,脚掌着地,左膝微屈,脚前掌点地成左虚步,右手由右肩上方向前下方斜插出,力达指尖。掌心向左,左手由腹前向前,经左膝向左后搂出至左胯旁。眼看右手。(图151、152)

Lift the left foot and move it forward with the sole touching the ground, and then bend the leg to make the foot void-forced (the front sole on the ground). Poke down with the right hand to the front from above the right shoulder with force exerted on fingertips and the palm facing left. The left hand moves forward from before the belly, passes the left knee, and draws back to the side of the left hip. Set eyes on the right hand.

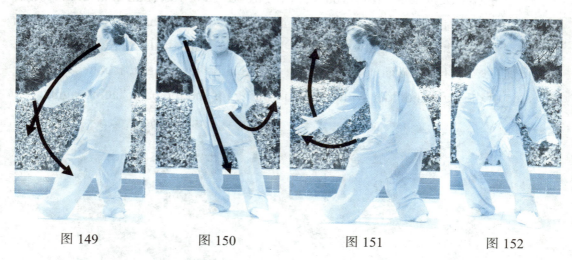

图149　　　　图150　　　　图151　　　　图152

口诀:①跟半步松手;②后坐转体划弧;③虚步提掌;④搂膝插掌。

Mnemonic lines: ① Follow half a step forward and loosen the right hand; ② Squat backward, turn the body and wave hands in arc-lines; ③ Make the left

第一章 简化24式太极拳

foot void-forced and lift the right hand up; ④ Brush the left knee and poke with the right hand.

要求：向下插掌上体不可前倾，不可低头突臀，两手划弧要在腰的转动下完成。

Demands: In poking with the right hand, the upper body does not lean forward; the head is not lowered; and the buttocks do not move out. The hands are led by the waist's turning and thus wave in arc-lines.

（二十）闪通臂 Flashing Arm

1. 上体慢慢起身直腰立顶，上体微向右转，重心坐于右腿；右手随起身上提，举至右额前方，左手同时上提，指尖搭于右手腕内侧，掌心向外。（图153）

Raise the body up slowly; keep the waist and head upright. Turn the upper body slightly rightward and transfer the center of gravity to the right leg. As the body rises, lift the right hand up to the front of the right forehead; and at the same time the left hand is raised up till the fingers reach the inner side of the right wrist (palm facing outward).

图153

2. 上体右转，提起左脚向前迈出，正西偏南，脚跟着地，右掌内旋掌心向外。

Turn the upper body rightward, and put the left foot forward to the west (straying to the south), with the heel touching the ground. Twist the right hand inward to face out.

3. 左脚放平重心前移，左腿屈膝成左弓步，右手向上、向后弧形屈臂，上举至右额前方，左手向前推出，掌心向左；左右手虎口相对。胸向西偏北。眼看左手。（图154）

图154

学打太极拳

Set the left foot completely on the ground and bend the left leg into a bow-shape. The right hand goes upward and backward in an arc-line to the front of the right forehead; the arm is kept bent. The left hand pushes forward with palm facing left. The "tiger's mouths" (the arcs formed by thumbs and forefingers) of both hands face each other. Chest then faces northwest. Set eyes on the left hand.

> 口诀：①直腰搭手；②转身上步；③弓步分手。
>
> **Mnemonic lines:** ① Set the waist upright and have your hands together; ② Turn the body and step forward; ③ Make the bow-shape step and part hands.
>
> 要求：弓步、推掌、举臂要协调一致，左脚上步至西偏南，不可在一条直线上。定式时上体自然正直。
>
> **Demands:** Coordination should be kept along the bow-shape step, pushing forward the hand and raising of the right arm. Put the left foot forward to the west (straying to the south); do not keep the feet on the same line. In the still pose, the upper body should be kept naturally upright.

第八组：转身搬拦捶 如封似闭 十字手 收势

Group Eight: Turning to Carry, Block and Punch, Obstructing, Cross Hands, and Ending Pose

（二十一）转身搬拦捶 Turning to Carry, Block and Punch

1. 右腿屈膝，重心后坐于右腿，身体向右后转，左脚内扣，两臂随转体划弧，左手举至左额前，掌心斜向前，右手举至右额前方。（图155）

Bend the right leg, and place your body weight on it. Turn the body backward from the right side with the left tiptoe turned inward. Arms, as the body turns, move in arc-lines: the left hand reaches the

图 155

front of the left forehead, with the palm facing slantingly forward, while the right one reaches the front of the right forehead.

2. 重心后移,坐于左腿上,上体继续右转右手随着转体向右、向下握拳至左肋前,拳眼向内,拳心向下,同时右脚收至左脚内侧,胸向东北。(图156)

Transfer weight back to the left leg, and keep the upper body turning right, while the right hand (transforming into fist) moves rightward and downward to the front of the left costal region with the thumb-side facing in. Meanwhile, draw the right foot to the inner side of the left foot. The chest should face northeast.

3. 身微向右转,右拳由左肋经胸并外旋向前搬出,拳心朝上,左手向前、向下弧形落于左胯旁,掌心向下,指尖朝前,同时右脚随搬拳上步,脚跟着地,眼看右拳。(图157)

Turn the upper body slightly rightward. Move the right fist (twisting outward to make the thumb-side face up) from the left costal region to the front. Have the left hand falls forward and downward to the side of the left hip, with the palm facing down and fingers pointing forward. Meanwhile move the right foot (following the forward moving of the fist) forward with the heel on the ground. Set eyes on the right fist.

图156　　　　　图157

学打太极拳

4. 上体右转,脚尖外撇至 45 到 60 度角落实,右腿屈膝重心前移于右腿(此时脚尖与右膝同向)。右拳内旋,拳心朝下。(图 158)

Turn the upper body rightward. Turn the right tiptoe 45 to 60 degrees outward, and bend the leg while the weight is transferred to it (at this time, the tiptoe and the knee point at the same direction). Twist the right fist inward to face down.

5. 提起左脚向前迈出一步,正东偏北,脚跟着地,同时左手向上、向前划弧拦出,掌心斜向下,右拳同时向右外旋,拳心向上收至右腰旁,眼看左手。(图 159)

Take one step forward with the left foot (east, straying slightly to the north), with heel on the ground. In the meantime, move the left hand up and then forward in an arc-line for blocking, with the palm facing slantingly down; and twist the right hand simultaneously outward to face up and draws back to the right side of the waist. Eyes are set on the left hand.

6. 左脚放平,左腿屈膝成左弓步,同时右拳内旋,拳眼向上、向前打出,高与胸平。左手附于右前臂内侧,掌心朝外,眼看右拳。(图 160)

Set the left foot completely on the ground and bend the leg into a bow-shape. Meanwhile twist the right fist inward (thumb-side facing up) and strikes forward to the height of the chest. Attach the left hand to the inner side of the right forearm with the palm facing out. Set eyes on the right fist.

图 158

图 159

图 160

第一章 简化24式太极拳

口诀：①后坐转体划弧；②转体收脚握拳；③上步搬拳；④转体旋臂；⑤上步拦拳；⑥弓步冲拳。

Mnemonic lines: ① Squat backward, turn the body rightward, and wave hands in arc-lines; ② Turn the body rightward, draw back the right foot, and change the right hand into a fist; ③ Put the right foot forward and move the fist; ④ Turn the body to the right and twist the right arm; ⑤ Step the left foot forward and block with the left hand; ⑥ Make the left leg bow-shaped and punch with the right fist.

（二十二）如封似闭 Obstructing

1. 左手外旋掌心朝上，右拳外旋变掌掌心朝上，左手由右腕下向前穿出，(两手交叉)即两手同时左右分开，掌心向上同肩宽。（图161）

Twist the left hand outward to face up; and transform the right one back into the palm that is also twisted up. Take the left hand through from under the right wrist, and then move the hands simultaneously to their respective sides (as wide as the shoulders) with both palms facing up.

2. 右腿屈膝，重心后坐于右腿，左脚尖翘起，两臂屈肘，两掌在胸前同时内旋，掌心斜朝前下方收至胸前，掌心斜向前。（图162、163、164）

图161　　　　　　　图162　　　　　　　图163

学打太极拳

Bend the right leg where the weight is put. Bend the left tiptoe up. Bend the arms too; and the hands twist inward before the chest at the same time. With the palms facing down to the front, draw the hands back to the front of the chest. Change the palms to face slantingly forward.

3. 放平左脚，重心前移，屈膝成左弓步，同时两手经腹前，向上、向前弧形推出，腕与肩平，手心向前，眼看前方。（图165、166）

图 164

Set the left foot completely on the ground; move the center of gravity forward; and bend the left leg into a bow-shape. Meanwhile push the hands upward and forward from in front of the belly, with the wrists reaching the height of shoulders and palms facing forward. Set eyes on the front.

图 165　　　　图 166

口诀：① 穿掌分手；② 后坐收掌；③ 弓步按掌。

Mnemonic lines: ① Make the left hand go under the right one and then separate them; ② Squat backward and draw back the hands; ③ Make the left leg bow-shape and press forward with both hands.

要求：后坐时不可后仰突臀，两臂回收时要坠肘松肩，推出之两手不得超过肩宽。

第一章　简化24式太极拳

> **Demands**: Do not lean back or project your buttocks out when squatting backward. Keep the elbows and shoulders drooped and relaxed when drawing the arms back. The distance between the forward-pushed hands should not be wider than that of the shoulders.

（二十三）十字手 Cross Hands

1. 右腿屈膝后坐，身体重心移于右腿，向右转体，左脚尖内扣至正南，右手随转体，外撇至西南方；左手向左弧形平摆，两臂成弧形，左右分开，掌心斜朝前。（图167）

图 167

Bend the right leg (to which the center of gravity is transferred) to squat backward. Turn the body rightward, and turn the left tiptoe inward (to the south). The right hand, following the body turn, waves out to the southwest, while the left hand waves in a horizontal arc-line to the left. The arms are in arc-shapes and separated to each side; both palms face slantingly forward.

2. 左腿屈膝后坐，重心移于左腿，上体微左转，右脚尖内扣，提起脚跟，收至左脚内侧，两脚距离同肩宽，成开立步。（图168）

Squat backward on the bent left leg, and transfer the center of gravity to it. Turn the body slightly leftward. Turn the right tiptoe inward, and then the heel is lifted and drawn back to the inner side of the left foot, which makes the parted step (feet parted as wide as shoulders).

图 168

3. 两手同时向下划弧，经腹前向上交叉，合抱于胸前，两臂撑圆，右手在外，左手在里，成十字手，手心均向里，眼看前方。（图169）

学打太极拳

Hands simultaneously move down to the front of the belly, and go up to cross before the chest (with the right hand on the outside). Extend the arms into rounded shapes and have the palms face inward. Eyes are set on the front.

4. 两腿逐渐蹬直起身,两臂前掤。(图 170)

Stretch the legs gradually to stand straight and move the arms forward before the chest.

图 169　　　　　　图 170

口诀:①后坐转体划弧;②后坐转体扣脚;③收脚合抱;④起身掤臂。

Mnemonic lines: ① Squat backward, turn to the right, and wave hands in arc-lines; ② Squat backward, turn to the left, and make the right tiptoe turned inward; ③ Draw the right foot back and cross the hands; ④ Stand up and move the arms.

要求:身体保持中正,不可前倾,要做到立身中正,眼平视前方。

Demands: Keep the body upright and balanced. Do not lean back or forth. Look straight at the front.

第一章 简化24式太极拳

(二十四) 收势 Ending Pose

1. 两手同时内旋,左右分开同肩宽,掌心朝下,两肘下垂成弧形,两臂慢慢下落,两手放回两腿外侧,掌心均朝里。(图171、172)

Both hands are twisted and separated to a width as that of the shoulders, and remember to keep the palms facing down and elbows drooped into arcs. The arms fall down slowly to send the hands back to the outside of the thighs, both palms facing inward.

2. 提起左脚收于右脚内侧,并步站立,眼看前方。(图173)

Lift the left foot and draw it back to the inner side the right foot. Stand with the feet close to each other. Look at the front.

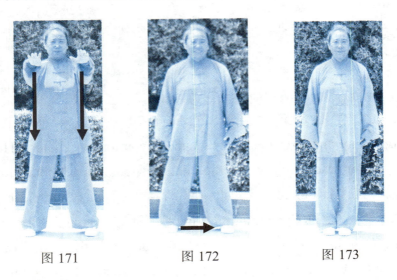

图171   图172   图173

口诀:①垂肘下落;②并步收脚。
Mnemonic lines: ① Have the elbows drooped and the arms fall down; ② Draw the left foot back to be juxtaposed with the right one.

要求: 收势时要全身放松,呼吸平稳,气息下沉。
Demands: Relax the whole body, breathe smoothly, and keep the air inside the body reserves deep.

学打太极拳

六、简化 24 式太极拳之新练法：反正结合之练法
Combination of the Original and Reversed Directions: A New Practicing Method

简化 24 式太极拳易学易练，很受广大爱好者的欢迎和喜爱，特别是初学者，但是经过一段时间的练习，大家发现和体会到，在练拳过程中左腿和右腿的负重，左右难以匀称，主要是这套太极拳"简化"的限制。如白鹤亮翅，单鞭，手挥琵琶，海底针都是右式，三个野马分鬃有 2 个是右腿负担体重，左腿负担体重只占三分之一，锻炼一段时间后人们发现右腿支撑的能力要比左腿好，两条腿难以得到平衡发展。于是我在教授简化 24 式太极拳时，面对学员，与学员面对面就像照镜子一样，如野马分鬃，学员出左脚我就出右脚，经过一段练习，我掌握了这一反打太极拳的技巧。学员也学会了 24 式太极拳的练法。于是，我采取了正打和反打结合进行锻炼，即面向南打一遍，再面向北打一遍，使左右姿势完全对称，较好地解决了这个问题。

Because of its easiness, the Simplified 24-Step *Taiji Quan* has gained a wide popularity among *Taiji* lovers, especially among beginners. However, one may find, after practicing for a while, that the weight is not being equally put on the legs. This is out of the restraints caused by the "simplification." For example, "The Crane Spreading Its Wings," "Single Whip," "Playing the Lute," and "Picking the Needle from the Seabed" are all of the right form only, and, among the three forms of "Splitting the Horse's Mane," two require the right leg to support the weight; therefore, it may be noted that the right leg gains more supporting force than the other one, which means unbalanced development between the legs. When I was teaching this set of *Taiji Quan*, I learned to do it in the opposite direction as I faced my students (who were practicing in the original direction) and moved with them like a mirror image. Thereafter, I combined these two ways by practicing in alternative directions, which provided a good solution to the problem mentioned above.

第一章　简化 24 式太极拳

我经过试教,这种反正结合的打法,使学员也掌握了反打的技巧,学员反映很好。具体作法下:甲组面向北,乙组面向南。①起势同时动,做到屈蹲按掌,甲组向左转体,收脚抱球,乙组向右转体,收脚抱球;②甲组向右转体,抱球上步;乙组向左转体,抱球上步,以此类推,使两组动作姿势完全对称,待第一遍打完收势,两组再重新起势,即甲向右转,收脚抱球,乙组向左转,收脚抱球;甲组向左转体,抱球上步;乙组向右转体,抱球上步,以此类推。待收势时两组又回到原位。全套共做 48 个式子,需要 11 分钟左右。这样反正练习解决了姿势动作中左右不对称的问题。

I tried and taught this new way to my students, who mastered it and highly praised it. Here are the steps:

Group A faces north; and Group B faces south (The two groups are set face to face).

① The two groups begin at the same time to squat and press hands; and then group A turns left, draws the foot back and make the ball-holding gesture, while Group B turns right to finish the movements.

② Group A turns right, makes the ball-holding gesture and step forward, while Group B turns left and makes the same movements. The rest is all finished in this way with the two groups responding completely to each other.

After the first round is finished, the two groups begin again. At this time, Group A turns right, draws back the foot and make the ball-holding gesture, while Group B turns left and makes the same movements. This pattern is continued until the end, at which point the two groups find themselves back to their original positions. The whole set (including two rounds) contain 48 steps, which take about 11 minutes. Thus the problem of uneven development of force can therefore be solved.

由于反打一改过去的习惯,开始会感到别扭,只要坚持几天就会习惯了,一旦习惯了,会感到非常舒服,有兴趣的朋友可以尝试一下。

At the beginning, one may find it unnatural to practice in the opposite direction; however, after a few days of adjusting, he/she will get used to it and feel very comfortable doing it that way. Those who are interested in this are suggested to have a try.

第二章 太极文化
Chapter Two The *Taiji* Culture

一、《太极拳论》（王宗岳）[①]
"On *Taiji Quan*" (by Wang Zongyue)

1.《太极拳论》原文

太极者，无极而生，动静之机，阴阳之母也。动之则分，静之则合。无过不及，随曲就伸。人刚我柔谓之"走"，我顺人背谓之"黏"。动急则急应，动缓则缓随。虽变化万端，而理唯一贯。由着熟而渐悟懂劲，由懂劲而阶及神明。然非用力之久，不能豁然贯通焉！

虚领顶劲，气沉丹田，不偏不倚，忽隐忽现。左重则左虚，右重则右杳。仰之则弥高，俯之则弥深。进之则愈长，退之则愈促。一羽不能加，蝇虫不能落。人不知我，我独知人。英雄所向无敌，盖皆由此而及也！

斯技旁门甚多，虽势有区别，概不外乎壮欺弱、慢让快耳！有力打无力，手慢让手快，是皆先天自然之能，非关学力而有为也！察"四两拨千斤"之句，显非力胜；观耄耋能御众之形，快何能为？

立如平准，活似车轮。偏沉则随，双重则滞。每见数年纯功，不能运化者，率皆自为人制，双重之病未悟耳！

欲避此病，须知阴阳，黏即是走，走即是黏；阴不离阳，阳不离阴；阴阳相济，方为懂劲。懂劲后愈练愈精，默识揣摩，渐至从心所欲。

[①] 王宗岳，清代康熙、乾隆年间山西绛州（今新绛县）人。武术理论家。著有《太极拳经(谱)》、《阴符枪谱》等，其中《太极拳论》影响很大，奉为经典。

第二章 太极文化

本是"舍己从人",多误"舍近求远"。所谓"差之毫厘,谬以千里",学者不可不详辨焉!是为论。

2.《太极拳论》的白话译文

太极是由无极生成的,又孕育着阴阳变化,运动的时候阴阳分开,静止的时候,阴阳相合,合成一体。动作不要过分,也不要不足,要随对方变化而伸展。对方刚劲打来,我要以柔化迎接,这就叫做走,我变成顺势占据主动,使对方陷于被动,处于劣势,这就叫做黏。对方快我反应也要快,对方慢,我随之也要慢。

Taiji, originating from *Wuji*, is the process of movement and stillness and contains the changes of *Yin* and *Yang*. In moving, *Yin* and *Yang* are parted, while in stillness, they are one. Movements should not exceed or go short of what is required. They are deployed according to the opponent's actions. Resolving the opponent's firm and strong force with softness and gentleness is what we call "*Zou*" (retreating); while "*Nian*" (following) means seizing advantages to go after and corner the opponent. If the opponent moves fast, we move fast, and vice *versa*.

虽变化千千万万,然而道理始终如一。随着法的熟练而逐渐明白劲力的规律。再由明白规律进而达到像神明一样运转自如。(这里将"着"与"劲"分别解释如下:"着"是武术的一种术语,拳术中的一腿、一脚、一掌、一拳,皆可说是一"着",也可说是一法,即攻击和防御的方法。)待着术动作纯熟后,便可慢慢练习各种推手,以求懂"劲"的功夫。懂"劲"之后,对于对方之来力的意向企图一黏手,即可明了,便可应付自如。"着"是有形的动作,容易了解。但"劲"是无形的,非有相当的功夫是不易了解的。所以,太极拳的功夫,以着术为入手的初步,其注意的是懂劲的功夫。"着"练熟了再学推手,推手日久,方能渐悟懂劲。懂劲之后,才能愈练愈精,进而达到神而明的境界,即随心所欲,得心应手,随便一动,无不恰到好处。如果不是长期用功锻炼,决不能一下子精通。头要向上自然地顶起,气要向下沉至小腹,所谓丹田。身体不可俯仰歪斜,动作要忽隐忽现,变化莫测。对方攻我左侧,我在左侧变虚,攻我右侧,我把右侧隐蔽。对方向上仰攻我,我升得要更高,使他摸不到;对方向下攻击我,我要变得更低,使对方感到深不可测。对方进我就退,使其长不可及,对方退我就乘势近逼,使对方感到更急促的压力。力量要判得

学打太极拳

准,一根羽毛的重量也要能察觉出来,感觉要十分灵敏。蚊虫落在身上也要有反应。要做到人不能知道我,而我却能知己知彼,对其了如指掌。

There might be thousands of changes, but they are governed by one rule. All *Taiji* learners follow this course of development: from grasping the skills (*Zhuo*) to gradually understand the rules of force (*Jin*), and finally conduct every move completely at will. ("*Zhuo*" is a term in *Kongfu*. Each movement of the leg, foot, palm, or fist can be called "*Yi Zhuo*", meaning one skill, or a method of attack or defense.) After the skills are well mastered, one may begin to practice all kinds of hand pushing in order to gain a gradual understanding of "*Jin*", or force, which makes it easy to know the opponent's intentions at the very beginning of engagements and how to deal with them. "*Zhuo*" or skill is the visible movement that is easy to master; however, "Jin" or force is invisible, and therefore is hard to be understood without years of practice. Hence, skills are made in the beginning of *Taiji Quan*, which, in fact, emphasizes the importance to the understanding of "Jin". When skills are mastered, one begins to learn hand pushing, and only after a long time of practicing, he/she is able to have a gradual perception of the rules of "Jin" or force. After that and with still more years of practice, he/she may reach the level of taking every move at complete will and ease. In conclusions, this is not to be mastered within a short time.

The head should be kept upright, and the air inhaled down to the belly or the pubic region. Do not lean the body back or forth, and the movements are constantly changing without being detected. If attacked on the left, make the left void; if attacked on the right, make the right untouchable; if the opponent comes up from below, rise higher to make the strike negligible; and if he/she strikes down, manage to get lower to exert a feeling of being bottomless on the opponent. In short, one should retreat to be untouched when the opponent charges, and approach to exert pressure when the opponent draws back. A *Taiji* master possesses sharp judgment of force: so sharp that even the weight of a feather could be measured exactly; and he/she is sensitive: so sensitive that a mosquito resting upon him/her would arouse response. The *Taiji* master has the ability to know

everything about the opponent while remaining unknown. This is probably the reason why a true hero is unconquerable.

英雄所向无敌于天下,都是由这个缘故取得的。拳法的流派很多,架势虽然不同,但大多都是以强欺负弱,以快压倒慢,有力打无力,手慢输给手快,这是人的先天自然之能,不是什么练功后取得的本事和作为。仔细分析一下太极拳歌诀中"四两拨千斤"之句,显然不是说大力取胜,而是要以巧取胜。再看看练太极拳的那些七八十岁的老人,能够抵抗一群人,战胜一群人,单纯靠速度怎么能办得到呢?

Kongfu contains various styles, and most of them seek to win by strength and speed, which, as a matter of fact, is the nature of human beings instead of one's learned skills. A better understanding of the line "to turn around hundreds of tons of weight with the slightest force" would make clear that winning is not out of strength but skillfulness. And a glance at the old with mastery of *Taiji Quan* who defeat a bunch of people single-handedly would make one believe that speed is not a huge factor.

身形身法要像水平仪一样中正,转动要像车轮一样灵活。对方用力进攻我要放松,将力量偏向另一侧,就会随对方的来势变化。反之,如果我也用力相抗就形成了双重,造成对方顶牛的局面,就会停滞不前。常常看到下了多年苦功仍然不能柔化运转的人,一律都是自己造成了受制于人的局面,就是没有领悟到双重这个毛病的危害。

The body is constantly kept balanced, and the turning and twisting are as agile as wheels. Parrying a forceful strike by moving one's own force away from the point of interaction to another side would help change positions smoothly because of the opponent's movements. On the contrary, taking the strike with force forms "double force", which causes engagements of wild strength and unsmooth movements. I often encounter people who have practiced for many years and yet cannot manage to resolve the opponent's attacks; this is because they have not understood the harm of "double force" and therefore cause themselves to be controlled by their opponents.

学打太极拳

要避免双重这个毛病，必须明白阴阳统一对立的辩证关系。要取得主动就必须走化劲，以退为进，只有走化运转才能变被动为主动，控制对方以柔克刚，走和黏密不可分，正如阴阳，阴不能离阳，阳不能离阴，阴阳相辅相成，互相补充依托才能懂得拳法的规律。明白规律后，才能越练越精，通过牢记和反复思考实践，就会逐渐得心应手，随心所欲。

To avoid the "double force", one has to understand the dialectic relation between *Yin* and *Yang*. The two, though in opposition, are closely connected, supporting and complementing each other. *Taiji Quan*, therefore, requires that *Zou* (retreating) and *Nian* (following) connect with each other closely. If one wants to change from passiveness (being attacked) into aggressiveness (attacking), he/she has to firstly resolve the attacking force by retreating (or with softness and gentleness) and then turn to follow and corner the opponent. *Zou* and *Nian* constantly transfer from one to the other, supporting and complementing each other as *Yin* and *Yang*. Achieving this means mastery of the rules of force, and only after mastering the rules of force can one gradually take moves at will and ease through times of practice.

本来这种战术的原则是舍己从人，随机应变，依客观而变化。然而，很多人错误理解为抛开对方，舍近求远，正如人们所说的，离开真理毫厘，就会谬误千里。学拳的人不可不仔细分辨。

The principle of this tactic was originally meant to make adjustments according to the practical situation. It, however, is misunderstood by many people as departing from the opponent and abandoning the short cut to go along a roundabout course. People often say an inch from the truth would lead to huge mistakes; therefore, it is necessary to distinguish closely between the right and wrong.

第二章　太极文化

二、太极拳在京城的发展简史
A Short History of *Taiji Quan* in Beijing

太极拳是我国武术中著名的内家拳种之一。据前辈考证大约起源于元朝,太极拳的发展有一个萌生、发展和成型的历史过程。经过无数先辈的总结、实践、推广才逐渐发展起来的。可分为形成期、套路形成期和流派形成期。

Taiji Quan is one of the renowned Chinese *Kongfu* styles which benefit the internal organs. According to records, it originated approximately in the Yuan Dynasty, and underwent a process of budding, development, and maturity through the summarization, practice, and promotion of numerous forerunners. The history could be roughly divided into the following three phases.

基本形成期:从陈王廷到陈长兴,其理论著作有《拳经总歌》、《太极拳十大论》、《用武要言》讲的都是技击方法,在拳论中运用了阴阳哲理、中医的理论来解释拳理。用中医的养生、气血、气化和阴阳平衡来练功实践。

The Budding Phase (from Chen Wangting to Chen Changxing): Theoretically works as a *General Guideline for Taiji Quan in Rhymed Lines* (*Quan Jing Zong Ge*), *Ten Theories on Taiji Quan* (*Taiji Quan Shi Da Lun*), and *Necessary Points for Attack and Defense* (Yong Wu Yao Yan), which are all about methods of attack and defense, and were written by either Chen Wangting or Chen Changxing, who used the philosophy of *Yin* and *Yang* and the theories of traditional Chinese medicine to explain their *Taiji Quan* theories and to guide their practice.

套路形成期:从陈王廷的七个套路传至陈长兴,陈有本一代,发展中逐渐取舍,形成了陈氏太极拳的一路和二路(炮捶),扬弃了原有的一些高难度动作,形成了现代意义上传统太极拳的雏形,朝着群众性的养生和健身方向发展,为演变和形成不同风格流派打下了基础,但仍然是以技击功夫为基本功。

The Phase of Movement Formation: Chen Wangting created seven sets of skills and tricks that were refined by Chen Changxing and Chen Youben's

学打太极拳

generation into the first and second sets of the Chen-Style *Taiji Quan*, which, by discarding some movements of high difficulty, formed the rudiments of the traditional (in modern sense) *Taiji Quan*. Though still employing the art of attack and defense as their basic concepts, these two sets of skills and tricks showed an emphasis to building health and laid a foundation for the future development of varied styles.

流派形成期：从杨露禅到陈家沟学拳，到孙禄堂晚年定型孙式太极拳，确立今天流传的杨式、武式、吴式、孙式太极拳。

The Phase of Style Formation: This phase roughly began from *Yang* Luchan's learning *Taiji Quan* in Chenjiagou and ended with Sun Lutang's finalization of his own style in his late years. The styles that are taught and learned presently—*Yang* style, Wu style, Woo style, and Sun style-were all formed in this phase.

太极拳发展到清末是鼎盛时期，在北京聚集了太极拳众多名师，太极拳理论探讨和学术研究是很有成果的。如太极拳谱、拳经、拳论以及手抄本广为流传，南北武术人相互之间的交流活动也很频繁。

Taiji Quan reached its prime time in the last years of the Qing Dynasty. A great number of *Taiji Quan* masters flocked in Beijing and made great progresses in theoretical exploration and scholarly studies. Books of *Taiji Quan* skills or theories and their hand-written copies were widespread. Communication among masters from all over the country was very frequent.

本书仅举杨式太极拳和陈式太极拳为例：

This book will take the *Yang* style and Chen style to illustrate the development of *Taiji Quan*.

1. 杨式太极拳 Yang Style

杨露禅在太极拳的发展历史上占据重要地位，他在河南学艺，有杨无敌之称，他最大的贡献是继承发展了传统拳技，开创了杨式太极拳，将太极拳体用双

第二章 太极文化

修向前大大地推动了一步。此举震惊了武坛，震惊了全国，使太极拳运动得以蓬勃发展。杨露禅大师对太极拳的重要贡献是打破了传统学艺的封建主义框框，敢于改革创新，改变了传统练法，从村野山沟走向京城，并设武馆公开传授太极拳武艺。从此太极拳从保守到开放，杨露禅之后又有了吴、武、孙式等各式不同风格不同练法的五家拳式的太极拳，太极拳从京城跨越长江，向全国推广，进而走向世界。

  Yang Luchan played an important role in the history of *Taiji Quan* because he went to Henan Province to learn *Taiji Kongfu* and brought it to the capital from the countryside. The greatest contribution he made, however, was that he invented his own style by refining the traditional styles and thus improved greatly both the functions of health building and fighting. This aroused thundering applause among *Kongfu* masters all over the country and helped the practice of *Taiji Quan* bloom. Master Yang was famous not because he defeated other masters, or because he was named "Yang the Unconquerable," but because he managed to break the traditional customs and rules by setting up schools to teach *Taiji Kongfu* publicly. *Taiji Quan*, from then on, went from relative isolation into public life. After him, five other styles appeared, including the Wu style, Woo style, Sun style, and so on. Thereafter, *Taiji Quan* began to flourish, being practiced all over the country and even the world.

2. 陈式太极拳 Chen Style

  陈式太极拳创于明末清初，距今已有300多年的历史。河南温县陈家沟陈王廷，是陈家沟陈氏九世。他综合性地继承和发展了明代军队中流行的各家拳法，结合古代的导引术和吐纳术，吸取了古典哲学的阴阳学说和中医基本理论的经络学说，创造了一种内外兼修的太极拳。并编写了《拳经总歌》，"纵放曲伸人莫知，诸靠缠绕我皆依……"。概括地说明太极拳独有的竞技方法"掤捋挤按，采列肘靠"的八种劲别方法，以黏连不脱，引进落空为技术训练的基本原则，这是我国武术史上具有独创性的成就。自陈王廷之后，陈家沟历代相传陈氏太极拳，练拳之风盛行，经久不衰且很少外传，直到陈长兴（陈氏十四代）才传给杨露禅。陈氏太极拳因陈家沟偏僻，处河南之一隅，交通不便，仅在陈家沟流行，没有得到发展。

学打太极拳

The Chen-style *Taiji Quan* was invented between the Ming and Qing dynasties-more than 300 years ago. Chen Wangting, belonging to the ninth generation of the Chen family in Chenjiagou, Wen County, and Henan Province, invented a kind of *Kongfu* boxing. It was a breakthrough because it would exercise both internal and external organs by combining the popular boxing arts during the Ming Dynasty, the ancient force-guiding and respiring methods, the philosophical theories of *Yin* and *Yang*, the theories about the body channels in traditional Chinese medicine, and his own rich experience. He also wrote the *General Guideline for Taiji Quan in "Rhymed Lines"*, which outlines the unique attack-and-defense skills, including the eight force-wielding methods—*bing*, stroking, squeezing, pressing, picking, breaking, elbowing, and leaning—and the basic principles of attack and defense—sticking fast and rendering the opponent's attacking force effortless by drawing it in. This was an achievement of great originality in the Chinese *Kongfu* history. Since Chen Wangting, the Chen-style *Taiji Quan* was passed on from generation to generation without decline, but it was seldom taught to people who were not within the family until Chen Changxing (of the fourteenth generation) passed it on to Yang Luchan. The Chen style did not get full development because it was practiced only in Chenjiagou, an isolated corner in Henan Province.

陈氏十七代宗师陈发科(1887—1957年)陈长兴四世孙,与陈氏十八代陈照丕自1928年来京教拳,对陈氏太极拳的传播做出了杰出贡献,开创了陈氏太极拳在全国发展的新纪元,是近代陈氏太极拳的杰出代表。陈发科逝世后,由他的弟子着手编写了《陈氏太极拳》一书,于1963年由沈家桢、顾留馨编著出版。陈发科弟子们继承师志,在北京设点教拳,有弟子侯志宜、雷慕尼、孙枫秋、田秀臣、冯志强等。

In 1928, Chen Fake (1887—1957) of the seventeenth generation and his son Chen Zhaopi began to teach the Chen-style *Taiji Quan* in Beijing, which contributed greatly to the spread of this style and opened a new era for its development. Chen Fake was considered an outstanding representative of the modern Chen style. Even upon his death, his disciples compiled the book "Chen-Style *Taiji Quan*", which was published in 1963 by Shen Jiazhen and Gu Liuxin. Some of his disciples, such as Hou Zhiyi, Lei Muni, Sun Fengqiu, Tian Xiuchen, and Feng Zhiqiang, took over their master's endeavor and continued the teaching of the Chen style in Beijing.

3. 太极拳在北京发展简史（见表）Diagrammatical Illustration the development of *Taiji Quan* in Beijing

【陈式】

陈发科（1887—1957）⟶ 冯志强（1928— ）

田秀臣 ┐　田秋田 ⟶ 白淑萍
雷慕尼 ┤　田秋信 ⟶ 曲志远
李经梧 ┘　田秋茂

顾留馨

邓　杰

沈家桢

唐　豪

陈照奎

李剑华

肖庆林

【Chen Style】

Chen Fake(1887—1957) ⟶ Fengzhiqiang(1928—)

Tian Xiuchen ┐　Tian Qiutian ⟶ Bai Shuping
Lei Muni ┘　Tian Qiuxin ⟶ Qu Zhiyuan
Li Jingwu　　Tian Qiumao

Gu Liuxin

Deng Jie

Shen Jiazhen

学打太极拳

Tang Hao
Chen Zhaokui
Li Jianhua
Xiao Qinglin

【杨式】
张三丰(明) ⟶ 王宗岳(清乾隆间) ⟶ 蒋发 ⟶ 陈长兴 ⟶ 杨露禅

杨露禅 ┌ 杨班侯(1837—1892)—吴全佑—吴鉴泉—吴图南
       │ 杨琦
       └ 杨建侯(1839—1917) ┌ 杨少侯(1862—1930)
                            │ 杨兆元
                            └ 杨澄甫—杨铭(守中)(1910—1985)
                                     杨振基(1921—)
                                     杨振择(1926—)
                                     杨震国(1928—)
                              高徒   崔毅士——吉良晨
                                     刘高明(1931—2003)
                                      └白淑萍(1947.12—)
                                     吴文考
                                     段建尼
                                     张海涛
                                     杨俊峰
                                     王永桢
                                     李 鸿
                                     黄永德
                                     陈连宝
                                     崔 彬
                                     邱佩如
                                     孙 正
                                     沈德丰

第二章 太极文化

$$\left\{\begin{array}{l}曹彦章\\李连生\\陈\ \ 雷\\和西青\\方\ \ 宁\\秦茂桐\\王守礼\end{array}\right.$$

崔毅士之女：崔秀辰(1918—1992)

孙子：崔仲三(1948—　)

外孙：张勇涛(1943—　)

【Yang Style】

Zhang Sanfeng（Ming Dynasty）—Wang Zongyue（Emperor Qianlong in Qin Dynasty）—Jiang Fa—Chen Changxing—Yang Luchan

Yang Luchan $\left\{\begin{array}{l}\text{Yang Banhou}(1837—1892)—\text{Wuquanyou-Wu Jianquan-Wu Tunan}\\\text{Yang Qi}\\\text{Yang Jianhou}(1839—1917)\quad \text{Yang Shaohou}(1862—1930)\end{array}\right.$

$\left\{\begin{array}{l}\text{Yang Zhaoyuan}\\\text{Yang Chengfu}\end{array}\right.$ ***Yang*** Ming(or Yang Shouzhong)(1910—1985)

$\left\{\begin{array}{l}\text{Yang Zhenji}(1921—\quad)\\\text{Yang Zhenze}(1926—\quad)\\\text{Yang Zhenguo}(1928—\quad)\\\text{Student: Cui Yishi}\quad\text{Ji Liangchen}\end{array}\right.$

　　　　　　　　　　　　Liu Gaoming(1931—2003)—

　　　　　　　　　　　　Bai Shuping

　　　　　　　　　　　　(1947.12—　)

　　　　　　　　　　　　Wu Wenkao

　　　　　　　　　　　　Duan Jianni

　　　　　　　　　　　　Zhang Haitao

学打太极拳

                                    Yang Junfeng

                                    Wang Yongzhen

                                    Li Hong

                                    Huang Yongde

                                    Chen Lianbao

                                    Cui Bin

                                    Qiu Peiru

                                    Sun Zheng

                                    Shen Defeng

                                    Cao Yanzhang

                                    Li Liansheng

                                    Chen Lei

                                    He Xiqing

                                    Fang Ning

                                    Qin Maotong

                                    Wang Shouli

           Cui Yishi's daughter：Cui Xiuchen(1918—1992)

                 Grandson：Cui Zhongsan(1948—　　)

                 Grandson：Zhang Yongtao(1943—　　)

三、太极拳(太极文化)的传播和影响

Spread and Influence of *Taiji Quan* (and the *Taiji* Culture)

    历史文化是一个民族生命力的传承和延续，是一个民族智慧和传统文化的积淀和结晶，是国家统一、民族团结的精神支柱,时刻都在影响着我们现在和未来的发展。当今世界人们越来越为博大精深、神秘莫测的东方文化所吸引,而太极文化则是东方文化中一颗璀璨的明珠。随着太极文化在世界的迅速传播,许多西方专家学者把太极文化之代表——太极拳称之为"人类健身之宝","是一项充满奥妙的运动","东方文化的瑰宝"。并预言:"太极拳将成为二十一世纪最受欢迎、最容易叫人们接受、影响面最大的运动方式。"

第二章 太极文化

Culture, as the carrier of a nation's vitality, the collection of its wisdom and tradition, and the spiritual support of its unity, exerts a great influence on a nation's present and future development. The present world shows a constantly deepening interest in the rich and mysterious Chinese culture, of which the *Taiji* culture is a shining pearl. As the *Taiji* culture spreads quickly in the world, *Taiji Quan*, the representative of the Chinese culture, is praised by Western experts and scholars as "the treasure for human health," "a sport with great profoundness," and "the gem of Eastern culture." They predicted that "*Taiji Quan* will become the most popular, acceptable and influential exercise in the 21st century."

1. 太极拳的传播经历了一个从民间到宫廷(由杨露禅父子)又到民间的过程
Spread of *Taiji Quan*: from society to the royal court (through Yang Luchan and his son) and back to the society

新中国成立后,太极拳得到广泛普及,经历了从民间至学府,从学府又到民间的过程。太极拳参加人数之多,流传地区之广,是任何体育项目都不能比拟的。1978 年 11 月 16 日,邓小平同志应日本众议院院长三宅正一之请,为日本太极拳爱好者题写了"太极拳好"四个字,揭开了太极拳运动新篇章。1990 年在第十一届亚运会开幕式上,中日 1400 名多太极拳爱好者 24 式太极拳表演激动人心,1998 年天安门万人 24 式太极拳表演以及 2007 年 11 月 11 日第九届北京国际武术比赛开幕式上千人 24 式太极拳表演,使太极文化得到了进一步传播。

Taiji Quan began to be widely accepted after the PRC was established, undergoing spreading from the folk to the school and back to the folk. No other sport is comparable to *Taiji Quan* in terms of the number of students and the growth in popularity. In November 16, 1978, Mr. Deng Xiaoping inscribed "Splendid *Taiji Quan*" (Tai Ji Quan Hao) upon the request of Shoichi Miyake, Speaker of the Japanese House of Representatives, which inspired *Taiji* learners greatly. On the opening ceremony of the 11th Asian Games in 1990, 1400 *Taiji* lovers gave a wonderful performance of the 24-Step *Taiji Quan*. In 1998, about ten thousand *Taiji* learners performed the 24-Step *Taiji Quan* at Tian'

学打太极拳

anmen Square, and in November 11, 2007, more than one thousand *Taiji* lovers performed the 24-Step *Taiji Quan* on the opening ceremony of the 9th International Wushu Contest in Beijing. All these were great advancements to the spread of *Taiji Quan*.

2. 太极拳在20世纪70年代开始向国外传播 Going overseas: from 1970s

特别是改革开放以后，太极文化逐步走向世界。在世界各国都可以看到练习太极拳的人群，西方一些国家把太极拳作为一个正式项目，每隔一段时间举办太极拳锦标赛。东南亚一些国家把太极拳列入了学校课间操加以普及，美国前总统老布什夫妇、澳大利亚前总理霍克、日本前首相田中角荣都是太极拳爱好者，他们曾来中国向我的导师刘高明先生学习太极拳。尤其是日本，不仅拥有几百万太极拳爱好者，而且还有近百个太极拳组织和一定的研究机构；在俄罗斯有太极拳武术馆，欧洲每年都要举行太极拳比赛。加拿大、澳大利亚派代表团来中国学习太极拳。美国航天员把太极拳列入训练项目等等。太极拳已走出国门向世界各地传播，为世界人民所认识与喜爱。世界诺贝尔奖获得者多人齐聚瑞士发表宣言，称二十一世纪将是太极拳风行全球的世纪，他们说属于世界的太极拳源于中国，中国是太极拳的根。太极拳的治病、防病、延年益寿的功效以及技击的科学性也日益为世人所瞩目。太极拳不仅是中华民族的珍贵文化遗产，也成为全人类的共同财富。

People around the world began to practice *Taiji Quan* during the 1970s, especially after the Policy of Reform and Opening-up was launched. People now are seen all around the world practicing *Taiji Quan*. In some Western countries, it is made a normal sports project, and Championships are held occasionally. In some Southeast Asian countries, *Taiji Quan* is added to the exercises between school classes. Among *Taiji* lovers are former US president George Bush and his wife, former Australia Prime Minister Bob Hawke, and former Japan Prime Minister Kakuei Tanaka, who have learned *Taiji Quan* from my master, Mr. Liu Gaoming. In Japan, especially, there are not only hundreds and thousands of *Taiji* fans, but also dozens of *Taiji Quan* organizations and even several research institutes. There are even *Taiji Quan* schools in Russia and contests are held every year in Europe. Delegations from Canada and Australia were sent to China specifically for learning this art, and it was even added to the training programs for astronauts in the US. All of these examples provide the evidence that *Taiji Quan* has been accepted and loved around the whole world. Several Nobel Prize Swiss winners have spoken highly of it by claiming that *Taiji Quan*, which had its roots in China, would become a great fashion around the world in the 21st century. Rising attention has been paid to its health building and scientific analysis of attack and defense. It is now not only a cultural legacy of China, but also a treasure shared by the whole world.

3. 太极文化的价值蕴含 Values of the *Taiji* Culture

太极文化博大精深、奥妙无穷,是中华优秀传统文化的精华之一。它融合技击性、健身性、艺术性于一体,涉及多种学科领域,具有多种综合价值蕴含。

As an essence in Chinese traditional culture, the *Taiji* culture is characterized by its richness and profoundness. It is a combination of the art of attack, defense, health building, and artistry. It is endowed with various values involving several branches of learning.

(1) 太极文化和保健医疗价值 Medical Values

生命在于运动,如果不运动,气血不周就容易生病,太极拳运动轻松自由,缓慢柔和,不论男女老少,体质强弱,均适宜习练。即使活动量过些,也没有副作用和危险。太极拳是一个"一动无有不动"的功夫,在运动中,除开合、隐现使周身骨节和肌肉群进行开展、收缩运动外,它还每式结合"开呼,合吸"使横膈肌升降,起到上承、下压的作用,促使胸、腹、脏、腑亦随着蠕动起来这样就形成了周身骨节、肌肉群五脏、六腑的运动,就使人体机能的各个系统如经络、神经、血液循环、呼吸、消化、内分泌等系统自然地、平衡地、协调地运转,激发人体自身抗御疾病、自愈再生的内在机制,有效地调动人体潜在的生命力,所以太极拳运动有防病治病、养生医疗保健的独特医疗价值。

Life is maintained and enhanced by exercises; otherwise, people would get illnesses due to the unsmooth circling of *qi* and blood. *Taiji Quan* is suitable to

学打太极拳

all kinds of people thanks to its gentle, slow, relaxing free movements. No danger or side effects would arise even if the demands of an exercise were somewhat high. *Taiji Quan* is a kind of *Kongfu* that requires great cooperation: if one part of the body moves, other parts move, too. Apart from stretching or folding joints and the muscles opening, closing, concealing, and revealing movements, it combines every movement with respiration according to this principle: "inhale when stretching and exhale when folding". This makes the diaphragm rise and fall to force the internal organs move in sync. Thus, all organs are now in motion, which ensures the natural, balanced, and harmonious working of all physical systems such as the main and collateral channels, nerves, blood circling, respiration, digestion, incretion, and so on, arousing the inherent immune and reproductive systems within the human body to awaken its potential vitality. This is the reason why *Taiji Quan* has medical value.

(2) 太极文化的哲学价值 Philosophical Values

太极拳创立的理论基础来自"周易"和道家老子的学说。《周易·繋辞》说:"易有太极,是生两仪。"老子说:"道法自然。""易"是易变;"道"是老子的根本思想。它说明宇宙间一切事物内部存在着阴阳两个对立而又统一的因素,永远在变动之中,并循着必然的法则而变化发展。太极拳与易学、经络学、医学为一体,体现在太极拳的拳势始末之间,蕴含着丰富的哲理价值。

The theoretical foundation of *Taiji Quan* came from "*Zhou Yi*" (*The Book of Changes*) and Taoism. Notice that in the prologue of *Zhou Yi*: "In the system of the Yi (changes) there is the *Taiji* (great supreme), which gives birth to the two elementary forms (*Yin and Yang*)." Lao-Tzu said: "The law of the Tao is it being what it is." "*Yi*" means change; and "*Tao*" is the essence of Lao-Tzu's thoughts. This is to say, everything contains the two opposing and unified elements, *Yin* and *Yang*, which change constantly according to certain laws. *Taiji Quan* is an integration of the doctrines of Yi and the theories about the body channels and medicine, which are implied through the movements; and therefore, has profound philosophical values.

第二章　太极文化

（3）太极文化的艺术价值 Artistic Values

太极拳本身是一门高雅的艺术，它的技击动作与形体表现是种美的享受，所以近年来许多学者把舞蹈、美术、书法等结合起来，产生了一系列特殊的艺术作品，对进一步研讨太极拳具有重大价值。

Taiji Quan itself is a type of noble art. Its movements and body poses are aesthetically pleasurable to view by its audience. In recent years, many scholars produced a series of special art works by combining *Taiji Quan* with dancing, fine arts, and Chinese calligraphy, which is another of important value in the deep study of *Taiji Quan*.

（4）太极拳的力学和生命科学价值 Values in Mechanics and Life Science

太极拳要求"用意不用力"是说多思想少用力，就是"以小力胜大力"的效能。其动作都是在划圆、弧形运转，发力则是圆中求直，也就是拳论所曰："曲中求直，蓄而后发"。太极拳的推手能把劲力任意集中在一点发放到身体的任何部位，如肩、肘、膝、手、掌、脚、腿都可打人，这些都是力学和生命科学上的问题，具有重大的研究价值。

Taiji Quan demands one to "use mind, not force," which means one should think more and use less force in order to "defeat the strong force with little force." Its movements are all in arc-shapes, and the force is exerted in a rounded way, as is pointed out in the theories: "Seek straightness in roundedness; reserve and then send the force out." The hand pushing in *Taiji Quan* is able to concentrate force on any point of the body for striking, such as shoulder, elbow, knee, hand, palm, foot, and leg. These are all valuable issues concerned with mechanics and biomechanics.

从生命科学来讲，太极拳又是一种高级气功，通过用意、练意、运气、练气，是运动中的气功，太极拳说揭示：人也是自然界的产物，故有"天地人合一"之说，因而被列入人类生命科学领域，太极拳讲究精气神的积聚和运转，对生命科学的研究具有极大价值。

学打太极拳

Speaking from the perspective of life science, *Taiji Quan* is a type of advanced Qigong that is practiced in motion through wielding and exercising the mind, along with guiding and exercising qi (air force). According to *Taiji Quan* theories, human beings are products of nature, and there is the doctrine of "the trinity of heaven, earth, and human." *Taiji Quan* pays attention to the gathering and moving of the energy and force. Therefore, it is of great value to life science.

(5) 太极文化的精神文明价值 Values in Spiritual Civilization

1) 太极拳具有顺其自然的和谐精神。太极拳的基本特征是圆的运动,圆即是和谐,练太极拳时,强调圆活自然,形象高雅,动作如行云流水,运作舒展大方,形象优美,气质高雅,具有顺其自然的和谐精神。

2) 太极拳具有谦让、含蓄精神。太极拳是道德拳,具有武德、口德和手德。追求道德之高尚,扶助弱者,讲究以柔克刚,后发制人,不伤体,以艺服人,在技击上点到为止,留有余地的斗智斗勇而不逞勇,它的谦让和礼仪是中华民族的优良传统。

Taiji Quan implies the spirit of harmony and nature-following. The basic characteristic of *Taiji Quan* is its rounded movements; and "roundedness" stands for harmony. It is required that the movements are rounded, agile, and natural, with one's figure elegant, poses, and gestures decent.

Taiji Quan also implies modesty and courtesy. *Taiji Quan* is a kind of a moral *Kongfu*; it demands high morality in practicing, speaking, and fighting. *Taiji* masters are supposed to root out the daring and protect the weak. During engagements, one should not initiate to attack, or hurt the opponent intentionally. They should defeat the opponent by using their skills, and they win with modesty, not ruthlessness or desperateness. The modesty and courtesy is shown within the Chinese traditional value.

(6) 太极拳在军事科学上的价值 Values in Military Science

太极拳精神博大精深,把"以静制动"、"以柔克刚"、"彼进我退,彼退我黏"、"引进落空合即出"、"牵动四两拨千斤"的战术用于军事上,极符合《孙子兵法》的军事科学。所以太极文化在军事科学上也有着极其重要的研究价值。

第二章 太极文化

Taiji Quan contains a profound fountain of thoughts. Its tactics are in closely related to that of Sun-Tzu, for example, "restrain the moving with stillness," "defeat the strong with softness," "retreat when the enemy charges, and follow when the enemy retreats," "draw in the force to make it effortless and then attack back immediately," "move hundreds of tons of weight with the slightest force," and so forth. Therefore, it is obvious that *Taiji* culture is of great value to military science.

四、太极拳之阴阳浅识
A Simple Introduction to *Yin* and *Yang* in *Taiji Quan*

《易经》中关于无极生太极。太极生两仪,两仪生四象,四象生八卦之说,这说的是什么呢?指的是太极图,我们看到的太极图是一圆,为无极,圆中有黑白两个鱼形图,即为阴阳,即两极也。

It is mentioned in *Yi Jing* (*Zhou Yi*, or *The Book of Changes*) that *Wuji* gives birth to *Taiji*; *Taiji* gives birth to *Liangyi* (the two elementary forms); *Liangyi* gives birth to *Sixiang* (the four directions); and *Sixiang* gives birth to *Bagua* (the eight trigrams). This refers, as a matter of fact, to the symbol of *Taiji*, which is composed of a circle-*Wuji*, and two fish-like patterns, one black and another white, in the circle-*Yin* and *Yang* (the two elementary forms).

(一) 从为什么取名太极拳说起 The Naming of *Taiji Quan*

我们先分析一下"太"和"极"二字的含义,"太"是大、无限;"极"是顶点、尽头,是终极、是根基、是枢纽,地球的南北两端。太极分阴阳,是大地万物的根本,万物由阴阳而生,所以太极拳取名为太极。正在于以虚实为本,掌握阴阳变化之机,可谓掌握拳术之精华,而成拳术之尖端——太极拳。

学打太极拳

Let us firstly explain the meanings of "*Tai*" and "*Ji*." "*Tai*" means great, limitless; while "*Ji*" means the end, the ultimate, the root, the pivot, or the poles of the earth. *Taiji* is divided into *Yin* and *Yang*, which gave birth to all things in the universe. *Taiji Quan* was named just because it was based on the concepts of void and solid (responding to *Yin* and *Yang*) and grasped the law that rules the changes of *Yin* and *Yang*. This means it got hold of the essence of the *Kongfu* boxing and therefore became the best of all.

(二) 太极图 The *Taiji* Symbol

太极是由无极而生的,此时的圆圈称之为无极圈。待阴阳分出后即有 S 曲线,我们称之为中级线,内含阴和阳两个半弧形的类似鱼形的图像,即为太极图。太极拳采用这个名称,象征着太极拳是圆形、弧形的,一阴一阳、刚柔相济的拳术。太极拳是以太极圈为体,以阴阳学说为灵魂的拳种,所以练太极拳必须首先懂得拳中的阴阳之理。

Taiji was born from *Wuji*, which is represented by the circle (before it is divided by the S-line) in the symbol; the S-line, called the middle line, divides the circle into two fish-shape patterns standing for *Yin* and *Yang*; thus gives us the *Taiji* symbol. *Taiji Quan* (*Taiji* boxing) uses the word *Taiji* to differentiate itself as a kind of *Kongfu* boxing that is characterized by its rounded and arc-shaped movements, its composition of *Yin* and *Yang*, and its emphasis on the mutual support between firm and soft forces. *Taiji Quan* takes the *Taiji* circle (after it is divided by the S-line) as its form and the theories of *Yin* and *Yang* as its soul; therefore, one has to grasp the true nature of *Yin* and *Yang* first if he/she wants to master *Taiji Quan*.

(三) 太极拳中的阴阳 The *Yin and Yang in Taiji Quan*

《太极拳论》中讲到:"阳不离阴,阴不离阳,阴阳相济,方为懂劲"这句话,说

第二章　太极文化

明了太极拳是由阴阳学说演变而来,要想掌握太极拳的真功夫,须知阴阳变化和配合,方为懂劲。

Wang Zongyue emphasized in On *Taiji Quan*: "*Yang* does not part from *Yin*, and *Yin* does not part from *Yang*. Only when one understands the mutual support and complementation between *Yin* and *Yang*, can he or she grasp the rules of force." These words make it clear that *Taiji Quan* based on the theories of *Yin* and *Yang*; therefore, one has to understand the transformation and cooperation between them for grasping the rules of force and thus mastering the real art of *Taiji Quan*.

"阴阳"二字从字义上讲是对所有对立面的概括,如虚实、快慢、刚柔、开合、进退、收放、急缓、黏走、内外、上下、动静、呼吸等矛盾关系。矛盾的双方既对立又统一,虽然依存却又相互制约,消长与共,阴阳互根。我们常说:阴是暗,阳是明;阴是反面,阳是正面,阴是黑,阳是白等。那么从太极拳的理论上讲,太极的阴阳是指开与合、虚与实、刚与柔、内与外、进与退、上与下、呼与吸、快与慢等等。从"阴阳"在拳术的作用上讲阴为合、为化、为蓄、为黏;阳为开、为放、为发。正如拳论上所讲的"阴中有阳,阳中寓阴"也就是"开中寓合,合中寓开",这就是太极阴阳从对立过渡到统一,形成阴阳相济的演变。怎样做到阴阳相济呢?

Literally, *Yin* and *Yang* refers to all opposite things, such as void and solidity, fastness and slowness, firmness and softness, opening and closing, advancing and receding, withdrawal and expanding, following and retreating, inside and outside, up and down, moving and stillness, exhalation and inhalation, and so forth. Each pair is in the dialectic relation, depending on and at the same time restricting each other; the opposite sides share the same root, and no one side can exist without the existence of the other. Usually we refer *Yin* to darkness, the reverse side, or the black, and *Yang* to brightness, the obverse side, or the white. According to the theories of *Taiji Quan*, *Yin* and *Yang* refer to the same opposite and dialectic relations mentioned above. As to the functional meanings of *Yin* and *Yang* in *Taiji Quan*, *Yin* refers to the closing, dissolving, reserving or following, while *Yang* refers to the opening, stretching or releasing. *Taiji Quan*

学打太极拳

theories mention that, "*Yin* contains *Yang*, and *Yang* contains *Yin*" or "Opening contains closing, and closing contains opening," explains the evolution of *Yin* and *Yang* from opposition to mutual support and complementation. How can we achieve this?

1. 注意自身的阴阳配合，如两条腿的虚与实，两个手的开与合，腰的左右旋转和呼与吸在动作上的配合等，王宗岳的《太极拳论》讲："左重则左虚，右重则右杳"，"立如平准，活似车轮"，身手圆活如车轮旋转，又能支撑八面。杨澄甫《太极拳十要》中讲："上下相随"、"分清虚实"的教导，说明了阴阳的相济和配合，只有阴阳同时变化才为相济。这是太极拳练功和进入技击的重要法则，要掌握好是很难的，处处要以先辈拳论为指导，再有老师的严传口授和自己的刻苦努力，方能有所得。做到自身的阴阳相济，这只是一个知己的功夫。

Pay attention to the cooperation between *Yin* and *Yang* on ourselves, such as the cooperation between the void and solidity of legs, the stretching and withdrawing of hands, the left and right turning of the waist, or exhaling and inhaling. Wang Zongyue mentioned in *On Taiji Quan*: "if attacked on the left, make the left void; if attacked on the right, make the right untouchable"; and "the body is constantly kept balanced, and the turning and twisting are as agile as wheels." Yang Chengpu said in "*Ten Essentials for Taiji Quan*": "the upper and lower body parts should be coordinated" and "the void and solid should be distinguished." These remarks explain that the support and cooperation between *Yin* and *Yang* happen only when they change simultaneously. This is one important rule in practicing and using *Taiji Quan*. It is hard to get full hold of the rule without the guidance of forerunners' theories, the instruction of the master and one's own assiduity. It is only the first step to get control of the cooperation between one's own *Yin and Yang*.

2. 还要做到知彼的功夫，就是两个人在接劲或推手中的阴阳相济，才是真正懂得了太极拳术阴阳相济的演变，才可在太极拳的技击中得到引进落空和借力打人的奥妙，也就是"阴阳相济，方为懂劲"的功夫，拳论中讲的"不丢不顶，舍己从人，沾连黏随"就是讲关于两人在接劲和推手中的论述。如：两人在接劲中，对

第二章 太极文化

方用力向我打来，我借用阴走化对方的来力，这就形成了两个人的阴阳相济，否则不是丢劲就是顶劲，如果两个人的力形成对抗都属于阳，为顶劲，两个人的力黏合不住和随不上对方为丢，产生顶劲是两阳相对，得不到借力和省力的效果。丢劲是光阴没有阳，起不到黏制发力的效果，阴阳得不到平衡，就不算阴阳相济，也不能算为懂劲。

The next step is to get control of the cooperation between the *Yin* and *Yang* of two opposing people, which means the support and complementation between *Yin* and *Yang* in the force-receiving or hand-pushing between two people. Achieving this level means understanding of the true changes in *Yin* and *Yang* that support and complement each other. Only until now can one manage to wield the skills of "drawing in the attacking force to make it effortless" and "attacking with the opponent's own force". On the topic of force-receiving and hand-pushing, these remarks are found in the theories of *Taiji Quan*: "Do not lose nor confront directly; adjust to the opponent's movements; stick and follow closely." For example, in the force-receiving, dissolving the opponent's forceful strike (*Yang*) with softness (*Yin*) forms the cooperation between *Yin* and *Yang*; otherwise, either "losing" or "direct confrontation" happens. When two forces meet and collide directly (both forces becoming *Yang*), we call it "direct confrontation"; and the "losing" means the failure to follow and stick to the opponent's force. Direct confrontation-both forces being *Yang*-makes it impossible to borrow the opponent's force and save one's own, while losing-both forces being *Yin*-renders it impossible to follow and launch effective strike. Both situations reveal imbalance and non-cooperation between *Yin* and *Yang*, and therefore show how one can fail to grasp the rules of these forces.

学打太极拳

五、太极拳与外家拳的不同
Differences between *Taiji Quan* and External-Exercising *Kongfu* Boxing

太极拳与外家拳的区别：Differences between *Taiji Quan* and external-exercising *Kongfu* boxing:

内家拳的名称，首见于明末清初学者黄宗羲（公元1610—1695年）撰《南雷文集·王征南墓志铭》。

The term, internal-exercising *Kongfu* boxing, first appeared in the "Epitaph of Wang Zhengnan" in *The Nanlei* Documents compiled by a scholar living in between the Ming and Qing dynasties named Huang Zongyi (1610—1695).

《王征南墓志铭》一文作于康熙八年（1669年），收入《南雷文集》，是最早记载"内家拳"史料，从此中国拳术分成内外两家。这是中国武术史上划时代的大事：武当武术与少林武术泾渭分明，于志钧老师说："这是任何人都否定不了的"。

The "Epitaph of Wang Zhengnan", written in the 8th year of Emperor Kangxi's reign (1669) and collected into The *Nanlei Documents*, was the first document with the record of the internal-exercising *Kongfu*. From then on, Chinese *Kongfu* boxing was divided into two schools. This was an epochal event in the history of Chinese Wushu. The Wudang School of Wushu is obviously different from the Shaolin School. This, as Master Yu Zhijun said, is a fact that no one can deny.

在中国武术历史上，"以静制动"是内家拳首先提出的。"以柔克刚"、"以小力胜大力"、"以慢制快"等技击思想都是从"以静制动"衍生出来的。

In the history of Chinese *Kongfu*, the School of the internal-exercising *Kongfu* first proposed to "subdue the moving with stillness," gave birth to these thoughts as "to subdue the firm with softness," "to defeat the powerful with little force," and "to conquer the fast with slowness."

第二章　太极文化

　　张三丰为武当道士，被尊为内家拳的创始人。武当派武术的始祖。张三丰成了内家拳派崇拜的偶像，被尊为太极拳的创始人。《王征南先生传》最重要的内容是记载了内家拳的创造方法，写道："张三丰既精于少林，复从而翻之，是名内家，得其一二者，已足胜少林。"话虽不多，意已明了，内家拳的基础是少林拳。张三丰把少林拳翻（反）过来创造了内家拳。内家拳是专门对付少林拳的。

　　A Taoist priest at the temple on Wudang Mountain named Zhang Sanfeng was renowned and admired as the founder of the Wudang School of Wushu, the internal-exercising *Kongfu* and *Taiji Quan*. The most important thing in "A Biography of Wang Zhengnan" is its record of the invention of *Taiji Quan*: "Zhang Sanfeng, by reversing the Shaolin style of *Kongfu* which he mastered, invented a new style which he named the internal-exercising. A preliminary mastery of the internal-exercising would be enough for defeating the Shaolin *Kongfu*." These few words have made it clear that the foundation of the internal-exercising *Kongfu* boxing is the Shaolin *Kongfu*: that Zhang Sanfeng invented it to go exactly against the Shaolin style.

　　少林拳的特点是：①注重筋骨皮的外部锻炼；②注重力量的训练，所谓"一力降十会"，风格是勇猛、凶狠、快速、直取；③注重先天自然之能的训练，主动、主力、主快、主直、主刚。

　　The characteristics of Shaolin *Kongfu* boxing are: ① emphasizing the exercising of external organs; ② emphasis on force training, seeking to gain the force which would "break ten realms of paper (about 5000 pieces) into pieces at one strike," and assuming to be powerful, fierce, fast, and direct; ③ emphasis on enhancing innate human powers, advocating active motion, power, speed, directness, and firmness.

　　内家拳则是其反面：①注重精、气、神的内部锻炼；②注重意念的训练，即"用意不用力"，风格是文雅、安逸、慢、圆；③注重后天克服本能的训练，主静、主意、主曲、主柔。内家拳是用"以静制动"、"以柔克刚"、四两拨千斤、以弱制强、"以慢

学打太极拳

制快"来对付少林拳的。在内家拳之前,古今中外的技击术都是尚力的强者哲学,内家拳反其道而行之,以静制动,以弱胜强。这一伟大的思想为后来的武术大家王宗岳、陈长兴、杨露禅、武禹襄等宗师追求、发展、完善,最终形成了中华民族之粹——太极拳。

The internal-exercising *Kongfu* boxing has the opposite characteristics: ① attention to the exercising of internal organs, energy, and *qi* (internal air force); ② emphasis on the mind's training, seeking to "sing the will rather than force," assuming to be elegant, peaceful, slow, and rounded; ③ emphasis on the training of acquired skills, advocating tranquility, will-rule, indirectness, and gentleness. The internal-exercising *Kongfu* boxing deals with the Shaolin *Kongfu* boxing by adopting the principles as "to subdue the moving with stillness," "to subdue the firm with softness," "to move the weight of hundreds of tons with the slightest force," "to subdue the strong with softness," and "to defeat the fast with slowness." Before this style of *Kongfu* appeared, all arts of attack and defense adopted the philosophy which stressed strength. The internal-exercising *Kongfu* boxing, however, took the opposite way. This philosophical thought was later pursued, developed, and polished by masters as Wang Zongyue, Chen Changxing, Yang Luchan, Wu Yuxiang, and so forth, for the maturity of *Taiji Quan*, a great legacy of the Chinese nation.

六、练习太极拳"十大要领"
The "Ten Essentials" for Practicing *Taiji Quan*

杨澄甫先生流传下来的"太极拳十要"给我们练习太极拳指明了方向,点出了精华。这十大要领即:

Yang Chengfu's *Ten Essentials for Taiji Quan* shows us the correct way for practicing *Taiji Quan*. These essentials are:

1. **虚领顶劲**:太极拳要求虚领顶劲,即头颈正直,头顶的"百会穴"要向上轻轻顶起,好似一根绳将头顶悬挂起来一样,下颚微收,颈部放松,舌舔上颚,时时

第二章 太极文化

保持精明轻妙的感觉,有头顶青天,脚踩大地的气概。不过这全是意念,不是用力量向上顶。练拳时,只要能时时保持虚领顶劲的感觉,精神自然能提得起。

Keep the neck relaxed and the head upright: It is required that the head and neck be kept upright with force, so that in a sense, the head is hung up to the vertex as it is hung up with a string. The chin is slightly withdrawn; the neck is relaxed; and the tongue sticks up to the maxilla. One should always have the feelings of lightness and alertness, and keep the lofty spirit as if standing steadily on the ground with head pointed up against the sky. All these, however, are done within the mind (by thinking or will) instead of pushing up practically with force. It is easy to get the spirit refreshed as long as the feeling of neck relaxed and head upright is kept.

2. **含胸拔背:** 所谓含胸拔背,即是胸部向内涵虚,舒松自然,使气能下沉丹田。如果胸部外挺,则气易阻滞于胸际,妨碍呼吸的畅通。但也不能故意内缩,故意内缩则易驼背。驼背则使胸腔缩小,使横隔肌受到活动的限制,妨碍呼吸和血液循环。

Keep the chest withdrawn and the back extended straight: The chest is drawn in a relaxed way to let the air go deep down into the pubic region, because if it is projected out, the air would be blocked at the chest, and that would make smooth breathing would be impossible. However, it should not be intentionally withdrawn, because that may cause the crookback that hinders respiration and blood circling as the result of the shrinking thoracic cavity and restricted diaphragm.

3. **松腰敛背:** 腰为全身之主宰,是上下身转动的关键。如果腰能放松,两足有力,则全身既能沉稳有力,又能转动灵活,虚实的变化也是由腰的转动表现出来的。定势时,腰胯要放松,则有利于沉气和贯劲四梢,下盘也更加稳固。故曰命意源头在腰隙。有不得力,必于腰腿求之也。

Keep the waist relaxed and the back restrained: The waist rules over all other body parts and is the hinge for turning the upper and lower body. Relaxing the waist renders the feet powerful, so that the whole body is kept steady and turning agile at the same time. The changes between void and solidity are also realized by the waist's turning. In a still pose, the relaxation of the waist is helpful for making the internal air fall deep and propelling force to the limbs; meanwhile the lower body is made steadier. This is why we say the source of all movements is in the waist. Whenever there is an error, it must be related to the waist and legs.

4. **划分虚实**：太极拳术以分虚实为第一义。如全身皆坐在右腿，则右腿为实，左腿为虚。全身坐在左腿，则左腿为实，右腿为虚。虚实能分，则转动轻灵平稳，毫不费力。如不能分，则迈步重滞，自立不稳，而且被人所牵动。所以身法、手法、步法、腿法的虚实变换，要求做到内外相合、上下相随，上下左右能分清虚实，动作就能圆转自如。

Cut a clear line between the concepts of void and solidity: The clarity between the void and solidity is of the most importance in *Taiji Quan*. If the body is laid on the right leg, the right leg is solid and the left void; vice versa. Once the void and solidity is made clear, the turning becomes agile, steady, and effortless. Otherwise, the stepping would be heavy and unsmooth; the body would be unbalanced; and it is easy to be brought under control. Therefore, the transfer between the void and solidity of the body, hands, steps, and legs needs to be highly cooperated and clear-cut so that all movements are flexible and smooth.

5. **沉肩坠肘**：沉肩者，也就是肩部放松下沉，若不能松沉，两肩耸起则意气上浮，妨碍内气的运行和气血的流畅，全身皆不得力。坠肘者，肘往下松坠下沉之意。肘若悬起，则肩不能沉，放人不远。练拳时，两臂微屈呈弧形，感觉两臂有一种内在的沉劲。

Keep shoulders and elbows drooped: Shoulders need to be drooped naturally; otherwise, the circling of the internal air force and blood would be hindered to make the whole body forceless. Elbows are drooped naturally, too, because if they are lifted up, the shoulders are unable to droop down, which renders effective attacks impossible. When practicing, keep the arms slightly bent into arc-shapes and you may feel internal drooping forces in them.

6. 用意不用力：练太极拳时全是用意不用力。全身放松，松透，四肢百骸柔若无骨，不使有分毫之拙劲，节节贯穿，则力由意生，出劲自然。每一动作的运行都须有意识的指导。拳经所谓："意气君来骨肉臣。"这就说出了意的重要性。

Use will (or consciousness) instead of force: Let the whole body completely relax as if there were no bones in it; maintain utterly smooth transfers between gestures, poses, and movements; in this way, force is brought out by consciousness naturally. Every flow of movement should be guided by consciousness or will. A line mentioned in *Taiji Quan* theories, "the will is like the emperor and the body the minister," which points out the importance of the will.

7. 上下相随：练太极拳时，每一个动作都要求做到上下相随，协调完整。拳经所谓："一动无有不动，一静无有不静。"每个动作都要以腰为轴带动四肢，决不可局部自动，或先手动而后腰动。运动时须根于脚，发于腿，主宰于腰，行于手指。由足而腿而腰至手，总须完整一气，腰脊领动，手足随动，眼神随之，上下连贯，浑然一气。有一不动，即散乱矣。

Keep the upper and lower body in sync: Every movement in *Taiji Quan* needs to be in sync and have coordination on all body parts, as is said in *Taiji Quan* theories, "If one part moves, others move, too; and if it stops, others stop, too." Each movement needs the waist to lead the limbs instead of certain body parts moving by themselves, or the hands moving before the waist does. The movements should be rooted in feet, delivered from legs, controlled by the waist, and launched by hands. The process needs to be done with utter continuity, in which the waist and the back take the lead, and the hands, feet, and eyes follow, to make it a complete whole. Even one part failing to move, it would make the action disheveled.

8. 内外相合：太极拳所练在神。练太极拳要求上下相随，内外相合。故云神为主帅，身为驱使。精神能提得起，自然举动轻灵。拳架不外虚实开合，所谓开者，不

学打太极拳

但手足开,心意亦与之俱开。所谓合者,不但手足合,心意亦与之俱合。能内外合为一气,则浑然无间矣。

Keep the internal and external highly coordinated: *Taiji Quan* emphasizes the importance of exercising the spirit (or will, consciousness). Therefore, we often say the spirit rules, and the body is ruled over. The movements become agile as long as the spirit is high. The basic framework of *Taiji Quan* includes nothing but void, solidity, opening, and closing. In the opening, not only the hands and feet are stretched out, but also the spirit. And the same is true with the closing. Once the internal and external are coordinated, a harmonious, integral whole would come into being.

9. **相连不断**:太极拳整套动作演练起来如行云流水,连绵不断,如长江大河滔滔不绝,以心行气,以气运身,劲断意不断,意断劲相连,周而复始,相连不断。

Keep the movements continuous: The whole series of movements should be done with great continuity just as water flows or clouds float. The mind guides the internal air force to circle around the body; both move in cycles continuously, and even if one of them is interrupted, the other one goes on so that the continuity is kept.

10. **动中求静**:外家拳者,以跳跃为能,用尽气力,故习练后无不喘气者。太极者以静御动,虽动犹静。故练拳架愈慢愈好。慢则呼吸深长,气沉丹田,不可忽快忽慢,忽高忽低,要保持同样高度,这样在动中也求得了静。

Seek stillness in moving: The external-exercising *Kongfu* makes jumping as one of its essentials; therefore, one would be breathless after the practice that takes all of one's energy. *Taiji Quan*, however, seeks to restrain the moving with stillness, and even the moving is endowed with the quality of stillness. Therefore, in practice, the slower the movements the better, because in slow motion, the breaths are deep and the internal air is able to gather at the pubic region. Sudden changes of speed or height should be avoided. In this way, stillness can be gained in moving.

第二章 太极文化

七、太极拳基本功
Basic Skills of *Taiji Quan*

练好太极拳要重视基本功的训练。

To master *Taiji Quan*, one needs to pay great attention to the training of basic skills.

(一) 身体素质之腿功 Physical Qualities: Basic Leg Skills

身体素质有五大类：力量、速度、耐力、灵敏和柔韧。24式太极拳所要求的素质以灵敏和柔韧为主，对灵敏素质的练习没有具体的要求。我们这里讲的是柔韧素质，是由关节的骨结构，关节周围组织体积的大小，胯关节的韧带、肌腱、肌肉与皮肤的伸展性三个因素来衡量。第三个因素对提高柔韧素质关系极大。此外，肌肉活动协调性，关节活动幅度加大，都有助于柔韧性的发展和完善。发展柔韧性，一般采用静力性拉长肌肉、韧带结缔性组织的方法收效较快。

Physical qualities include five aspects: strength, speed, stamina, nimbleness, and pliability. The 24-Step *Taiji Quan* requires high nimbleness and pliability. However, there are no specific instructions for the training of nimbleness. The pliability mentioned here is measured by three factors: the structure of joints, the size of the tissues around the joints, and the elasticity of the ligaments, tendons, muscles and skin around the hip joints. The third factor is of the most importance to the building of pliability. In addition, the coordinated moving of muscles and the enlarged moving degree of joints are both helpful for the development and perfection of pliability. The most common and effective way of pliability building is to stretch connective tissues as muscles and ligaments with still force.

关于上肢和腰的柔韧性练习，这里从简。对于下肢的柔韧性练习，这里也只提几个主要方法仅供参考。

The current book will skip introducing the pliability training methods of arms and the waist; as for the leg's liability training, a few methods are provided below.

学打太极拳

1. 正压腿：面对扶手，并步站立，左脚提起，脚跟放在相当胯高的扶手上，脚尖向上用力勾起，两手扶按在左膝上，两膝伸直，立腰，收腹向前下振压。左右脚交替进行。

Front leg-pressing: Stand to face the handrail which is hip-high; raise the left leg and put the foot on the handrail; force the tiptoe to bend up; put hands on the left knee which, together with the right one, are stretched straight; bend the upper body forward and downward for pressing. Take turns to exercise both legs.

2. 侧压腿：侧对扶手，左腿在里，两脚并立，左腿举起，脚跟放在扶手上，脚尖向上用力勾起，右臂上举，左臂胸前平屈，上体向左振压，右手扶左脚，左臂从胸前向右振动，眼看上方，左右脚交替进行。

Sideway leg-pressing: Stand with the handrail on the left side; raise the left leg and put the foot on the handrail; force the tiptoe to bend up; raise the right arm up and put the left arm in front of the chest; press the upper body leftward with the right hand touching the left foot and wave the left arm rightward; eyes look up. Take turns exercising both legs.

3. 仆步压腿：两腿左右大开立，右腿屈膝全蹲，右脚向右45度角，与右膝同向，全脚着地；左腿挺膝伸直，全脚着地，左脚尖内扣，身体左转，两手同时扶在左脚背外侧，或左手扶在左脚外侧，右手扶在右脚面上，做蹲压起伏动作，两腿交替进行。

Leg-pressing in the crouching way: Stand with feet fully parted sideways; squat completely on the right leg with the foot (completely on the ground) turned 45 degrees rightward to point at the same direction with the knee; stretch the left leg straight; put the whole left foot on the ground with the tiptoe turned inward; turn the body left; meanwhile put hands on the outside of the left instep, or the left hand on the outside and the right top of the instep; make up and down movements for the pressing. Take turns exercising both legs.

第二章　太极文化

4. **正踢腿**：并步直立,两臂侧平举成立掌,左脚向前半步踏实站稳,右脚尖勾起,向前额处猛踢,两眼平视前方。上踢要猛,下落要控制慢落。两腿交替进行。

Front kicking: Stand straight with feet juxtaposed; raise arms to horizontal positions on both sides with hands erect; put the left foot half a step forward and stand on it steadily; kick with the right leg forcefully up to the direction of the forehead with the tiptoe bent up; set eyes on the front. The upward kicking should be sudden and forceful, while the falling should be made slow. Take turns exercising both legs.

5. **侧踢腿**：侧对前进方向,左侧对前,两臂侧平举,掌心向上,右脚从左脚前向左跨半步,左脚勾起,用力向左侧上方猛踢;左臂内旋屈肘,经右摆动至胸前,掌心向下,右臂内旋,向头上方摆动,掌心向上,连续练习,折回时交换,右侧对前。

Sideways kicking: Stand with the left side facing the forward advancing direction; raise arms to horizontal positions on both sides with palms facing up; put the right foot half a step to the left (from before the left foot), and kick with the left foot (tiptoe bent up) suddenly and forcefully up to the left; twist the left arm inward, bend it, and wave it before the chest with the palm facing down; the right arm is twisted inward and waved towards above the head with the palm facing up. Keep going this way, and when turning around, face the front with the right side of the body.

6. **弓步压腿**：左脚向前迈出一大步,屈膝成左弓步,右腿伸直,右脚尖成45到60度角,身体向上下起伏压腿。再换成右弓步压腿,此动作主要是拉长胯根内部的韧带。

Bow-shape leg-pressing: Take a large step forward the left foot and bend the leg into a bow-shape; stretch the right leg straight with the tiptoe turned 45 to 60 degrees inward; move the body up and down for the pressing. Then turn to the right form of bow-shape leg pressing. The purpose is mainly to stretch the ligaments inside the hips.

学打太极拳

7. **外摆腿**：面对前进方向站立，两臂侧平举，成立掌，右脚向前半步踏实，左脚尖向上勾起，从左侧向右向上猛力踢起，然后经面前向左方外摆，直腿落于右脚内侧；两腿交替进行。左腿向左摆时，左手即拍打左脚外侧击响，右腿向右摆时，两手同时击响右脚外侧。

Outward leg-waving: Stand to face the front; raise arms to horizontal positions on both sides with hands erect; step a half step forward with the right foot and stand steadily on it; wave the left leg (foot bent up) forcefully rightward, upward, and then out to the left, then finally falling down beside the right foot. Take turns exercising both legs. When waving the left leg to the left, pat the outside of the left foot with the left hand; the same is true with the right foot.

8. **里合腿**：面对前进方向站立，两臂侧平举，成立掌，右脚向前半步踏实，左脚尖向上勾起，从左侧向左向上猛踢起，然后经面前向右方内摆，左腿向右内摆，右手击拍左脚内侧击响，直腿落于右腿内侧，两腿交替进行。

Inward leg-waving: Stand to face the front; raise arms to horizontal positions on both sides with hands erect; take half a step forward with the right foot and stand steadily on it; bend the left tiptoe up, kick forcefully up to the left, and then wave the leg in to the right; as the left leg waves rightward, pat on the inside of the left foot with the right hand; set the left leg (stretched straight) beside the right one. Take turns exercising both legs.

9. **控腿**：在正压腿的基础上，左腿离开扶手上举，控制其腿平举，在此基础上，平举之腿屈膝收回，小腿再向上平举，两腿交替进行。

Leg-controlling: Upon the pose of the front leg-pressing, raise the left leg up from the handrail and keep it on the horizontal position; then bend the knee to draw the foreleg back and raise it up again. Exercise both legs by turns.

（二）桩功 "Piling" Skills

常言道："练拳不练功，到老一场空。"太极拳的基本功除腿功的训练外还有哪些呢？又从何练起呢？

第二章 太极文化

The old saying goes: "Learning *Kongfu* would be in vain without practicing the basic skills." What basic skills do we have to practice apart from the leg skills? And which one should we start from?

王宗岳《太极拳论》第一句话即是"太极者,无极而生"。太极十三势的"掤、捋、挤、按、采、列、肘、靠、进、退、顾、盼、定。"我们从哪个基本功练起呢?从多年的练拳实践中,我体会到要练好太极拳,首先要注重基本功的锻炼,站桩是太极拳的入门功,也是贯穿始终进入高级阶段的高级功夫,是重要的练习内容之一。

Wang Zongyue emphasized in the first sentence of his "On *Taiji Quan*" that "*Taiji* was born from *Wuji*." There are thirteen basic skills of *Taiji Quan*: *bing*, stroking, squeezing, pressing, picking, breaking, elbowing, leaning, advancing, retreating, attending left, attending right, and stabilizing. So from which one should we start? In my years of practice, I realized that one should focus on the most basic skill first-the "piling" (standing or moving by assuming the body as a pile on the ground which implies steadiness-translator), which, as not only an entrance skill, but also an advanced skill throughout the practice of *Taiji Quan*, is one of the more important training projects that we learn.

那么我们首先的功法即为无极桩,也就是十三势中最后一个字"定"开始练起。站桩功法过去仅为养身之术,后来人们在锻炼中逐渐发现了站桩可以培养出超乎寻常的技术能力,故将其引入太极拳作为基本功。桩功分以下几种:

The "piling" was originally regarded as a body nourishing method; only later was it discovered to be able to nurture unusual skills and abilities, and therefore was introduced into *Taiji Quan*. The "piling" skills contain the following types:

1. 静功 Still Skills

(1) 无极桩 The *Wuji* Piling

The *Wuji* Piling is the first thing that we are seeking, which corresponds to the last of the thirteen basic skills: stabilizing.

学打太极拳

1）两脚开立同肩宽,身体直立,头正悬顶,即百会穴虚上顶,收下颚,竖颈椎,两肩松沉,两肩自然下垂,手指微屈舒展,指尖轻附两腿外侧,含胸拔背,收腹敛臀,松腰松胯,两膝微屈放松,脚趾微微抓地,脚掌微含力点于涌泉穴。呼吸自然平稳,意守丹田,目视前方。要求:练习此桩功领悟心静体松,身正安舒。

Separate the feet as wide as that of shoulders; keep the body and head upright; withdraw the chin; keep the cervical vertebra upright; droop shoulders naturally; have the fingers slightly bent with tips touching the sides of thighs; keep the chest withdrawn and the back extended upright; keep the belly and buttocks in; relax the waist and hips; slightly bend and relax the knees; toes are slightly bent in (in a relaxed way) on the ground; soles are made shallowly hollow with force collected at the center. Breaths are natural and smooth. The mind is focused on the pubic region. Eyes are set on the front.

Requirements: When practicing this skill, try to experience the feelings of a peaceful mind and the relaxed, uprightness, and easiness of the body.

2）二会一点,即百会、会阴、二涌泉中点与地面垂直。

The line through the center of the head, the crotch and the central point between the feet should be perpendicular with the ground.

3）全身松透,肌肉、骨关节、五脏六腑放松。

Keep the whole body, including muscles, joints and internal organs, completely relaxed.

4）意念活动要求:无思无虑,无我无他,无天无地,拳无拳意无意,只有这样才能无意之中出真意,空空洞洞,虚虚实实,混沌中有一点真气。

Requirements for the mind (consciousness): Utterly void; thoughtless; surroundings kept completely out. Only in this way can the true consciousness be born from the unconscious and a bit of pure air force kept within the "Chaos".

5）时间要求:1小时以上或更长的时间,无极桩的功效不可思议。小成者祛病延年；中成者在此基础上修炼太极拳时得心应手，随心所欲，太极十三势收发自如；大成者可开发人体智慧和潜能，对生命产生新的体验，实现天人合一。只有坚持不懈，持之以恒地站桩，才能进入内不知有身心，外不知有世界的无极态，从而达到内气不悟而自悟，神精不养而自养，筋骨不练而自练，这种状态能使大脑皮层的活动得到很好的抑制，从而调整人体阴阳平衡，气血运行，实现内气彭荡，以意导气，以气运身。

Time requirement: more than one hour or longer. The *Wuji* piling has unimaginable effects. A preliminary mastery is helpful for health building; a medium mastery makes *Taiji Quan* practice a lot easier; and a complete mastery is able to awaken human wisdom and potential, so much that one gains new experience about life and the union of self and nature. Persistence to this leads to the state in which one is completely unaware of the existence of the self and the surroundings, so as to get spontaneous nurture of the internal force and the body. The state is effective to restrain the activities as the pallium, and therefore manages to regulate the balance of physical systems and the smooth circling of the internal air and blood to make the body energetic.

(2) 马步桩 The Bucking Squat

两脚相距三脚远，平行或小八字步，重心落于两脚中间，屈膝下蹲，大腿与小腿的夹角为120度为宜，上体要求同无极桩。两手屈臂呈弧形，手指微屈自然展开，指尖相对掤于胸前，掌心朝里，劳宫穴对于乳峰。脚趾五趾抓地，掌心微含，力点于涌泉穴。时间要求同无极桩。请大家牢记太极筑基要言：足踏大地头顶天，怀抱朝阳背靠山，马步蹲裆气逆行，尾闾中正经络通，前似海潮翻巨浪，上如瀑布汇涌泉，呼吸深长心入静，神臻仙境飘飘然。

要求：上体中正，意守丹田，呼吸自然平缓，初练时每次三至五分钟，久练后每次练习时间可逐渐增加。

Stand with feet separated (on parallel lines or both feet turned outward slightly) as wide as the length of three feet; place the center of gravity in the center of the two feet; squat with legs bent into approximately 120 degrees angles. The upper body shares the same requirements with the *Wuji* piling. Arms are bent into arc-shapes in front of the chest; fingers are slightly bent; with the palms, pointing at each other with fingertips, face inward with the center in opposition to the breasts. Toes are slightly bent in (in a relaxed way); soles are made shallowly hollow with force collected at the center. The time requirement is the same as the *Wuji* piling. Please keep in mind these guiding lines for foundation building: Rest the feet steadily, and point the head to the sky; shape the bosom as if embracing the sun, and stretch the back upright as if leaning against a mountain; squat as a horse bucks, with the air force circling in the opposite way; keep the hips centralized to make the channels unblocked; hands move as waves rolling around at the front, and the spirit converges into the head from above like a waterfall; breathe deep, and keep a peaceful mind; the consciousness attains a fairyland on wings.

Requirements: Keep the upper body upright; focus the mind on the pubic region; keep smooth breaths. Practice for three to five minutes once at the beginning, and prolong the duration gradually.

(3) 开合桩 Opening and Closing

在马步桩姿势的基础上,两臂做向外掤开与内收合的练习。要求:两臂向外掤开时为"吸气",用逆式呼吸法,小腹内收,两手臂意识如抱"汽球"充气一般;两臂向内收合时为"呼气",小腹放松,两手臂意识如抱"汽球"排气一般,初练学时呼吸力求自然、平缓、畅通,不要憋气。久练之后逐渐加大呼吸深度,做到呼到再不能呼时变为"吸气",吸到再不能吸时变为呼气。每次可练习三至五分钟,久练后每次练习时间可逐渐增加。

目的:两手臂外掤与里收培养"开中寓合,合中寓开",逐渐形成意到、气到、力到、内外合一,内劲浑厚圆满的意识。

Extend the arms out and then draw back to the chest upon the pose of the bucking squat. Requirements: Inhale in the reversed breathing way (the belly draws in) when extending arms out, as if holding a balloon that is being inflated; and exhale with the belly releasing out when drawing arms back, as if holding a balloon that is being exflated. At the beginning, try to breathe in the natural, smooth way; do not hold breaths. After practicing for a long time, deepen the respiration to its greatest extent: inhale when exhalation has reached its peak, and *vice versa*. For beginners, three to five minutes at a time is appropriate, and the duration should be gradually lengthened.

Purposes: Arms extend out and draw back to the chest for "Opening implies closing and closing implies opening", gradually readiness of the mind, the qi, and force and coordinating the internal and external force.

(4) 升降桩 Rising and Falling

升桩：在马步桩姿势的基础上，两手臂缓缓向前平举至肩高，同肩宽，此时两腿随举臂同时起立。两肘微下垂，手指微屈掌心内含向下；目视两手。两臂平举时为吸气，用意念将丹田气提升贴于脊背，此式为升桩。用意不用力，自然由蹲慢慢起身直立。

降桩：当两手臂升至肩高时，两腿屈膝下蹲，同时两手臂垂肘，下按至腹前方，屈膝下蹲时为呼气，用意行气沉入丹田，此式为降桩。一升一降反复练习。

要求：初练升降桩，呼吸力求自然、平缓、通畅，不要憋气，久练后可逐渐加大呼吸深度。当两臂升至肩高吸气到达极点，改为呼气。同样，两手臂下按至腹前时，呼气达到极点，改为吸气。一升一降为一次练习。初练时可练习三至五分钟，久练后每次练习时间可逐渐增加。目的是达到使劲力起于脚，通于背，达于手的协调练习，理解"升"练"掤劲"，"降"练"采"的目的。

Rising: Begin with the bucking squat. Lift arms (with distance as that of shoulders) forward to the horizontal level of shoulders, and in the meantime extend legs gradually straight to stand up. Elbows are slightly drooped, and the palms a little concaved, faced downward with fingers slightly bent. Eyes are set on both hands. Inhale when raising the arms, and lift up (in consciousness) the air at the pubic region to the back. Use the mind (consciousness) instead of force. Stand up slowly in a natural way and alternate between rising and falling.

Requirements: At the beginning, try to breathe in a natural, smooth way; do not hold breaths. After practicing for a long time, deepen the respiration gradually. When arms reach the height of shoulders, inhale the most you can before exhaling; likewise, when arms reach the front of the belly, exhale the most you can before inhaling. A round is composed of a rising and a falling. For beginners, three to five minutes at a time is appropriate, and the duration could be gradually lengthened. One of the purposes is to train the force, which is supposed to start from the feet and reach the hands through the back. Another purpose is to let one have a true grasp of the meanings of "the rising exercises the *bing* force, and the falling exercises the picking force."

（5）虚步桩和独立桩 The Void-Step Piling and Single-Legged Piling

1）虚步桩 The Void-Step Piling

① 两脚平行分开，与肩同宽，身体中正自然，两肩松沉，两手臂自然松垂手指尖轻附两腿外侧，目视前方。

② 两手臂缓缓向前，平举至肩高肩宽，两肘微下垂，手指微屈，掌心向下，两手臂缓缓向前，平举时为吸气，用意行气由丹田上升贴于脊背，此式为"升式"。

③ 当两手臂升至肩高时，两腿屈膝下蹲，同时沉肩坠肘，两手下按至腹前，掌心向下，舒指展掌；目视两手前下方。屈膝下蹲，两手下按时为呼气，用意行气沉入丹田，为"降式"。

要求：松腰敛臀，两手下按和屈膝下蹲时要求协调一致，两手要向下沉，用意下"采"。

① The feet are separated on parallel lines as wide as the shoulders. Keep the body upright and relaxed. Shoulders are drooped. Arms hang naturally with fingertips touching the sides of thighs. Eyes are set on the front.

② Arms (separated as wide as shoulders) rise forward to the height of the shoulders with elbows slightly drooped, fingers slightly bent and the palm facing down. Inhale when the arms rise, and lift (in consciousness) the air force up from the pubic region to the back. This is called the "rising form."

③ Bend the legs to squat the moment the arms reach the height of the shoulders, and move the hands down to the front of the belly in the pressing way with palms facing down; extend the palms and fingers. Look down to the front of the hands. Inhale when squatting and pressing, and lower (in consciousness) the air force down to the pubic region. This is called the "falling form."

Requirements: Relax the waist, and do not let the buttocks project out. The hands' pressing and the squatting are required to be in coordination. The hands should fall down with the intention of "picking" in consciousness.

④ 重心移于右腿，左脚跟提起，上体微右转。两手臂微微向两侧上方分开，两手略低于肩，目视左前方。

Move the center of gravity to the right leg; lift the left heel up; and turn the upper body slightly rightward. The arms go up to each side (a little lower than the shoulders). Look at the left-front side with your eyes.

⑤ 提起左脚向前方迈出半步，脚跟着地，脚尖翘起，左膝微屈，同时两臂向左胸前相合，左手指尖同鼻高，掌心向右，右掌在左肘内下方掌心向左，掌心斜相对，指尖均朝前上方，目视左掌方向，如同手挥琵琶。

Take a half step forward with the left foot and with the heel set on the ground and the tiptoe bent up; the left knee is slightly bent. At the same time, draw the arms close to each other at the front of the left chest; face the left palm rightward with the fingertips as high as the nose, and the right palm, facing leftward, is under the inner side of the left elbow. The palms face each other slantingly, and all fingers point up to the front. Eyes are set on the direction of the left palm. This is similar to the pose of "Playing the Lute."

⑥ 左脚收回成两脚平行开立步，与肩同宽，两腿屈膝，两手臂胸前平举。两肘微下垂，手指微屈，掌心微合，掌心向下，而后两腿伸直起身，两臂上升同肩高，目视两手。两臂上升平举时为吸气，用意行气由丹田上升贴于脊背。

Draw the left foot back to form the parallel parted step (as wide as the shoulders); bend the legs; and raise the arms levelly before the chest with elbows drooped slightly, fingers bent a little, and with the palms concaved and facing down. Then extend the legs straight to stand up and raise the arms to the height of shoulders. Set eyes on both hands. Inhale when raising the arms, and lift the air force from the pubic region up to the back.

⑦ 两腿屈膝下蹲,同时沉肩坠肘,两手下按至腹前,掌心向下,舒指展掌;目视前下方。屈膝下蹲时为呼气。

Bend the legs and squat down; and at the same time, droop the shoulders and elbows while the hands press down to the front of the belly with palms facing down; extend the palms and fingers while the hands go down. Look at the front and exhale when squatting.

⑧ 重心移于左腿,右脚跟提起,上体微微向左转。两手臂向左右微微分开,两手略低于肩,目视右前方。手臂要有"开中寓合,合中寓开"的意识,产生掤的内劲。

Move the weight to the left leg; lift the right heel; turn the upper body leftward slightly. Move the hands to their respective sides a little, to a position slightly lower than shoulders. Look at the right-front. There should be a sense of "opening implies closing and closing implies opening" in the moving of arms, thus producing the internal force of *bing*.

⑨ 右脚向前迈出半步,脚跟着地,脚尖翘起,右膝微屈,同时两手臂微屈向右胸前相合,右手指尖同鼻高,左掌在右肘内下方,目视掌方向,如同右琵琶式。

Take a half step forward with the right foot and set the heel on the ground and the tiptoe bent up; keeping the knee slightly bent. Meanwhile the arms are slightly bent and drawn close to each other in front of the right chest, with the right fingertips as high as the nose and the left palm under the inner side of the right elbow. Set eyes on the right hand. This is similar to the right form of "Playing the Lute."

左右式反复交替进行练习,收式还原时,两脚平行开立步与肩同宽,身体中正自然,两手臂松垂,两掌轻附于两腿外侧,目视前方。

第二章 太极文化

Take turns to practice by repeating the left and right forms. In the ending pose, the feet are parted on parallel lines as wide as the shoulders, the body is upright in a natural way, and the arms hang relaxed with the palms attached lightly to the outside of thighs. Eyes are fixed on the front.

要求：头虚领顶劲，下颚微收，沉肩坠肘，含胸拔背，上体中正，收腹敛臀。定势时前手指与前脚尖、鼻尖三尖相对，肩、肘、手与胯、足一一相合。精神集中，用意领气，吸气贴于背，呼气沉于丹田穴，意气运转须换得灵，周身务求自然舒松，不用拙力，两腋下虚空，两臂用意内合。

Requirements: Keep the neck void-forced and the head upright with force propelled to the vertex (in consciousness). Draw the chin slightly in. Shoulders and elbows droop downward. Keep the chest withdrawn and the back extended upright. The upper body should not lean to any side. The belly is withdrawn and so are the buttocks. In a still pose, the tip of the fingers of the hand, the tip of the toes and the nose correspond to each other; and coordination should be maintained among shoulders, elbows, hands, hips, and feet. Maintain concentration, and lead the internal air force with the mind. Inhale to lift the air force up to the back, and exhale to lower it down to the pubic region. The transfer of the internal air force should be nimble. The body must be kept relaxed and natural without any sudden use of force. The armpits are hollow and arms contain the sense of closing.

目的：每次练习不论时间长短，都要持之以恒，领悟意、气、形的协调配合；气贴背敛入脊骨，力由脊发，步随身换，久练之后，对周身内劲及腰腿功夫的增长，都有很大的促进作用。此功法含有太极十三势中的前进、后退、左顾、右盼、中定以及攻守等势，所以在太极拳桩功练习中极为重要，亦称太极拳的"技术桩"。

Purposes: However long or short it is for each time of practice, persistence is strongly recommended for grasping the coordination of the mind, the internal air force and the body. The air force is attached to the back and then gathered into the spine; then it is sent out from the back; and the steps change according to the turning of the upper body. Practicing for a long time in this way greatly enhances the inner force along with the waist and leg abilities. This kind of "piling" contains several of the thirteen basic postures in *Taiji Quan*—advancing, retreating, attending left, attending right, stabilizing, and other postures of attack and defense; therefore, it is of great importance among the "piling" skills. This is probably why it is also called the "technical piling" in *Taiji Quan*.

2）独立桩：Single-Legged Piling

立正站立，重心移于右脚，左腿屈膝提起，小腿放松，脚脖放松，脚尖自然下垂，膝关节高过胯，与腰平，左掌立掌指尖向上屈臂上举，掌心向右，高与眉齐，左膝与左肘相对，右手按于右胯旁，手心朝下，虎口向前，右腿全脚着地，微屈站稳，意念下沉，自然呼吸，眼看前方。左右独立桩交替练习，如金鸡独立。此桩有转侧之精，独立之能，争斗之勇。具有独立平稳之特性，又有俯身屈腿踏远，变化敏捷之特征。

Stay attentive and move the center of gravity to the right foot. Lift the left leg up, with the knee bent to let the foreleg and the ankle relax and the tiptoe droop naturally. The knee is lifted on the same level with the waist. Make the left hand vertical with fingers pointing up and lift the arm up until the right-facing palm reaches the level of the eyebrows. The left knee corresponds to the left elbow. Place the right hand at the side of the right hip with the palm facing down and the "tiger's mouth" facing the front. The right leg, slightly bent, is set completely and steadily on the ground. The will (or consciousness) moves downward. Eyes are set on the front. Repeat the left and right forms alternately. This type of "piling" is endowed with the essence of turning, the ability of standing single-legged with the vigor of attacking. It is characterized by the steadiness of single-legged standing, and the agility of downward leaning, leg bending, and large-pace stepping.

2. 动功 Moving Skills

也是太极功,先师杨澄甫先生曰："不动为无极,已动为太极。"怎么动起来呢？

第二章　太极文化

Moving skills refer to the *Taiji* skills, as Mr. Yang Chengfu put it: "*Wuji* is the state of stillness, while *Taiji* is the state of moving." The question is how to move?

（1）八种手法：Eight Hand Skills

1）掤、捋、挤、按（四正手）
2）采、列、肘、靠（四隅手）

1) *Bing*, stroking, squeezing, and pressing (the four central hand skills)
2) Picking, breaking, elbowing, and leaning (the four sideways hand skills)

（2）五种步法：进、退、顾、盼、定的训练。牢记筑基要言：太极原是无极生，阴阳虚实要分清，手捧八卦意领先，沾连黏随六合宗，掤、捋、挤、按懒扎衣，进、退、顾、盼、定五行，久练此桩秉元气，技击尽在此功中。

Five stepping skills: advancing, retreating, attending left, attending right, and stabilizing. Keep in mind these important lines for building a foundation: *Taiji* was born from *Wuji*; *Yin* and *Yang* (void and solidity) should be made clear; hands move in response to the Eight Diagrams, while the mind takes the lead; in following and sticking, coordination is of the most importance; shed, stroke, squeeze, and press with clothes loosely fastened; advancing, retreating, attending left and right, and stabilizing compose the basic skills of stepping; persist to practice this and the pneuma will be grasped, for all skills of attack and defense are included in it.

综上所述，告诉我们未经练拳，先练此桩，即练脚——太极脚。在没有手上动作干扰的情况下，(掤、捋、挤、按、采、列、肘、靠)用心专一地练习静功，练得其法。到练手上功夫时，有坚实的脚上功夫作基础，就能事半功倍，练拳先练脚是一条练拳的捷径。所以说站桩是走步的基础，走步又是站桩的继续。走步即走好太极步——猫行步。

As is told by the above lines, before we move on to the hand skills, we should first practice this type of "piling," the stepping skills or the *Taiji* steps.

学打太极拳

Concentrate on the stepping skills without the interference of the hand movements first, and later it will be a lot easier to master the hand skills with the foundation of solid foot skills. It is a shortcut to begin with the foot. "Pile" standing is therefore the groundwork of stepping. And by stepping we mean the *Taiji* stepping, or the cat-style stepping.

先师杨澄甫先生在《太极拳之练习谈》中所述:"两腿宜分虚实,起落犹似猫行";武禹襄在《打手要言》中又说:"迈步如猫行,运动如抽丝。"我们现在将太极拳上步及进步之步法、步型称之为"猫行步"或"蛇行步"、"虎步",这是我们习练24式太极拳主要而最基本的步法步型。常言道"先看一步走,再看一伸手",一言道破步法步型在太极拳中之地位,欲具有高素质的拳架者,则必须具有高质量的"猫行步"。

Master Yang Chengfu pointed out in his On the Practice of *Taiji Quan*: "Legs need to be differentiated as void-forced and solid-force; and the stepping should be like that of a cat." Master Wu Yuxiang also mentioned in his "Important Points for Striking": "Step as a cat does, and move as if reeling the silk thread off cocoons." The stepping is now named the "cat-style stepping," the "snake-style stepping," or the "tiger-style stepping," which is the most basic stepping skill in the 24-Step *Taiji Quan*. The saying, "Judge firstly by one's stepping, and then his/her hand moving," shows exactly the importance of the stepping skills. One has to master the "cat-style stepping" if he/she wants to have high-quality *Kongfu* postures.

3. 迈好猫型步的几点要求:Requirements for the Cat-Style Stepping

如何迈好太极步,即如何做到"迈步如猫行"需注意以下几点。以简化24式太极拳左弓步之后迈右步为例。

The following points should be paid attention to for making the correct *Taiji* stepping (stepping as in the cat walks). For example, the stepping with the right foot after the "left bow-shape step":

第二章　太极文化

（1）左弓步后，重心移至左脚跟，腰胯左移，向左撇脚，逐渐坐实左腿，重心百分之百在左脚，左膝与左脚尖上下相应，臀部与脚跟齐平。

After the left leg bows, move the center of gravity to the left heel; move the waist and hips to the left; the left foot turns outward; then gradually transfer the whole weight of the body on the left foot; the knee and tiptoe are on the same vertical line, so are the hips and heel.

（2）一动无有不动。当以左脚跟为轴外撇时，右脚跟应随之离地外展，以便身法、步法相随和，动作顺达。

If one foot moves, the other one moves too. When the left tiptoe turns outward with the heel as an axis, the right heel turns outward at the same time, so that the body and steps are in harmony and the movements are smooth.

（3）肩胯相合。腰左转时，肩与胯也要同时左转，如腰、肩转，胯不转，则成了扭腰，因此说腰、胯同时转。

Keep the shoulders, waist, and hips coordinated. When the waist turns left, the shoulders and hips should turn to the same direction. If the waist and shoulders turned and the hips did not, a twisted waist would be formed.

（4）内劲潜转。腰胯左转时产生的内劲，经腿、膝至脚跟，像钻头似地左旋入地，左腿稳固了，迈右脚方能做得轻灵、稳健。

The inside force is swirled downward. When the waist and hips turn left, they produce an inside force that drills into the ground through the left leg, knee, and heel. This makes the left leg fixed, so that the right foot movement can be agile and steady.

（5）两肩齐平。腰胯左转时，不能出现左肩低、右肩高的现象，以免破坏立身中正。

Shoulders are kept balanced. When the waist and hips turn, the left shoulder should not be lower than the right one; otherwise, the balance of the body would be broken.

（6）点起点落。提右脚不要蹬地而起，也不要擦地拖起，更不能全脚掌同时离地，而是脚跟外侧先离地，然后脚掌内侧离地，犹如从泥浆中轻轻地将腿拔起，点起点落是迈太极步的规律之一。

Gradually rise and fall. The right foot is not lifted by kicking the ground, or being dragged and rubbing the ground, or by taking the whole foot away at the same time. The correct way is: the right side of the heel leaves the ground first, and the left side of the sole leaves last, as if lifting the leg lightly from mud. Rising and falling by bits is one of the essential rules of the *Taiji* step.

（7）旋踝转腿。提右脚时，右腿应内旋，右脚前伸时，右腿要外旋，其旋转的幅度要比旋腕转臂小得多，不要做得太明显。

Twist the ankle and leg. Lift the right foot, twist the leg inward; then put it forward and twist it outward. The degree of twisting the leg is much smaller than twisting the arm; therefore, it should not be done too obviously.

（8）提脚不能过高。右脚不要提得过高，离地宜超过一拳，脚尖自然下垂。

Do not lift the foot too high. The right foot cannot be lifted too high; a fist's width would be appropriate for the distance between the foot and the ground. Keep the tiptoe naturally drooped.

（9）关节放松。提脚伸腿均以大腿带小腿，右踝关节和膝关节放松自然。

Keep the joints relaxed. Let the thigh lead the foreleg in either by lifting the foot or by stretching the leg. Keep the right ankle and knee naturally relaxed.

第二章 太极文化

（10）脚走弧形。右脚提起后不要直向前迈，应略靠近左踝旁弧形前伸。

Move the foot in an arc-line. After the right foot is lifted, do not move it straightly forward. Make it move in an arc-line with the top of the arc close to the left ankle.

（11）轻轻出步。左膝微屈，以最小的力送右脚前伸，轻起轻落，又是迈太极步的法则之一。

Step lightly. Bend the left leg slightly and put the right foot forward with the little force. Rising and falling lightly is another rule of the *Taiji* step.

（12）敛臀。右脚前伸时要敛臀，不可突臀或扭臀，影响立身中正。

Keep the buttocks withdrawn. Move the right foot forward and keep the buttocks retracted. Do not make them protruded or twisted, because it will affect the balance of the body.

（13）松胯。右脚前伸应与腰胯左转同时开始，右胯松开，使胯关节周围较紧的韧带松弛，腿膝则灵活，迈步会轻灵；另外，松胯后又不可使迈步开阔，以保持右弓步两脚的横向距离。

Keep the hips relaxed. The forward stepping of the right foot should happen at the same time with the left turning of the waist and hips. Relax the right hip (make the ligaments around the hip joint relaxed) so that the leg can be nimble so the step can be light and agile. Meanwhile, in order to keep the distance between the feet, the step should not be made too large after the relaxation of the hip.

（14）边伸边落。右脚前迈时，应边伸边落，当右腿伸直（非挺直）时，脚跟正好着地，切莫在空中伸直后再慢慢着地。

Put the foot downward while stretching the leg. When the right foot steps forward, it should be put down gradually as the leg is being stretched. The heel should touch the ground at the exact time that the leg is stretched naturally straight. Do not put the foot down after the leg is stretched straight.

学打太极拳

(15) 自然伸直。右腿伸直时,不可呈笔直状态,膝关节略弯曲,以免大腿肌肉紧张,影响腰胯转换。

Keep the leg naturally straight. When the right leg is stretched, it should not be completely straight. Keep the knee slightly bent, in order not to cause tension to the thigh muscles.

(16) 分清虚实。右脚跟着地要轻,如履薄冰,不要全脚掌同时着地,也不要同打夯一样落地有声,右脚落地一刹那,重心仍在左脚。

Distinguish between void and solid forces. The right foot touches the ground lightly as stepping on thin ice. Do not stand with the whole foot, or step heavily with loud noises. At the moment the right foot touches the ground, the center of gravity is still on the left foot.

(17) 方向准确。右脚前伸后的方向要正,不要外撇,脚尖朝前,以免影响右弓步的步型。

Keep the direction correct. The right tiptoe should be kept pointing to the front when the foot is put forward. Do not turn it outward or it will affect the correctness of the bow-shape.

(18) 平实踏地。右脚跟先着地,依次为脚掌、脚尖着地,待全脚踏平后,再蹬左腿,这样容易扎地生根。

Step on the ground steadily. Have the right heel touches the ground first, followed by the sole and the tiptoe. Extend the left leg after the right foot is firmly set on the ground, which helps make the whole body balanced.

(19) 步幅自然。迈步的幅度以右脚跟着地的距离为准。拳架高,步幅即小,易分清虚实,但运动量小;拳架低,运动量大,易患换步不灵、起伏和断劲等毛病。总之,步幅大小,要根据个人体质和技术而定。

第二章　太极文化

Keep an appropriate stepping pace, which is decided by how far the right heel steps on the ground. Small paces make it easy to distinguish between void and solid movements, but with less amount of exercise. Large paces cost more energy, but make unsmooth transition of steps, movements, and forces easy to happen. Nonetheless, the degree of pace is decided by one's physical condition and his or her mastery of the essentials.

（20）速度均匀。在迈步过程中，提脚和前伸速度要均匀，不可忽快忽慢，更不可在左踝旁停留或脚尖点地。

Maintain the same speed. In the process of stepping forward, the lifting and stretching should be in the same speed. Do not make it suddenly fast or low, not to mention stopping the left ankle.

（21）身体保持水平，不可起伏。在提脚前伸的整个迈步过程中，拳架要始终如一，不可忽高忽低上下起伏，以避免和减小运动量步幅忽大忽小。

Keep the body balanced. During the whole process of stepping, the height of the pose should be kept uniform, without rising or falling abruptly to avoid the changes of energy cost and paces.

（22）随遇平衡。右脚踏平后，重心才徐徐前移，其过程如同太极阴阳图慢慢、均匀地转变，即从无到有，从小到大，由30%、60%到100%坐实右腿，随遇平衡是正确调整重心的方法。

Balance is preserved in the whole process, from right after the right foot sets steadily on the ground that the center of gravity moves gradually forward. The transition is slow and smooth, as that in the *Taiji* symbol, from zero percent to completely setting the weight on the right leg. Preserving balance anytime is the right way to adjust the center of gravity.

学打太极拳

接下来迈左腿也是如此,即右脚百分之百的重心又渐渐变为零,这样往复转换,一步一太极,故前人把太极拳的迈步称之太极步。

The left leg moves in the same way, i.e., the weight on the right leg is transferred gradually to the left one. This process is repeated, with each step being a completion of the *Taiji*-style transition of force or weight; hence, the stepping in *Taiji Quan* was named the *Taiji* stepping.

第三章　教学随笔
Chapter Three Random Sketches on Teaching

一、练好太极拳具备的条件

Conditions for the Mastery of *Taiji Quan*

练好太极拳要具备"三要素"：即师资、天资、苦练。

There are three basic conditions for the mastery of *Taiji Quan*: a teacher, talent, and practice.

1. 师资 Teacher

师资为练好太极拳的首要因素。古人云：师者，所以传道授业解惑也。习文练武莫不如此。尤其是练习太极拳，老师是先决条件，无师自通的例子至今尚未见到。如果仅以习拳为娱、玩玩而已，自不在此列。要想练好太极拳，必须有一位品德高尚、技术精湛、理论精通、教学有方的老师，即真正懂太极拳的老师，才能引导学生步入正确途径，少走弯路，起到事半功倍的练功效果。如没有名师指导，一旦误入歧途，终身难登堂奥。即使练习多年，仍停留在照葫芦画瓢的阶段，即便是以后遇见名师指导，也很难改掉不正确的姿势。古语说得好：学拳容易改拳难。

A good teacher is the first condition for the mastery of *Taiji Quan*. Han Yu, a scholar in the past, defined the teacher as "the one who imparts morals and skills and dispels doubts." It is true in knowledge learning or in *Kongfu* practicing that the teacher is a decisive factor especially for the practice of *Taiji Quan*. No example has been discovered by now that one is able to master *Taiji*

学打太极拳

Quan all on his/her own. This, of course, excludes regarding *Taiji Quan* learning as merely an entertainment. Only under the guidance of a teacher who has high morality, masterly skills, theoretical conversance, and effective teaching methods can one practice *Taiji Quan* in the correct way with less effort. Otherwise, it is nearly impossible to attain true mastery of *Taiji Quan* once one is diverged from the right way; movement imitation would be all he/she can do after years of practice. And it is very hard to correct the wrong postures even if under the instruction of a master. That is why people say learning *Kongfu* boxing is much easier than correcting it.

2. 天资 Talent

天资是练好太极拳的关键因素。天资聪颖、接受能力强、思路清晰,能举一反三。太极拳精奥之处不仅靠老师指导,还必须亲身体验,用心琢磨,悟透拳理,达到较高境界,否则,虽有名师传道授业解惑,自己不肯下功夫苦练,可惜悟不透拳中精奥之处,也只能停留在二成功夫的水平上。

Talent is a key factor in learning *Taiji Quan*. A talented person is able to understand things quickly and draw inferences about other cases from one instance. Apart from the teacher's instructions, one has to experience and ponder the profound essences of *Taiji Quan* to reach higher levels. Otherwise, true mastery of *Taiji Quan* would never happen.

3. 苦练 Practice

苦练是练好太极拳的决定因素。自己天资聪颖,又得名师指导,还必须有吃苦耐劳精神,才能成功。有人天资稍差些,但肯下功夫苦练,在持之以恒的苦练中照样能深悟太极拳术之真谛。

Persistent practice is the decisive factor in learning *Taiji Quan*. Apart from a capable teacher and one's own talent, one has to persist and endure all difficulties to get success. Some less talented people can still master *Taiji Quan* through persistence and endurance.

第三章 教学随笔

二、关于简化24式太极拳的教学方法
Teaching Methods for the Simplified Twenty-Four-Step *Taiji Quan*

我从事太极拳教学工作近三十年,现将教授简化24式太极拳的方法提供给大家参考。

I have been teaching *Taiji Quan* for nearly 30 years, and I would like to provide for reference my teaching methods of the Simplified 24-Step *Taiji Quan*.

(一) 关于讲解、示范和领做 Explanation, Demonstration, and Practice Leading

1. 先用一个课时,向学员详细地讲解参加太极拳锻炼的意义和作用,以及有关太极拳的基础知识。

It takes only one hour of class to explain in detail the significance and function of *Taiji Quan* practice along with the basic knowledge of *Taiji Quan*.

2. 在教每个动作之前,先交代清楚动作的名称和它的含义。太极拳每个动作的名称都很有意思,或者是动作的形象化描述,如"白鹤亮翅",或者是动作要领,如"搂膝拗步"。讲清这些动作的名称便于学员理解和记忆动作,形成概念。

Before teaching a step, make clear its name and the meanings contained in the name. The names of *Taiji Quan* steps are interesting, some being picturesque descriptions, such as "The White Crane Spreading Its Wings," and some others being essential movements, such as "Knee Brushing and Twisting Step." Making these terms clear before hand helps students understand and memorize the corresponding movements.

3. 讲解与示范动作和领练时所站的位置很重要。我的体会是:教练的位置应随动作的变化而变化,有时站在队伍的正面(正前方);有时在左前方或右前方;有时是面向学生,有时是背对学生,有时是侧向。如教"左右穿梭"最好是在左前方,侧向学员;教"野马分鬃"则宜在正前方或面向学员等。为什么要这样不断变

学打太极拳

化呢？因有时来学拳的学员多，一般在二三十人以上，队伍较宽、较深，而太极拳各个动作之间都有紧密的连贯性，打的过程中又常变换方向，教练做示范动作，如果只站在同一位置上，就很难使全体同学都能看清每个动作。最初的示范要慢一些，动作幅度要适当大一些，路线要准确而清楚。领练时教练动作的速度应稍慢于一般同学的速度，以便他们一边思考一边做动作，一旦忘记下一个动作时，可以看看教练然后能够连续打下去。

Where the teacher stands is important when he/she does the explanation, demonstration, and practice leading. According to my experience, the coach's position changes according to the movements: sometimes in the front, and sometimes at the left-front or right-front; sometimes facing the students, and other times not. For example, it is better to stand laterally at the left-front of the students when teaching the "Shuttle Throwing"; while in the teaching of "Splitting the Horse's Mane," it is appropriate to stand right in front of the students. Why so? The movements of *Taiji Quan* are closely connected with constant turnings, and often there are many students (more than twenty to thirty on average); therefore, it is impossible for them to get a clear sight of each movement if the coach stays in one position. The demonstrations at first should be slower and larger-paced than the normal, and the moving courses should be exact and clear. In the practice leading, the coach's speed is a little slower than the average, so that the students have time to think while practicing, and regain their movements by resorting to the coach when they forget what to do next.

学员的队形、位置和练习场地的环境也应适当变换。初学者往往借助于周围固定的目标来帮助自己弄清不断变化的方向。如面向南起势练一遍简化24式太极拳，他在练的过程中就能很准确地找到野马分鬃、搂膝拗步是向东走。左右穿梭使向西南或西北运动。这种方法在初学是有利的，可是不能一直这样下去，因为这样实际上还没有能够独立地掌握太极拳各种转体动作的方向。所以在学员已经初学掌握动作的基础上，教练应当常变换学员的队形、位置，或用其他办法使学员不能借用周围固定的目标，以免在以后的比赛中找不到方向。

第三章 教学随笔

The students' formation, position, and practicing field should also be changed properly. Beginners usually identify directions by resorting to fixed objects nearby. For example, if they do a round of the Simplified 24-Step *Taiji Quan* by facing the south at the beginning pose, they can easily realize that they should move eastward in "Splitting the Horse's Mane" and "Knee Brushing and Twisting Step," while in "Shuttle Throwing" they need to move to the southwest or northwest. This is helpful at the beginning, but it should not always be done in this way, because it means the learners have not grasped the directions of all turnings. Therefore, after the students have learned the movements, the coach should change regularly their formation and position or make use of other methods to keep them from identifying direction by using fixed objects. This is to avoid the inability of direction identification in future contests.

(二）分解教学与完整教学 Dissembled and Complete Teaching

太极拳动作复杂，路线变化多，常常上下肢同时活动，运用分解教学的方法特别重要。一般说要把上下肢的动作分开练习，例如教"野马分鬃"，做上肢动作时，叫学员两脚左右分开，站立不动，先后练习左抱球——左分鬃，右边抱球——右分鬃等动作。上肢动作熟后，再练下肢。这时两手可叉腰不动，两腿连续练习左上步、左弓步、后座、撇脚、移重心上右脚，反复左右边的步法动作。上下肢的分解动作学会后，就合起来练习整个"野马分鬃"的动作。这种教法看起来好像要多用一些时间，实际上是省时间的。"云手"、"倒卷肱"等动作也是如此教法。这样做无论是先做下肢还是先做上肢的动作练习，重要的是使学员的动作容易准确，容易达到上下协调等要求。

The movements of *Taiji Quan* are complicated with moving courses constantly changing, which usually requires simultaneous action of both upper and lower limbs; therefore, to teach by dissembling the movements is especially important. The common way is to divide the movements of the upper limbs from that of the lower. For example, when teaching the "Splitting the Horse's Mane," the coach may have the students do the ball-holding gestures with feet fixed in a parted way. Then later when the upper movements are grasped, the training of leg and foot movements begins. At this time, with hands akimbo, the students may practice in sequence the left forward stepping, left bow-shape step, backward squat, outward turning of the foot, transfer of the weight, the right forward stepping, and other right forms of leg and foot movements. After this, all movements of both the upper and lower limbs are combined for praising the whole step of "Splitting the Horse's Mane." It may seem that this takes a longer time, but it actually saves time. This method can be used to other steps as the "Cloud-Waving Hand," the "Reversed Brachium Twisting", and so forth. The purpose is to make it easier for the students to attain standard movements and better coordination.

(三) 诱导性练习和辅助练习 Guided Practice and Assistant Practice

对于某些一下子较难掌握的动作，有必要采取诱导性练习的方法。例如教"云手"的两个手翻转时，大部分学员不能立即做得正确，我采取用"两手依次向外围绕"的诱导性练习后，同学们就较快地掌握了。辅助练习可以为正式练习准备条件，我经常引导同学做仆步式、下蹲式、向前走或向后退步等动作，有助于与上肢的配合。

It is necessary to use the guided practice for some difficult movements. For instance, most students will find it hard to do the circle waving of the "Cloud-Waving Hand" correctly; I, therefore, guided them by "waving the hands outward in circles by turns," and the students grasped it quicker. The assistance in the practice is to prepare for normal practices. I usually instruct my students to do movements as crouching step, squatting, and stepping forward or backward, which are helpful for the cooperation of the upper limbs.

(四) 信号刺激 Signal Stimulation

信号刺激是为了帮助同学们加强记忆。初学阶段的同学们容易出现忘记下面动作的情况，这时教练即做简单的提示就能帮助他们回忆已忘掉的动作，继续打下去。简化24式太极拳的全套动作都可以用简单的语言作刺激信号，以第一组而言，可用"起"、"屈蹲"、"抱球"、"分掌"、"跟半步"、"亮翅"、"搂推"等简单语言做刺激信号，其余类推。

Memorization through simple words as signals is to help students enhance their memorization. Beginners usually forget what follows next, and the coach (or teacher) at this moment helps them recollect it by giving simple signals. All the movements in the Simplified 24-Step *Taiji Quan* can be expressed by simple words as stimulating signals. Take the first group as example, the signals can be "begin," "bend, squat," "hold ball," "hands part," "follow half," "spread wings," "brush, push," and so forth.

(五) 矫正错误 Error Correction

俗话说:"习拳容易改拳难。"因此一开始就应注意矫正学员的错误或不规则动作。我在教学过程中发现同学们的错误或不规范动作主要有两类:一是动作的路线、方向不正确;二是打不出太极拳缓慢、柔、均与圆活等特点。纠正前一种错误比较容易,只要重新讲解、示范,做必要的诱导性、辅助性练习或分解练习,一般就可以帮助学生改正。纠正后一种错误或不规范动作则比较困难,用以上方法未必很快见效,我采用了另一些办法:

People often say, "Learning *Kongfu* boxing is much easier than correcting it." Therefore, the correction of errors and nonstandard movements should begin from the starting moment. The errors and nonstandard movements I found in teaching belong to two types. The first one is the moving courses and directions are incorrect. The second one is the lack of the characteristics of *Taiji Quan*, such as slowness, gentleness, smoothness, roundedness, and agility. Correcting the first type is easy; normally some re-explanations, demonstrations, and guided assistance or dissembled trainings will do. Correcting of the second type, however, is difficult, and the above methods might need a long time to be effective. Therefore, I adopted some other methods.

1. 在正式开始教学前,叫同学们跟我做一些放松的、柔和的动作,如手臂慢慢抬起,慢慢放下,柔和的前推等,使神经及身体各部分放松,不拘束、不僵硬。这还可以起到集中学生注意力的作用。

学打太极拳

   Before formal training, have the students do some relaxing and gentle movements, such as the slow rising and falling of arms, gentle forward pushing, etc. These movements are helpful for making the mind and body relaxed and natural. In addition, it also functions to make the students concentrated.

2. 有些同学因为性情好急好快，老做不好。对这样的同学要提出严格要求，并给以个别帮助。开始练习前可要求他们先深呼吸一至三次，我再来用信号刺激时的声音放慢、速度放长等。

   There are always some students who cannot do well because of their impatience. To them I propose strict demands, and give personal advice. I may ask them to take deep breaths for one to three times before the normal training, and then slow down the speed of signals during the practice.

3. 我发现有些同学的动作打得快而有顿挫，是因为脚步移动突然，身体重心变化太快的缘故。对这些同学就着重训练他们的脚步移动，例如要求他们跟着我的动作模仿前进、后坐、向左右转体、半蹲步走的练习，重心就可慢慢前移，慢收左脚向前迈步的练习，指出步子不宜过大也不宜过小，待重心全部移至左或右腿后，才能提起左或右腿向前迈出等等。

   Some students' movements are fast and unsmooth because of the quick transfer of the center of gravity caused by the abrupt moving of steps. As for them, I focus on training their stepping. For instance, I may ask them to follow my suit to do the movements as advancing, backward squatting, left and right turning, and stepping in the half-squatting way. In addition, I may have them step forward while drawing the left foot slowly, emphasizing that the step should be in proper pace, and that the forward stepping of the leg only happens after the whole weight transfers to another leg.

4. 更多的同学动作不圆活、不协调、不舒展，是因为不熟练的缘故。这就要求他们多练。至于眼神、呼吸等方面的要求，则不能一下子都要求同学们做到，以免"欲速则不达"。

第三章 教学随笔

A lot more students are unable to reach the standards of roundedness, coordination, and naturalness out of unfamiliarity. In this case, more practice is the only solution. As to the requirements for eyes and respiration, it is appropriate to have the students grasp them gradually, because urging causes negative effects.

（六）新旧教材的安排 Review and Learn

"温故而知新"这句话应当体现在太极拳教学中。熟练地掌握已经学过的旧动作,对于学习新的动作很有好处。因此在教授一定数量的教材后,应当做适当的复习。复习时要着重在某些难以掌握的重点动作上。我认为 24 式简化太极拳的"野马分鬃"、"搂膝拗步"、"云手"、"转身搬拦捶"、"倒卷肱"等动作是比较难学、难掌握的,应当注重复习。在教材安排中开始阶段教得少些、慢些,以后再逐步加快。

The spirit of "review and learn" should find expression in *Taiji Quan* teaching. Reviewing learned movements benefits the practice of new ones. It is necessary to do proper reviews after having taught a certain amount of the textbook. In reviewing, focus is placed on those difficult movements. In my opinion, the steps in "Splitting the Horse's Mane," "Knee Brushing and Twisting Step," "Cloud-Waving Hand," "Turning to Block and Strike," and "Reversed Brachium Twisting are hard to master in the Simplified 24-Step *Taiji Quan*, and therefore they need extra reviewing. As for the planning of the teaching material, make it less and slower at the beginning, and increase the amount and speed gradually."

我采用的复习方法有两种:一种是集体辅导,照顾重点。这种方法是在教练带领下集体复练习拳,对某些困难较多的同学由教练或指定学得比较好的学生专人帮助,形成一帮一;另一种是测验与个别练习相结合。测验能够督促学生自己练习。但测验是普遍进行的,在复习中对每位同学都进行测验,给以指导,并指出不足之处。此外,在安排太极拳教学之间,请练得较好的老学员作表演,以增加新学员的学习兴趣。

学打太极拳

I adopt two types of methods for reviewing methods. One is to give guidance collectively, and at the same time select the students who do well to help those who have the most difficulties. Another is the combination of test and personal practice. Tests can urge students to practice on their own. In reviews, I give tests to everyone, instruct them, and point out their deficiencies. Also, to increase the new learners' interest, I often invite the students who do better to give performances between classes.

三、浅谈太极拳技术教学法
Methods of Teaching *Taiji Quan* Skills

太极拳的普及和推广，各级太极指导员起着重要的作用。担负着教授太极拳，带领广大群众强身健体，培养优秀运动员的重任。为提高教学质量，笔者总结了几种教学方法，供大家参考。抓好太极拳基本规律技能的传授，是加快教学环节，保证教学质量和提高学员技术的首要条件。

All *Taiji Quan* instructors at different levels play an important part in the promotion and spread of *Taiji Quan*. They teach *Taiji Quan*, lead people to do the exercise, and train athletes and other instructors. To improve their quality of teaching, the present author provides here a summary of some methods for their reference.

A high-quality instruction of basic *Taiji Quan* skills is the prime component in accelerating the teaching process, guaranteeing the teaching quality and improving learners' skills.

（一）课型式训练 Training with Class Types

在组织教学训练必须有明确的课型，按太极拳要求进行明显的课型训练。即"要想打好拳，走步是关键"。俗话说"先看一步走，再看一伸手。"这就告诫我们在教授太极拳时的重点，先教太极拳的猫行步，即太极步结合身型的要求前进后退，和平行步的训练。第二节课在太极步的基础上进行手型、手法中的抱球、分掌，如野马分鬃、搂膝拗步、倒卷肱、左右云手至单鞭，这些最基础的训练。使学员的动作，由僵硬、不规范、不协调变为准确、规范、上下协调，对今后学习形成较复杂的技术技能是十分有利的。第三节课侧重于弓、马、扑、虚、独立、弹跳、内外摆腿、左右摆莲脚、拍脚、眼神协调等动作规律训练，有的放矢，给学员打下良好的基础。

There must be distinct class types, which are designed according to the requirements of *Taiji Quan*. In the first class, the stepping is the focus. We often say "the stepping is the key in *Taiji Quan* practice," and "judge firstly by one's stepping, and then by his/her hand moving." This tells us that *Taiji Quan* training should start with the "cat-style stepping," or the *Taiji* stepping, which includes advancing, retreating, and the parallel step in accordance with the requirements of the body. The second class focuses on the ball-holding gesture and the hand parting on the basis of the *Taiji* stepping, such as that in "Splitting the Horse's Mane," "Knee Brushing and Twisting Step," "Reversed Brachium Twisting," "Cloud-Waving Hand," and the "Single Whip." These are the fundamentals. Instructing students to make correct, standard, and coordinated movements greatly benefits the learning of the complicated skills. The third class may focus on the training of these movements as the bow-shape step, the bucking squat, crouching, force transfer, single-legged standing, jumping, inward and outward leg waving, the lotus-waving step, foot patting, eye movements, etc. Each training project is purposeful to help students lay a solid foundation.

（二）示范式训练 Training with Demonstration

指导员指导教学，必须通过正确的示范动作，给学员一个正确动作的概貌，这就要求不断学习，掌握动作要领，提高业务技术水平，训练教学才能把动作尽量做得准确、规范、可采用：

In teaching, the instructor must give students a vision of the correct movement through demonstration. This demands the instructor to improve his/her own skills by constantly learning. Only in this way can he/she make correct, standard, and adopted demonstrations.

学打太极拳

1. 位置示范 Positions

就是在讲解动作要领的基础上，站在队列的前列，左右斜向、中心点、侧面、正、背面等不同的位置，使学员清楚地看到指导员的示范动作。

When demonstrating different movements, the instructor should take different positions so that students can have clear sights of his/her demonstrations.

2. 动作示范 Movement Demonstration

指导员示范可采用先示范后讲解，或先讲解后示范整体动作或分解动作，或边讲边示范的方法。但每招每势要求规范正确，学员才能更好地去领会、模仿和训练。

The instructor may use different methods: to demonstrate before the explanation; to explain first and then demonstrate the complete or dissembled skill; or to demonstrate and explain simultaneously. Each movement or gesture should be correct and standard so that students have a better understanding, imitation, and training.

3. 攻防示范 Attack and Defense Demonstration

攻防示范是正确引导学员并弄清要领、发劲、防守之意。指导员可采用假设性攻防动作，如手挥琵琶。我右手管住对方右手之腕，左手管住对方右手之肘，两手是一合劲。又如，"搬拦捶"即一搬二拦三捶加进步，是一极为凶狠的招法，排在"太极五捶"之首。假设对方以右拳向我击来，我以右拳从左胁下向前搬出，由上往下压，化中有打、拦法，使整个手臂随腰行动，追封、打合一。如对方抽臂换步，我即将左手向前，随步追击，我左手拦其右手，速将我右拳向敌胸前击去。再如，搂膝拗步，设对方以手或足向我击来，我以左手护住自己的裆部，再往外将对方手或足搂开，右手向对方的胸部推去，这就是先防后打法。总之，示范训练是教学的必要手段。

The attack and defense demonstration is to let students grasp the ideas of force delivery and defense. The instructor may imitate the attack and defense skills. For instance, in "Playing the Lute," I assumingly control the opponent's right wrist with my right hand, and restrain his/her left elbow with my left hand, so that my hands form the blocking force. The "Carrying, Blocking and Punching" is a rather fierce skill. For example, suppose the opponent strikes with the right fist, I would move my right fist forward from under the left costal region to press the opponent's fist down, resolving the striking force with the simultaneous intention of blocking and hitting. The whole arm is in sync with the waist, and the blocking and striking are combined into one movement. Furthermore, if the opponent drew his/her arm back, I would follow up with my left hand, moving forward for an attack: blocking his/her right hand with my left hand, and punching quickly towards his/her chest. In "Knee Brushing and Twisting Step," suppose the opponent attacked with the hand or foot; I would firstly protect my crotch with the left hand, and move the hand on to brush the opponent's hand aside while pushing my right hand towards his/her chest. This is the so-called "defend and attack."

In short, demonstration is an indispensable means in *Taiji Quan* training.

(三) 启发式教学训练 Heuristic Training

首先,指导员在传授时做到精讲多练,进行启发式教学。如完成陈式太极拳的"搬拦锤"动作的发劲要整,可启发学员两手握住铲把铲沙装车,或铲麦扬场的发劲,此劲就在生活之中。又如,掩手肱捶的发劲,是发寸劲,发劲前是先蓄劲为慢,即把肱捶的距离分成三份,前两份为蓄劲,后一份为发劲,好比长跑的百米冲刺,迅猛爆发力强。

Firstly, the instructor needs to explain with simple but clear language, and to encourage students practice a lot. For example, the force delivery in the "Carrying, Blocking and Punching" of the Chen-Style *Taiji Quan* is supposed to be complete and even, as that of waving a shovel. While in the "Elbowing with Hand Concealed," force is delivered in a different way: it is stored up before the delivery. In other words, the distance of the elbowing is divided into three lengths; in the first two lengths, force is stored; while in the last length, force is delivered forcefully as that in a sprint at the finish.

学打太极拳

也可采取两组动作的对比方法,如"搂膝拗步",一组为比手画脚,没有转动腰胯,先弓好步再搂膝推掌,另一组以腰为轴带动四肢,上下相随,使学员明辨优劣,逐步掌握完成动作要领,达到启发教学和训练的目的。

In addition, the instructor may arrange comparisons by splitting the students into two groups. Take the "Knee Brushing and Twisting Step" as an example. Have one group move hands and feet without the turning of the waist and hips; make the bow-shape step first and then do the knee brushing and hand pushing. In contrast, another group of students turn the waist to lead the moving of limbs. The purpose is to let the students distinguish the standard from the nonstandard, so that they may get hold of the skills gradually.

教学语言要简练、通俗易懂,即口语式教学和训练。

在教学和训练中的语言式教学极为重要,直接影响学员情绪和效果。 首先指导员态度严肃,声音洪亮,富有魄力。可采用:

The language used in teaching is supposed to be simple and clear. Spoken language is strongly recommended.

The instructor's speaking is very important in teaching because it directly influences students' spirit and the training effect. Therefore, the instructor needs to be strict and speak loudly and forcefully. The following styles of spoken language are recommended:

1. 要领式口语 Guideline Style

如预备式,(1)两脚并拢,自然站立;(2)百会上顶,微收下臀、竖颈;(3)松肩两臂自然下垂;(4)含胸拔背;(5)收腹敛臀;(6)两膝放松;(7)两眼平视前方。又如起势,(1)两脚开立同肩宽;(2)两臂前平举肩高肩宽;(3)屈膝按掌,按在腹前。

For instance, in the preparation, we may say: (1) close feet and stand naturally; (2) head upright, neck straight; (3) relax shoulders, arms hang naturally; (4) withdraw chest, extend the back; (5) withdraw belly and buttocks; (6) relax knees; (7) look forward. In the beginning pose: (1) feet separated to shoulder length; (2) raise arms forward as high and wide as shoulders; (3) bend legs, press hands to the belly.

又如揽雀尾：(1)转体划弧；(2)收脚抱球；(3)开胯上步；(4)弓步前掤；(5)转体旋臂；(6)后坐下捋；(7)转体扬掌；(8)转正搭手；(9)弓步前挤；(10)抹掌分手；(11)后坐垂肘；(12)弓步按掌。使学员边学边掌握此动作的基本要领，逐步达到动作的规范化。

In "Grabbing the Bird's Tail": (1) turn and wave arms in arcs; (2) draw the foot back, make the ball-holding gesture; (3) step forward; (4) bend the leg bow-shaped, shed forward; (5) turn, and twist arms; (6) squat back, stroke down; (7) turn, wave hands; (8) turn to the front, attach hands; (9) bend the leg bow-shaped, hands squeeze forward; (10) split hands; (11) squat back, elbows droop; (12) bow-shape step, press hands. The words help students grasp the essentials and standardize their movements.

2. 命令式口语 Order Style

指导员严厉命令的"预备"、"开始"、"走"、"慢慢……快"！"蓄……发"！"松"等，都直接激发学员完成动作的紧迫感、节奏感和士气。

The strict orders as "set," "begin," "step," "slow, slow...fast!" "hold...release!" "relax", etc. are stimuli to the students' morale and senses of urgency and rhythm.

3. 节奏性口语 Rhythm Style

如完成杨式太极拳之揽雀尾，在要领式口语的基础上，用匀速的1、2、3、4……至12动。又如，完成陈式太极拳的掩手肱捶动作，可采用开、合、蓄、再蓄……发！再如陈式太极拳的闪通臂动作的1、2、3……4！（加重口语），如"蹬一根"动作的1、2……3！（加重口语），增强学员完成动作与套路的劲力、速度和明显的节奏感。

For example, when doing the "Grabbing the Bird's Tail" of the Yang style, we may say "1, 2, 3, 4... 12" at a constant speed to guide students, but in the

学打太极拳

"Elbowing with Hand Concealed," we may adopt "stretch, close, hold, and hold... deliver!" Other instances are the "1, 2, 3... 4 (stressed)!" in the "Flashing Arm," or the "1, 2... 3 (stressed)!" in the "Kicking". These are to nurture the students' force, speed, and sense of rhythm.

4. 形象性口语 Picturesque Language

如陈式太极拳的闪通背的转身180度，由弓步穿掌开始，指导员形象的口语，如右手抓住对方的手腕，左手管住对方的肘部，微向左蓄劲，再向右快速转身摔打对方是一摔劲。又如杨式剑的"野马跳涧"形象的比喻，骑着马从这一山涧跳到对面山涧时，空中勒马，落地刺剑，两腿似马一样腾空，跳跃山涧达到又高又远的要求，加深学员对动作的理解，较好地去完成它。

For instance, when teaching the "Flashing Back" of the Chen style, the instructor, beginning from the bow-shape step and forward piercing hand, can use picturesque language to explain the skill: hold the opponent's wrist with the right hand and the elbow with the left hand, store force slightly to the left, turn quickly rightward and throw the opponent on the ground. Another example is the "Wild Horse Jumping over the Canyon" in the Chen-Style *Taiji* Sword: jump as if riding a horse that leaps over a canyon, rein in the horse, fall down and stab with the sword; the jump should be as high and far as that of the horse. In this way, students are able to get a better understanding of the skill.

总之，口语式教学和训练，会鼓起学员的学习热情，提高训练效果，如果一个指导员的口语无力，则训练效果也不会很好。

In short, instructing with the simple and clear spoken language inspires students' passion and enhances the effect. Forceless and uninspiring speaking would not be able to bring out a satisfactory result.

（四）理论联系实际是搞好教学的关键 Combination of Theory and Practice

太极拳的理论是先辈们长期修炼的思想精华，它对太极拳的锻炼具有重要的作用。理论来源于实践，又需要在实践中加以验证，并不断地丰富发展。因此，我们从事太极拳锻炼，从事教学传授的人必须正确认识太极拳的理论和实践问题。

第三章 教学随笔

The theories on *Taiji Quan* were from the result of the forerunners' long-time efforts. They play an important role in *Taiji Quan* practice. Theories came from practice, and need to be realized and refined in practice. Therefore, it is necessary that *Taiji Quan* learners and teachers have a correct idea about the relationship between the theories and practice of *Taiji Quan*.

要正确认识太极拳的理论和实践。太极拳的前辈经过几百年的时间,用自己毕生的精力,反复研究,反复实践,反复总结,从感性认识逐步上升到理性认识,极大地丰富了太极拳的理论宝库,使我们后世练拳者有所遵循。特别是王宗岳、武禹襄、李亦畲的拳论,更具有很高的权威性,在太极拳界乃至整个武术界产生了重大影响。但是我们后来人要真正运用这些理论指导实践,也不是一件容易的事,必须认真研习、分析,弄通这些理论。

The forerunners, spending their whole lives on studying, practicing, and generalizing, made theories that would guide the later generations. Especially authoritative are those made by Wang Zongyue, Wu Yuxiang, and Li Yishe. However, it is not easy for us to use these theories as guidance of practice: we first have to understand them completely.

太极拳理论言简意赅,高度概括,有的一句话一个字都包含着极其丰富的内容,如果不能掌握正确的方法,进行太极拳的实修,在具体练习拳架时,就不知该怎么办,只能是照猫画虎,照葫芦画瓢。练习多年不知怎样用腰胯,不知上下相随,不知虚实,不知阴阳互转,更不知内三合、外三合这些最简单的太极理论。

The *Taiji Quan* theories are highly generalized; one sentence, or even one word, contains profound meanings. If one fails to understand the meanings, he/she can only imitate the dry movements without grasping the real essence; thus even those simplest theories are not within his/her sphere of understanding.

所以,一要通过练习太极拳架来验证太极拳的理论,验证的过程是一个长期的反复的实践、摸索的过程,如:怎样做才能立身中正,才能上下相随,才能做到外三合,才能逢左必右,逢右必左,才能虚实分清等。二要在拳架的基础上上升到

学打太极拳

太极推手,进一步验证太极理论的深刻含义。四两拨千斤,以静制动、以柔克刚……在太极拳理论的指导下,由招熟而渐悟懂劲,由懂劲而价及神明。在推手的高级阶段,才能随心所欲、得心应手。

Therefore: 1) we need to comprehend the *Taiji Quan* theories in practice, which is a long-term process of groping. For example, how one should make the body upright, to coordinate the body parts, to move to one side with the implication of moving to another side, and to make the void and solid clear; 2) upon the mastery of basic postures and skills, we need to practice the hand-pushing for a deeper understanding of the theories like "to move the weight of hundreds of tons with little force," "to restrain the moving with stillness and the firm with softness," etc. Under the guidance of theories, we are able to advance gradually from the lower level to the highest.

因太极拳理论渊博,拳势细腻,所以,在教授太极拳的过程中要由浅入深,使学员掌握理论与实践相结合的运动方法和要领,在太极拳理论指导下,奠定扎实的基础,是搞好教学的关键。

The *Taiji Quan* theories are profound, and the movements are full of subtleness. As a result, it is necessary that the teaching of *Taiji Quan* be designed as a process of gradual advancement, in which the students are directed to combine theories with practice. It is a key factor in teaching *Taiji Quan* to help students lay a solid foundation under the guidance of theories.

四、初学太极拳易犯的毛病及纠正办法
Common Errors among Beginners and the Ways to Correct Them

近年来,学练太极拳的人越来越多,由于太极拳博大精深,规范性强,初学者虽然热情很高,因对太极拳的特点和要领知之甚少,易出现这样那样的毛病,如不及时纠正,就会走偏,影响练拳的效果。根据二十年来的教学心得体会及有关

第三章 教学随笔

理论资料,现就初学者易犯的毛病,整理归纳出以下意见和纠正的办法,仅供参考。

Taiji Quan learners have increased greatly in the past decades. Beginners are often highly passionate; however, the profoundness and demanding standards of *Taiji Quan* make it easy for them to commit errors, which, if not corrected in time, would hinder the progress of *Taiji Quan* practice. The following summarizes the common errors and the ways to correct them according to my twenty years of experience and other theoretical works.

1. **思想不集中**。一些初学者在老师授拳时心静不下来,一边练拳一边想着别的事情。老师做示范动作或纠正别人的毛病时,他视而不见,听而不闻,在一边只顾自己低头想事或想动作,思想不跟着老师的指教思维。别人学会了,他还不会,产生了畏难情绪或丧失信心。学者应在老师授拳时,精神集中,排除杂念。精神集中,一招一式认真看老师的示范动作,并跟着老师的示范模仿动作,悉心体认。默记揣摩,照而行之。用意识指挥自己全身的实践,不可东张西望看着别人的动作模仿。

Lack of concentration. Some beginners tend to be absent-minded, thinking of other things while practicing. They do not heed the teacher's demonstrations and corrections, or think according to the teacher's instructions. When they fall behind, they lose confidence or regard mastering *Taiji Quan* as something impossible. It is suggested that learners concentrate completely on the practice, pay close attention to the teacher's demonstration and try their best to imitate and digest the skills. Remember to let the consciousness direct the practice. Do not look around and imitate the peer's movements.

初学者要树立"五心"。一曰"信心"。一是要有信心,坚信自己。别人会了我也一定能学会。自信心乃是练好太极拳的动力源泉。二是对人要真诚讲信义,信仰太极拳,信任授拳之师。只有这样,才能安定身心,一心一意,不致朝秦暮楚,见异思迁了。

学打太极拳

Beginners are suggested to nurture five qualities. The first one is confidence, including self-confidence and the confidence in *Taiji Quan* and the instructor. They need to believe that they are able to master *Taiji Quan* as others do. Self-confidence is the inner drive for learning *Taiji Quan*. In addition, they have to believe in *Taiji Quan* and the instructor. In this way, they are able to settle down and concentrate on practicing.

二曰敬心。培养良好道德品质,敬业敬师。学习太极拳不可不敬,不敬则外慢师友,内慢自己的身体。不敬老师,怠慢拳友,怎样学得拳艺？所以说,学拳先练德,即要有良好的道德品质。

三曰决心。学练太极拳要有练好太极拳的决心,方能立志学好、学深、学出水平、学出门道。才能不为外界所动,坚定不移,不达目的不罢休。

四曰恒心。就是要树立恒心,持之以恒的练习太极拳,几十年如一日地坚持下去,不可浅尝辄止,三天打鱼两天晒网。

五曰耐心。习拳没有耐心是不可能练好太极拳的。

学拳时由于自身悟性,学得比别人慢、记不住,产生急躁、失掉信心情绪。因此,要想把太极拳学好,就要有耐心,一遍二遍不会,要反反复复练习。修炼太极拳是一个长期的身心修炼过程,不能急于求成。否则,适得其反。要求每位学练太极拳的朋友,要不厌其烦、心平气和的循规蹈矩,在练习太极拳的过程中怡养浩然之气,达到身心双修,自然水到渠成。

The second quality is respect. Learners must show respect for the teacher, their peers, and themselves. Otherwise, it is impossible to master *Taiji Quan*. That is why we often say one should first possess good moral qualities.

The third quality is resolution. Learners have to be determined, so that they may not be influenced by other things.

The fourth quality is perseverance. Learners need to hold on to their determination until they have reached the highest level. Discontinuing practice leads to nothing.

The fifth quality is patience. Beginners tend to lose patience when they fall behind due to the deficiency of their own talent. They forget that *Taiji Quan* is a long-term process; any person who seeks to master it in a short time is doomed to failure. It is strongly recommended that learners keep their mind peaceful and follow the normal course of practice; thus, they are able to exercise both internal and external organs, and the mastery of *Taiji Quan* will happen naturally.

2. **身体不放松，动作僵硬**。初学者在学拳时，全身僵硬，即紧张。做起动作来全是拙力和笨劲。这就是全身放松不下来。"放松"二字听起来简单，实践很难做到，必须经过一段很长时间的努力才能做到。

The body is stiff, and the movements are unnatural. Beginners tend to be nervous, which makes the body stiff and the movements clumsy. In other words, they cannot relax their bodies. It sounds easy, but is in fact hard to get hold of without long-term efforts.

所谓的放松，就是要求全身放松，即思想放松，肌肉放松，所有的骨关节放松，全身不要有一点拙力和笨劲。但也不能松软，好像没了骨架子一样。学练太极拳用意不用力，全身放松，不使有分毫之拙劲。

The so-called "relax" refers to the relaxation of the whole body, including the mind, muscles, and joints. There is not even a bit of redundant force used. But this does not equate to flaccidity as if there are no bones in the body.

3. **迈步如砸夯，身斜脚无桩**。现在社会上无论是在公园，还是街区，教与学者大都是你学我就教，一上来便教动作，忽略了教授初学者"太极步"。多年来的教学经验告诉我教拳先教走——太极步。拳谚曰："未练拳，先练脚。"在没有上肢动作的干扰的情况下，用心专一地在老师的指导下练习太极步。正因在学拳过程中未练习太极步，使学者在习拳过程中总是迈出的脚如砸夯一样咚咚落地，支撑腿没有力量和根基，始终处于不稳状态，是两脚未分清虚实的具体表现。如：(1)有人在练拳中的两脚虚实不清，前进后退的方法不对，步伐迟滞不灵；(2)也有人虚实过渡太快，步伐笨重，重心不稳；(3)还有人虚实过渡的步子中途迟钝，甚至虚脚不贴近实脚的踝骨，直接地从后或前侧向前或后跨步等。

学打太极拳

The stepping is heavy, the body is unbalanced, and the feet are unsteady. *Taiji Quan* practice has become a common scene everywhere in China; however, some instructors are in fact unqualified, teaching movements from the very beginning instead of the "*Taiji* stepping," which, according to my experience, is what one should learn first. Because the *Taiji* stepping is not taught, learners tend to step heavily and unsteadily without much force on the supporting leg, which is a concrete example of messing up the void and solid forces. Specifically, the following situations happen commonly: (1) some people cannot make the feet clearly void-forced or solid forced; they advance or retreat in incorrect ways, and their steps are clumsy; (2) some people exchange the void and solid forces too fast, which leads to heavy stepping and unbalance; (3) some others may in the middle of the stepping which exchanges the void and solid forces, or step forward or backward directly without moving the void foot close to the solid one.

4. 低头弓腰臀后突。在学拳过程中凡是低头、偏歪、上体左右摇晃歪斜或突臀者，都违背了"外三合"（手与足、肩与胯、肘与膝相合）的要求。也违背了"虚领顶劲、含胸拔背、收腹敛臀、气沉丹田"的要求，使身体重心脱离了垂直线，偏向底盘边缘，身体始终处于不稳状态。正确做法是：头百会穴要轻轻向上领起，竖颈，微收下颚，面部肌肉放松，胸微含拔背，收腹敛臀，使自己的脊椎骨自然竖直，使之百会穴与裆下会阴穴成一垂直线，不容歪扭，使全身在练拳过程中始终保持立身中正安舒的状态。

The head is drooped, the waist bent, and the buttocks projected out. The violation of the "three external harmonies" (that between hands and feet, shoulders and hips, and elbows and knees) happen whenever there is the case of drooped head, leaning, waving of the upper body, or projecting of the buttocks. These cases also violate the requirements of "head upright and neck void-forced; back extended straight; chest, belly and buttocks withdrawn; air force down to the pubic region." The center of gravity goes astray, and therefore the body is constantly in an unsteady state. The right way is to propel force to the vertex to push the head slightly up; keep the neck straight and the chin withdrawn a little; relax the facial muscles; withdraw the chest slightly and extend the back upright; withdraw the belly and buttocks; keep the vertebra naturally straight and on the same vertical line with the centers of the head and crotch, so as to keep the body balanced, upright and natural.

有人问，照上所述，如在做蹬脚、金鸡独立或是海底针时怎样做到立身中正和百会上顶呢？

我们说有些动作要根据拳式的变化，做到"偏中求正"。如：(1)左右蹬脚：在上体要求下，可重心侧重于左右腿，做到"偏中求正"。(2)金鸡独立：要有意识地将重心偏于支撑腿一侧，使重心垂直，百会穴与尾闾会阴穴及脚跟成一垂直线，处于底盘中心部位。(3)海底针：身体需要倾时，切不可曲腰弓背，此时百会穴同会阴穴仍保持一条斜形的直线，以不失立身中正。

Someone may ask how one can keep the body upright and the head pushed slightly up when we do the kicking, the single-legged standing, or the "Picking the Needle from the Seabed."

Sometimes we need to "seek uprightness in deflection" according to the change of movements. For instance: (1) the left and right kicking: move the center of gravity to one of the legs in accordance with the upper body; (2) single-legged standing: transfer the center of gravity intentionally to the side of the supporting leg to be on the same vertical line with the heel and the centers of the head and the crotch. (3) "Picking the Needle from the Seabed": do not bend the waist or the back when the body needs to lean forward; at this time the center of the head and the crotch are still on a slanting straight line.

在初学太极拳时还容易出现扭臀或突臀。扭臀或突臀即臀部扭来扭去或向后蹶起。也叫扭臀摆尾。形成扭臀或突臀的毛病，表现在做动作时如左弓步，由于右腿形成僵直（挺直），右膝关节有形成跪膝（膝关节向下）右腿的大骨股头与骨盆相顶住，使臀部向左歪扭，反之又向右歪扭，或者向后蹶起。这种毛病一旦形成习惯，是很难纠正过来的。形成的主要原因是初学者不懂坐胯和敛臀的要领。纠正此病，首先要懂得坐胯和敛臀的基本要领。初学者要在明师的指点下，将下肢

学打太极拳

的三大关节：胯、膝、踝，即首先要松开胯关节，只有胯关节松开后，腰的动作才能灵活协调。杨澄甫说："一个松字，最为难能，如果真能松净，余者末事耳。"又曰："松要全身筋骨松开，不可有丝毫紧张。"掌握圆裆后的松胯，使胯关节与骨盆之间的缝隙扩大，后腿膝关节放松不可挺直，保持与脚尖的斜向相对，后脚脚尖朝45到60度角为宜，前弓腿之膝关节不可超出脚尖，松腰坐胯，收腹敛臀，才能做到尾闾中正神贯顶。只要自己在做动作时稍加注意不难纠正，否则严重影响身体中正安舒。切记杨澄甫所言："身躯宜中正而不倚，脊梁与尾闾垂直而不偏"的名言。

Beginners also tend to incline or protrude their hips. For example, in the left form of bow-shape step, the right leg is stretched stiffly straight, or the knee droops down too much so that the thighbone pushes against the pelvis to force the hips incline to the left (in the right form, the hips incline to the right) or protrude backward. It is hard to correct this error once it is formed. The fundamental reason for this is because beginners have not yet grasped the essentials of the squat and buttock-withdrawal. Therefore, one has to understand them first in order to solve the problem. Beginners should learn, under the instruction of a master, to relax the three set of joints of the lower body: hips, knees, and ankles. The hip joints should be firstly relaxed so that the waist can be flexible. Yang Chengfu pointed out that "relaxation is the most difficult; once it is reached, others are much easier;" and "the whole body should completely relaxed." Experience the relaxation of the hips after the crotch is made a rounded arc; it enlarges the gap between the hip joints and the pelvis. The knee in the back (in the bow-shape step) is relaxed and kept in the same direction with the tiptoe, which points 45 to 60 degrees outward; the bow-shaped leg does not go beyond the tiptoe; relax the waist and squat the hips down; the belly and the hips are withdrawn; thus, the hips are kept central and the force goes straightly up to the head. A little attention to this in the practice is enough to correct the error; otherwise, the body's upright ness would be affected. Do keep in mind Master Yang Chengfu's words: "It is appropriate that the body be kept upright instead of inclining, and the back on the same vertical line with the hips."

第三章 教学随笔

5. **抬肘耸肩身不正**。在练拳架时有许多人出现抬肘耸肩的毛病。如"抱球状"之野马分鬃,右手在上,左手在下抱球为例。即出现右肩耸起,抬肘上翻,而左肩又向左下歪斜,左臂夹腋,使上体身型歪斜而不正。此式反过来右野马分鬃时,又变成了左肩耸起,左肘抬肘上翻,而右肩又向右下歪斜,右臂夹腋。毛病在于上肢部分没有放松僵硬不灵,势必使气血阻塞于肩肘关节,难以达于手指;同时气血不畅,也不利于改善健康状况。杨澄甫曾指出:"若不能松垂,两肩耸起,则气亦随之而上,全身皆不得力矣。"

Lift the elbows and shoulders, and the upper body is inclined. The lifting of elbows and shoulders happen to many people in the practice of basic postures and movements. For instance, in the "ball-holding gesture" of "Splitting the Horse's Mane," when the right hand is above the left one, the right shoulder and elbow are lifted up, while the left shoulder inclines down to the left, and the left armpit is not made hollow, rendering the upper body inclined; and when the left hand is above the right one, the same thing happens, but in the reversed way. The problem is the upper body is not relaxed enough; therefore, the internal air and blood are blocked at the shoulders and elbows, unable to reach the fingers. Meanwhile, unsmooth circling of the internal air and blood affects the health condition. Master Yang Chengfu once pointed out: "If shoulders are not drooped naturally but lifted up, the internal air, in accordance, moves up, and the whole body loses its force."

要克服抬肘耸肩毛病,就要做好"虚领顶劲"、"松肩坠肘"、"含胸拔背"、"松腰松胯"等基本要求,全身关节都要做到节节松沉,不使有丝毫拙力僵劲占据经络,有利于气血通畅,使内劲顺达于肢梢。

To conquer this, one has to follow the requirements: "neck relaxed and head slightly pushed up," "shoulders and elbows relaxed and drooped," "chest withdrawn and back extended upright," and "waist and hips relaxed." All joints are in the relaxed state without any redundant force occupying the internal channels. This way, the circling of the internal air and blood is smooth, and the internal force reaches the ends of limbs unhindered.

学打太极拳

练拳时不自觉地抬肘,是没有掌握松肩,只有肩部放松了,肘自然松垂。前人云:肘若抬起,则肩不能沉,腕关节也难以松沉,交手时发人无力。两肘上翻,两肋侧面大开,易使敌方乘虚而入,是武家之大忌。所以在练拳架时,时刻保持"两肘往下松坠"之意,在做任何架式时,皆应做到"沉肩坠肘",肘尖有意识地下垂护肋,做到肘不悬起,但又要防止另一极端,使两肘夹住肋部,捆住自己而失灵活。因此,在沉肘的同时要使两腋下虚空有一拳之空隙,使两臂上下掤圆。

The lifting of the elbows is out of the fact that shoulders are not relaxed. The forerunners claimed that if elbows were lifted up that the shoulders then could not droop, and neither could the wrists, which rendered the attacks forceless in engagements. In addition, when elbows are twisted up, the costal regions become unprotected, which is a huge taboo for *Kongfu* masters. Therefore, when practicing the basic postures and movements, one should always maintain the sense of "drooping elbows." Each pose needs "shoulders and elbow to droop." The tips of elbows intentionally droop to protect the costal regions; and at the same time, the elbows should not press tightly on the costal regions, because flexibility is lost in that way. Keep the armpits hollow (a fist's space) to curve the arms.

6. **太极步法中的过劲与迭步 The over-force and piled-up steps in stepping**
(1) 在做太极之左右弓步的时候,前腿膝关节的垂直度超过了脚尖,身体的重量一部分压在左右膝关节上,使膝关节受力,同时也使上身前推之肘部也超过了膝关节,使肘膝不能相合,违背了外三合的基本要求。如与对方交手,则易被对方引进而前跌。

In the left or right bow-shape steps, the (left or right) knee goes beyond the tiptoe, and a proportion of one's weight is therefore placed on the knee to make it force-burdened; at the same time, the forward moving elbow goes beyond the knee, causing disharmony between them and therefore violating the requirement of "the three external harmonies." This makes it easy to be dragged forward and down on the ground in engagements.

第三章 教学随笔

正确的弓步：应在前腿弓步时，前脚尖朝前，后脚尖朝外约45到60度角，全脚着地，前后两脚的横向距离约在30公分左右，前后两脚不能在一条线上。前腿屈膝前弓，膝关节要超过与脚脖的垂直线，但不能超过脚尖。后腿自然伸直而不是僵直或挺直，是指后腿膝部微微有一点弯度。不能跪膝，即膝关节向下弯曲朝地，后腿膝部如向下弯曲，下盘支撑与后腿蹬地就无力，技击进攻就没有劲了。所以要保持膝关节的弹性和弓劲。

Correct bow-shape steps: The tiptoe of the bow-shape leg points forward, while the other tiptoe turns about 45 to 60 degrees outward. Both feet are set completely on the ground. The feet cannot be on the same line; the parallel distance between them are about 30cm. The front leg is bent forward to make the bow-shape; the knee should go beyond the vertical line of the ankle, but not that of the tiptoe. The other leg (in the back) stretches naturally but not stiffly, i.e., the knee is bent a little. Do not bend the knee too much down to the ground; otherwise, the supporting force of the lower body and the pushing force of the back leg would be lost, along with the attacking force. Therefore, the flexibility and bending force of the knee should be maintained.

(2) 在做太极步时，上步之脚落在与后脚的同一条直线上，称之为迭步。通俗讲就是拧麻花走独木桥。无论是弓步或虚步、还是前进或后退步，两脚都不可出现迭步。因这种步法使底盘过窄，重心不稳，练拳容易左右歪斜，与人交手时更无法应敌。

Piled-up steps refer to the forward stepping foot falling on the same line with the other one. Piled-up steps should not happen in any situation, because it makes the body unsteady.

正确步型应是：前后两脚不能落在同一直线上（中轴线），两脚的横向距离约在10—30公分左右，即约一肩宽。前进步或后退步均应走弧线，沿着中轴线前进或后退。后退步是在前进步的基础上沿着原来路线弧形退回去。即怎么走出去的再怎么退回来。请看下面的示意图。

学打太极拳

① 前进步（onward）：如野马分鬃、搂膝拗步：

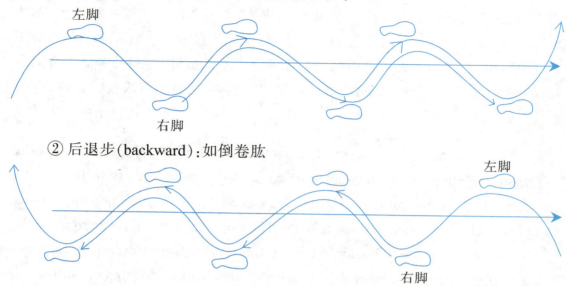

② 后退步（backward）：如倒卷肱

The correct stepping: The feet do not fall on the same line (the central line). The parallel distance between the feet is about 10-30cm (about the width of shoulders). Arc-lines should be followed (along the central line) by either advancing or retreating. The retreating course should be the reversed course of the advancing. Please consult the following illustration.

7. 软裆

(1) 指在弓步时膝关节之夹角小于 90 度角，使裆部低于膝关节；(2) 是指在动作过程中臀部低于两膝，如 24 式简化太极拳收势时，两膝屈成马步抱掌时，臀部低于两膝；(3) 是指做仆步时裆部全部下落，软弱无力地贴近地面，看起来好像式子很低，实际上是一种做过了头的动作，使之向上起身特别吃力，也易造成臀部左右摇摆。仆步的正确姿势，应略显拱形，裆下是一拱桥，以圆裆保持弹性和弓劲。起身时上体仍竖直头顶向上。仆步时体重大部分落在支撑腿上，支撑腿屈膝下蹲时注意膝关节要与脚尖同向。

Forceless crotch

(1) In the bow-shape step, the angle at the knee is smaller than 90 degrees, making the crotch lower than the knee. (2) It refers to any case of the buttocks being lower than the knee, as that in the ending pose of the Simplified 24-Step

Taiji Quan. (3) In the crouching step, the crotch is close to the ground. It looks as if the center of gravity is rendered low, but actually it is a movement overdone, which makes it hard to rise up and may incline the hips to either side. In the correct crouching step, the crotch is in an arc-shape that maintains the flexibility and force; the weight is mostly on the supporting leg with its knee and tiptoe on the same direction; in the rising up from crouching, the upper body and head are maintained upright.

8. 上下不相随。有些人在练拳时上肢与下肢的动作不协调,甚至两个上肢的动作也不协调。如搂膝拗步一式,有人往往是迈出的脚已落实成弓步,下肢和上身已不再动了,而上肢还在缓缓地运动。或上肢搂、推到位,而下肢还在缓缓蹬腿,把身体再往前送。野马分鬃一式也是如此,有人下肢弓步已到位,后腿也蹬直了,上身也不再动了,而两臂还在慢慢分开。24式简化太极拳由白鹤亮翅转第一个搂膝拗步后,再打第二个搂膝拗步时,腰胯还未转动,上肢右手已挥摆至左臂前,形成扭肩的动作,而且也未与下肢的右脚相配合。这些都是上下不相随的具体表现,违背了"上下相随"的要领。

The upper and lower bodies are not coordinated. Some people fail to maintain coordination between arms and legs, and even that between the two arms. For instance, in the "Knee Brushing and Twisting Step," the arms are still moving slowly while the legs and the upper body are held still; or the arms have reached their positions, while the legs are still stretching to send the body forward. In "Splitting the Horse's Mane," the arms are still being parted slowly while the bow-shape step is completed and the upper body is held still. Or in the second "Knee Brushing and Twisting Step" after the first one in the Simplified 24-Step *Taiji Quan*, the right hand moves to the front of the left arm before the waist and hips turn, forming the twisted shoulders and losing the coordination with the right foot. These are all cases that violate the requirement of "coordination between the upper body and the lower body."

杨澄甫指出,上下相随者,即太极论中所云"其跟在脚,发于腿,主宰于腰,形于手指,由脚而腿而腰,总须完整一气也。手动、腰动、足动、眼神亦随之动。如是

学打太极拳

方可谓上下相随,有一不动,即散乱也"。因此,练拳时全身各部动作,必须以意领先,以腰为主宰,做到一动无有不动,一静无有无静。

Master Yang Chengfu pointed out: the coordination between the upper body and lower body refers to force being "rooted in the feet, delivered by legs, controlled by the waist, and launched by fingers; the course circles again and again, forming a coordinated whole. Hands, waist, feet, eyes, all move simultaneously, and coordination is reached. If one part fails to move, the coordinated whole is broken." Therefore, in practicing *Taiji Quan*, the movements of all body parts should be led by the mind and controlled by the waist; so that complete coordination should be maintained: if one part moves, other parts move, too, and if one is held still, others are kept still at the meantime.

9. **眼睑下垂或眼无目标——野视或死盯前手**。有人在练拳时眼睛无精打采,眼神提不起来,眼睛下垂看地面,有人死盯住运动之前手不放,眼光发呆;也有人不知看哪好,目光乱看(野视);甚至还有面目紧张,两眼怒目圆瞪或闭眼合目。

Eye problems. Some people cannot show any energy or passionate spirit in their eyes; they tend to look down at the ground. Some people are inclined to stare at the moving hand at the front. Some others have no idea where to look at, and they just look around. There are people who even have nervous-faced eyes that are either closed tightly or opened wide with assumed anger.

杨澄甫先生曾指出:"目光虽然向前平视,有时当随身法而转移","神出于心,目眼为心之苗。"说明眼法是练太极拳之手、眼、身法步五法之一,极为重要。因此,我们在练拳时精神要提得起,眼神要平视,根据拳式的变化、意念的方向之需要,动作的方向目视前方较远处,做到随视或注视法。从而做到精神贯注,意动势随,内固精神,外示安逸,神态自然之境界。

Master Yang Chengfu has pointed out: "Although it is requested that one should look horizontally at the front, sometimes the eyes should follow the body movement and make proper adjustments;" "the spirit comes out of the heart (or mind), and the eyes are the outpost of the heart (mind)." These words emphasized the importance of the training of eye movements. When we are practicing *Taiji Quan*, we need to keep a high spirit, look horizontally at the front, and make adjustments according to the changes of the movements and the direction of the mind. In this way, the spirit is lifted, the mind takes the lead, and the person gets into a completely natural state.

10. **动作不连贯,速度忽快忽慢。**有人在练拳架时,往往出现动作不连贯,忽快忽慢,速度不均匀,甚至时断时续,有意无意地出现一顿一顿或一晃一晃的动作,故而练拳时全身不协调。也有人为了追求慢,形成动作迟滞、呆板,这些都是不符合太极拳的基本要求的。

If the movements are not continuous, then the speed is not steady. Some people tend to move in a discontinuous way with intentional or unintentional pauses or sways, and the speed is not even; therefore, the body is not moving in the coordinated way. Some other people make their movements sluggish and stiff in their pursuit of slowness. Both cases go against the basic requirements of *Taiji Quan*.

杨澄甫先生曰:"太极拳用意不用力,自始至终绵绵不断,周而复始,循环无穷",原论所谓'如长江大河,滔滔不绝',又曰:"运动如抽丝,迈步如猫行"。皆言其贯串一气也。我们在练拳时应做到"如行云流水,滔滔不绝,连绵不断"。这是太极拳的独特风格。为我们后来人指出了太极拳的"功蕴于内,劲不外露的特点"。我们在每一定势时,表现为前势之末,后势之开始的似停非停状态,而绝不可有一停一顿、断断续续、迟滞的痕迹。从而我们在练拳时要达到:松柔为主、柔中寓刚,刚柔相济、均匀而连贯的境界。

Master Yang Chengfu said that "*Taiji Quan*, which wields the mind instead of force, goes continuously and circles round and round... just as the continuous flow of rivers," and that "the stepping is like a cat walking, and the moving is like reeling the silk thread off cocoons." All these words refer to the continuous whole of *Taiji Quan*, pointing out *Taiji Quan*'s "characteristic of reserving force inside the body". When practicing *Taiji Quan*, we need to express its special style of "continuous flow as that of the cloud and water." Every still pose is a seemingly pausing but actually moving state, indicating the end of the former movement and the beginning of the coming action: there is never a trace of pausing, discontinuity, or sluggishness. These requirements are supposed to be reached: gentleness and relaxation taking the priority, firmness imbedded in softness (supporting and complementing each other), even-speed, and continuity.

11. 只见四肢动,练拳不动腰。有人练拳确不会动腰,更不懂得腰裆结合的妙用,所以练起动作来,只是一味地比手画脚,或者用腰过度,形成扭腰晃肩摆胯,身法不稳。如由白鹤亮翅转搂膝拗步,只见两臂左右挥摆,不见腰的转动。揽雀尾的左右掤转捋式时,只见两臂向上扬起,确不见腰的转动。在理论上,太极拳是圆象,练拳之时,可以见到手以走弧形为主,但功夫稍深者,则是主动地运用腰胯,四肢不过是腰胯动作的外在延伸,或称之为腰胯动作的外在表现形式。但功夫浅的人眼力也浅,每每只见手脚的运动形式,不见腰胯的运动规律。

Limbs move without being led by the waist. Some learners have absolutely no idea about how to turn the waist, not to mention the incredible functions of the waist and crotch combined. Their practice contains either mere imitations of hand-and-foot movements, or the overuse of the waist, which causes the twisted waist, inclining shoulders and hips, and an unbalanced body. For instance, in the "Knee Brushing and Twisting Step" transferred from the "White Crane Spreading Its Wings," we may see the arms waving left and right without the turning of the waist. In "Grabbing the Bird's Tail" (when the *bing* transfers to the stroking), we may see the arms waving upward without the turning of the waist. Theoretically, *Taiji Quan* is a rounded *Kongfu* boxing. It is obvious that most hand movements follow arc-lines, but someone on a higher level uses the waist and hips actively, for they know the limb movements are merely extensions or outside representations of the movements of the waist and hips. The student on a lower level, however, may pay attention to limbs instead of the waist and hips.

第三章 教学随笔

在太极拳练习中,腰的转动是有规律的,动作欲向左则腰先向右转;欲向右则腰先向左转;只有掌握了这一规律,运用"以腰为轴带动四肢"练习太极拳的腰劲就不难了。

以上所述,是在教拳实践中的亲眼所见,是针对易出现的毛病而述,不当之处请读者予以纠正。但主要是为了使学者少走弯路,所以学者择师至关重要。若有良师指授,益友切磋,加之勤学苦练,刻苦钻研、揣摩,一定会掌握正确的姿势、方法。

In *Taiji Quan*, the waist turns according to a certain rule: it turns rightward first if the movement intends to go left, and *vice versa*. It will be much easier to train the waist force according to "the waist leading the limbs as an axis" if this rule is understood.

The above is a summary of the common errors seen in my teaching and their respective correcting ways. If any mistakes are found, please let the author know. The main purpose is to keep learners from going the wrong way. As mentioned, the author thinks that choosing a good teacher is very important. One is surely able to attain the correct poses and ways if he/she combines the guidance of a good teacher, the exchanges among peers, along with his/her own diligence.

五、练习太极拳要防止膝关节损伤

Preventing Knees from Being Hurt

(一)练太极拳容易损伤膝关节之原因 Why Knees Are Easily Hurt?

练太极拳我们常在屈膝状态下做缓慢而均匀的动作,始终是一条腿的膝关节担负承受着全身的重量,支撑全身重心。一般膝关节会出现疼痛,还伴有大腿肌肉及小腿肌肉疼痛。这对初练太极拳的人来说是一正常现象,一般经过二、三周的时间,大小腿肌肉疼痛即可自然消退。但由于初学者没有掌握要领,加之一些指导老师未讲其理,使学员盲目练习;或是在运动前没有做好充分的热身运动,有些练习太极拳的人膝关节发生扭伤后问一位教授:"老师,我们的膝关节痛

学打太极拳

是怎么回事？"回答："练得少,还要多练。"结果学员一味地苦练,确不知怎样去练,结果膝关节肿胀,不能屈膝下蹲了,结果适得其反。甚至有的老师看到学员仆步下不去,不讲动作要领硬要学员下势,同样使学员的膝关节损伤。

When practicing *Taiji Quan*, we often move slowly and evenly with legs bent, and most of the time the whole weight is put on one bent leg. Therefore, the knee joints, along with the muscles on thighs and forelegs, tend to be painful at the beginning. It is normal for beginners. In two or three weeks, the pain in the muscles will fade away. Some learners may hurt their knee joints because they fail to get hold of the correct way, having not done enough warm-ups, or practice blindly out of the fact that the instructor has not made the essentials clear. It happens that after being hurt, some learners asked their teacher about the reason, and the answer was that they needed more practice. They practiced more, without knowing how, until they could not bend their legs due to the swelling on their knees. Some instructors even force learners to crouch down without explaining how, which also hurts the knee joints easily.

(二) 造成膝关节损伤的主要原因 Major Causes to the Knee Hurts

太极拳的健身作用人人皆知,但在练太极拳的人中却出现了程度不同的关节损伤,我在教学中发现,许多初学者练太极拳的姿势不正确,使半月板有不同程度的损伤,更严重的是有很多人以不正确的姿势教授太极拳。教与学大都停留在照猫画虎、照葫芦画瓢的基础上,这不得不引起大家的重视。造成膝关节损伤有以下几个方面的原因。

Taiji Quan is renowned for its function of health building, but there are people who hurt their knee joints when practicing it. Why? I found in my teaching that many beginners hurt their menisci due to the incorrect postures. What is worse, many teachers cannot teach the correct postures. Attention should be paid to the fact that most teaching and learning are dry imitations of the movements. Specifically, the knee joints are hurt out of the following causes.

第三章 教学随笔

1. 练拳时，由于全身的重量都由下肢承担，拳式越低，膝关节承受的压力越大，如虚步是最典型的步伐，即全身的力量落于一足之上，并屈膝下蹲，另一脚虚着地，这样必然调动更多的肌肉纤维参与工作，才能支持膝关节维持支撑。否则虚步时就变成了双重。所以说，以健身养生为目的人，练拳的姿势略高一些为好，不要蹲得太低，也尽量避免一足承重，虚步时可两脚承重各三七开，即前足三分，后足七分。

Since the whole body is supported by legs, the lower the postures are the more pressure the knee joints receive. The void step is the most typical, in which the whole weight falls on one bent leg, while the other foot is set void-forced on the ground. This, in consequence, needs more muscles to support the knee; otherwise, the void step becomes "double-forced." Therefore, for those who practice *Taiji Quan* for health building, it is better that the general frame of postures is a little higher, and the weight does not fall on one leg only (in the void step, the void-forced foot may support about 30 percent of the weight, and the other foot supports about 70 percent.)

2. 练拳时姿势不中正。如挺胸、突臀、下蹲时两膝超越足尖，夹裆、使膝关节加重压力，是造成半月板损伤的第二个原因。所以练拳时要全身肌肉放松，关节松开，但这种放松必须建立在保持各关节的正常功能和正确位置的基础上。在肌肉放松的同时做到虚领顶劲，含胸拔背，沉肩坠肘，松腰敛臀等练拳的要求。反之，就会造成关节的损伤，(如脚关节、膝关节、髋关节)。

The body is not kept upright. The second cause to the hurt of the menisci is the incorrect body gestures: projected chest and buttocks, knees going beyond tiptoes, closed crotch, etc., which all cause increasing pressure on the knee joints. Therefore, the muscles and joints need to be relaxed on the basis that they are kept the right position. At the same time, these requirements are to be followed: neck straight, head upright, chest withdrawn, back extended upright, shoulders and elbows drooped, waist relaxed, and buttocks withdrawn. Otherwise, joints (e.g., ankles, knees, and hips) are inclined to be hurt.

学打太极拳

练拳时的后坐，扑步下势、弓步时后腿跪膝，前膝内扣或外撇是造成膝关节损伤的主要原因。膝关节不是万向节，它的主要功能是顺着胫骨（小腿）和股骨（大腿）的方向弯曲，侧向扭动的余地不大，扭动过大就会损伤半月板，而这种扭动比受压迫更为严重。所以练习太极拳：1）虚步要求开裆或圆裆，使胫前脚尖朝前，后脚尖外撇45到60度角。骨、胫骨和脚尖三者的方向一致。2）后坐时后腿膝关节先去找脚尖。3）扑步下势时膝关节与脚尖同向。4）弓步使前膝关节同时找准脚尖，不可内扣或外撇呈扭曲状态，否则会严重损伤膝关节。

The knee joints also tend to hurt during backward squatting, crouching, or in the bow-shape steps, because when the back leg is bent too much down, or the front knee is turned inward or outward. The knee joint cannot be bent in all directions. It bends only according to the directions of foreleg and thigh, and bending sideways would hurt the meniscus in a more serious way. Therefore, in *Taiji Quan* practice: 1) for the void step, the crotch is in an arc-shape, the shin and tiptoe at the front point forward, and the tiptoe at the back turns 45 to 60 degrees outward; the knee, shin, and tiptoe share the same direction; 2) for the backward squatting, the knee of the back leg point at the same direction with the tiptoe first; 3) for the crouching step, the knee of the bent leg shares the same direction with the tiptoe; 4) for the bow-shape step, the knee of the front leg points at the same direction with the tiptoe the moment the leg is bent; do not turn the knee outward or inward to make it twisted; otherwise, it would be severely hurt.

（三）怎样预防膝关节的损伤 Ways to Prevent the Knee Joints from Being Hurt

1. 练习太极拳前的准备活动：练习太极拳一般是在早晨，经过一夜的睡眠，全身肌肉及韧带尚处休息状态，所以练拳前先要活动下肢、腰部的肌肉，使腰部及膝关节周围的韧带、股四头肌及股二头肌等适应伸展屈曲及旋转运动。除做腰、膝部位的活动外，还要通过压腿、踢腿、外摆和内摆腿等活动，使全身的肌肉、韧带处于兴奋状态。

Warm up activities. Normally, *Taiji Quan* is practiced during the morning, at which time, the muscles and ligaments are still in the rested state after a night's sleep. Therefore, before the practice, it is necessary to activate the muscles and ligaments of the waist and legs. Also, one should waken the muscles and ligaments of the whole body by leg pressing, kicking, and leg waving (outward and inward).

2. 在练习动作时,无论是弓步、后坐,还是仆步下势,膝关节与脚尖应做到同向,即膝关节找脚尖。如(1)弓步时前腿膝关节与脚尖垂直,但膝关节不可超过脚尖。(2)后坐即重心后移时,后腿膝关节先屈开裆圆胯,膝关节找脚尖。(3)仆步下蹲时,屈膝下蹲之膝关节也同样去找脚尖,才能仆下去。

When practicing movements, the knee is kept in the same direction with the tiptoe, no matter how it is in the bow-shape step, the backward squatting, or the crouching step. (1) In the bow-shape step, the front knee is on the same vertical line with the tiptoe instead of going beyond it. (2) In the backward squatting, i.e. the backward moving of the center of gravity, the knee of the back leg bends first (sharing the same direction with the tiptoe), and the crotch is made arc-shaped. (3) In the crouching step, the knee of the bent leg should also point at the same direction with the tiptoe; only in this way can the crouching be done.

3. 运动量由小到大,由浅入深。太极拳架的步幅可由小到大,经过一段时间的锻炼,腿部肌肉发达了,有力量支撑全身的重心了,步幅自然会大,不可追求拳架低,步幅大而使膝关节损伤。运动量要根据个人的身体条件,适度加大。运动量的大小,一是练习拳架时可连续3到5遍,二是步幅大,低架练拳,使之运动量加大。

Follow gradual advancements. The stepping pace can be gradually enlarged as the muscles on legs to gain increasing force to support the body weight. Do not intentionally seek a large stepping pace at the beginning or the knee might get hurt. The amount of exercise should be increased properly according to one's own personal physical conditions. One way of increasing the amount is to do the practice for 3-5 rounds; another is to enlarge the stepping pace and to lower the general frame of postures.

学打太极拳

4．"左倒卷肱"容易扭伤右膝关节且不合拳理之练法是：继 24 式简化太极拳的"手挥琵琶"左虚步之后，左退步中，左腿抢先形成后坐步，而不是随左臂倒卷而重心由右腿蹬劲渐渐后移，如此使胸腹面过早对向东北方向，而右脚尖、右膝关节还处于指向东南方向，胯关节前侧位早已对向东北方，使三者活动位置之改变不一致，致使右膝关节承受不正常向应力之损害，此种先坐实左腿再倒卷左臂、手动而腿不动之练法较为多见。

The left form of the "Reversed Brachium Twisting" tends to get the right knee hurt. The reason why is: after the left form of the void step in "Playing the Lute" of the Simplified 24-Step *Taiji Quan*, the center of gravity is not moved gradually backward by the pushing of the right leg when the one twists the left arm in the reversed way; instead, the left leg is drawn back too quick to form the backward squatting step; thus, the chest and belly, together with the front side of the left hip joint, face the northeast too early, while the right tiptoe and knee still point at the southeast; these three are therefore not changed accordingly in position, which causes abnormal pressure to the right knee joint. This practicing way—the left leg squats before the left arm is twisted—is common among learners.

5．"进步搬拦捶"一式，容易扭伤右膝关节且不合拳理之练法：

（1）以 24 式简化太极拳之"闪通臂"后"转身搬拦捶"为例，右脚向前迈出时，不是以脚尖领劲在前，脚跟在其后向前迈步，而是右脚内侧在前之横侧位向前迈步，如此右脚尖、右膝关节偏向外，而右胯关节前侧位则向正前，使三者活动位置不相一致。当右脚落地时，致使右膝关节承受异常向应力之压迫，有人称这种练法是用右脚横向蹬踹或蹬踩对方小腿。

The "Advancing to Carry, Block, and Punch" tends to get the right knee hurt if not practiced correctly. The incorrect way may be the following reason.

(1) Take the "Turning to Carry, Block, and Punch" after the "Flashing Arm" for example. When the right foot steps forward, the inner side of the foot, but not the tiptoe, faces the front. In this way, the right tiptoe and knee are turned outward, while the front side of the right hip faces forward; thus, the three do not

move to the same direction, and when the foot is set on the ground, the right knee receives abnormal pressure. This is referred to as kicking sideways with the right foot or stepping on the opponent's foreleg.

（2）右脚向前迈步时，由于过早向外撇，落实脚尖，重心尚未充分前移，坐实后腿，右脚尖、右膝关节、右胯关节前侧位尚未一致对向东南方向，右脚尖早已落实地面，才提左腿上步，使右膝关节内侧承受异常向应力的损害。这种在后的一条腿，脚跟尚未提起，在前的一条腿边抢先落实脚尖的迈步方法，违反了人类平时走路的自然规律，在练习太极拳复杂多变的太极步中，岂有不使膝关节受伤之理？

When the right foot is put forward, the tiptoe is turned outward and put on the ground too early, while the weight is not moved completely forward and the way of stepping the front tiptoe is set on the ground before the back heel is lifted up, which goes against the normal way of human walking; therefore, it is possible that the knee gets hurt in the practice of the complicated *Taiji* stepping.

（3）右脚向前迈步之弓步时，这时由于脚尖与中轴线不是45到60度角，所以当左腿上步在前，右腿在后向前蹬成左弓步时，后腿感到不得劲才挪动右脚跟来调整没有到位的角度的步型。后腿在前蹬的同时挪动脚跟之练法，在一些套路中普遍存在，它不但为右膝关节带来损伤隐患，更违反了拳理、拳论所言："其根在脚……"，右脚挪动调整步型之练法，即为拔根，实乃武术之大禁忌。

When the right leg bends forward to form the bow-shape step and the tiptoe does not form 45 to 60 degrees angle with the central line is a common error. Therefore, when the left foot is put forward and the right leg is stretched to form the left bow-shape step, the right heel is moved to adjust to the new step. This is commonly seen in some skills. It not only brings potential injury to the right knee, but also goes against the theory: "the root is in the heel." Adjusting the foot by moving the heel is referred to as "uprooting," which is huge taboo in the realm of Wushu.

综上所述，膝关节扭伤，是只因在练拳架中不符合拳理之练法所致。习拳者

学打太极拳

要得拳理要领练拳,是防止膝关节损伤之关键。

In conclusion, the hurting of the knee is caused fundamentally by incorrect practicing ways. Therefore, the key to preventing the knee from being hurt is for learners to practice according to the *Taiji Quan* guidelines and essentials.

六、浅谈太极拳的腰裆功
The Waist and Crotch Skills in *Taiji Quan*

太极拳的普及和推广,使更多的人乃至外国人步入了这一运动行列,然而更多的人练习太极拳多年,却不知道用腰或不会用腰,更不懂得腰裆结合的妙用。所以练起拳架来,只是一味地比手画脚,且越练越觉得枯燥无味。有的人在练拳中用腰过度,形成扭腰晃肩,身法不稳,正如拳论所云,"有不得机不得势处,身便散乱,必致偏倚,其病必于腰腿求之。"我们在练拳过程中每一转动,每一招式,或左或右,或上或下都是有意图有目的,动作欲向左则腰先向右转动,欲向右则腰先向左转,只有这样掌握了规律,练习太极拳的腰劲就不难了。

As *Taiji Quan* becomes popular, increasing numbers of people, including even foreigners, it becomes necessary to learn it. However, many of them, having practiced for years, have no idea about either wielding the waist or the way to wield it, not to mention the incredible functions of the waist and the crotch combined. Therefore, the practice of skills is merely imitation of the movements and gestures, which becomes increasingly boring as time passes. Some learners move the waist exceedingly, which causes the waist and shoulders to incline and the body unsteady, as is said in the theories of *Taiji Quan*: "When chances and advantages are lost, the body becomes clumsy, and the mind gets disturbed. The reason is found in the misuse of the waist and legs." Every move in the practice is with certain intentions and purposes. The waist turns rightward first if the movement is heading to the left, and vice versa. Grasping this rule makes it easy to build up the waist force.

另外,在练拳走架中,腰一定要直起来,身法要做到"立身中正","不偏不倚"。不能出现前俯后仰,左右倾斜的不良姿势,而腰部的左右旋转和腿部的虚实转换,是靠膝关节松活来实现的。如果两个胯关节不松活,死顶住骨盆,腰也就难以起到车轴的作用,所以松胯活裆是腰劲训练的关键。

In addition, the waist must be kept upright so that the body is "upright and central." Any inclining is not allowed. The turn of the waist and the transfer between the void and solid forces on legs are realized by the relaxation of the hip joints; otherwise, the waist cannot play the role of the axis. In this sense, the relaxation of the hips and crotch are crucial to the building up of waist force.

另外,旋转关节换劲时,不要单独地去扭腰,否则会造成身体摇摆,下盘不稳,只有结合两胯放松,裆劲撑圆,才能使腰胯左右转换"轻灵圆活",形成悬腕转膀,旋踝转膝,旋腰转背的立体螺旋缠丝动作,整套动作练起来才能圆转自如,顺其自然。

Furthermore, when transferring force, do not only twist the waist; otherwise, the body would be made unsteady. Only by combining it with the relaxation of hip joints and the arc-shape extension of the crotch can the waist be turned agilely, which further leads the turning and twisting of other joints in a spiral way. In this case, the whole set of skills can be done with naturalness, roundedness, and smoothness.

太极拳对裆部的要求是:圆虚松活。即两胯根与两膝盖撑开撑圆,又要有虚虚相结合之意,裆虚圆则下盘有力,支撑八面,两胯放松则裆可松活,虚实转换也就轻灵快捷。要避免出现尖裆、塌裆和死裆的毛病。

The crotch is required to be rounded, void-forced, relaxed, and flexible. The thighs and knees are extended open to make the crotch in a rounded arc-shape, containing the sense of void and solid forces combined at the same time. If the crotch is rounded and void-forced, the lower body is steady and has to support the whole body. When the hips are relaxed, the crotch becomes relaxed and flexible, and the transfer between the void and solid forces gets agile. The peak-arched, the flat, or the rigid crotch should be avoided.

学打太极拳

尖裆——即人字裆,是动作虚实不分,两膝不开,跪膝。

塌裆——是臀部低于膝盖,膝关节有了死弯,易犯转换不灵的毛病。

死裆——是不结合腰劲,不松胯使上下之劲不能相随。

  Peak—arched crotch—the inverted "V"-shape crotch, which surfaces because the void and solidity are undistinguished with the knees not opened wide enough.

  Flat crotch—formed by getting the buttocks lower than the knees, hence causing stiff bends at the knee joints which make transitions unsmooth.

  Rigid crotch—the result of the rigid hips and the separation from the waist force, which makes the forces in the upper and lower body uncoordinated.

腰劲与裆劲之间有着密切的联系,不能顾此失彼,要相互结合,协调一致。腰与裆的结合在练拳过程中表现为,每个动作定势要做到塌腰、合裆,可使动作气沉丹田、下盘稳固,在运劲走势过程中,要做到活腰松裆,可使动作流畅连贯、轻灵自然,在发劲放劲时要做到拧腰、扣裆,腰劲旋拧,裆劲扣住,可使发劲快猛迅疾,力达梢节。

综上所述,腰裆劲在太极拳中的重要位置是显而易见的,是其他劲所不能相提并论的,所以,腰裆劲的训练不可忽视。

  The waist and the crotch are closely connected, cooperating and coordinating with each other. In each still pose, the waist is completely relaxed and the crotch is closed, which helps the internal air fall down to the pubic region and steadies the lower body. In moving, the waist should be flexible while the crotch is relaxed; in this way, the movements are smooth, continuous, agile, and natural. In delivering or releasing force, the waist is twisted and the crotch is crossed, so that the force is delivered or released in a fierce, end-reaching way.

  In summary, compared to other skills, the waist and crotch skills are obviously crucial in *Taiji Quan*; therefore, great attention needs to be paid to their training.

第三章 教学随笔

七、练太极拳动作与呼吸的配合
Cooperation between Movements and Respiration

练太极拳结合呼吸是根据动作的变化而自然形成的。初练太极拳往往采用不与动作结合的自然呼吸法,坚持练拳久了,也就会不自觉地使动作与呼吸结合起来,先将呼吸与动作相配合的一般规律归纳如下:

The inclusion of respiration into *Taiji Quan* happens naturally according to the changes of movements. At the beginning of practice, learners usually do not try to combine respiration with movements: they breathe in the natural way. After a long time of practice, they would find themselves unconsciously breathing in cooperation with their movements. A summary is made here about the general rules of combining respiration and movements.

(一) 自然呼吸法 Natural Respiration

要求练太极拳时精神贯注于动作中,呼吸顺其自然,不加任何勉强和干扰,但这种呼吸又与不运动时自然呼吸不同,与一般的剧烈运动呼吸更不一样,其巧妙处则在于全身运动极轻松和缓,协调自然,动作活泼而严肃,在安详中兼带全神贯注。这样动中有静、精神极其镇定的状态下匀缓动作,呼吸就会自然变得深长,这种呼吸方法适应范围很广,便于太极拳的普及和推广,是初学太极拳的人所必须采用的。也适用于经常打太极拳的中老年人、体弱者或其他以医病、健身为目的的人采用。

This demands concentration on movements, while the breathing is completely natural without any interference. This kind of breathing, however, is different from either the natural breathing in a leisure state or panting in strong exercises. Its exquisiteness lies in the fact that it is done when the body moves in a way that is extremely relaxed, gentle, coordinated, natural, lively but serious, and serene but concentrated. Breaths become consequently deep and smooth when the movements are in a state in which the moving is endowed with the quality of stillness and the mind is completely calm. This kind of breathing is entitled to

学打太极拳

a wide range of people, and therefore is helpful for the spread of *Taiji Quan*. Learners must adopt it at the beginning. It is also suitable for the middle-aged and old people who exercise *Taiji Quan* often, people with unsatisfactory physical condition, and those who seek to cure illnesses or build health.

练习太极拳要求呼吸深长、细匀,纯任自然,不必故意以呼吸配合动作。太极拳呼吸之道,主要是气沉丹田,鼓荡丹田内息,以连绵不断之动作相应。因内息之鼓荡不停,亦自能抽动外面呼吸之气往来不辍,且深长气匀,如漆似胶。但我们不去注意它,需让它自然出入,出则势开而放,入则势合而收,且身势开放收合到极点,或转换时更往往与呼吸首尾相应。如身势由合而开,气即随之由吸转呼,当开到极点时,则为一呼之尾,也可能为一吸之首。如24式之起势,开立步时,当左脚跟抬起时,向左横跨时为吸,脚掌落踏实时为呼,但还有一开之中,可能不只一呼,需加一吸(即一开势呼起吸止),或需再加一呼(即一开势中两头呼中间吸)。一合之中,可能不止一次吸需加一呼,或再加一吸。如24式的野马分鬃:(1)转体划弧为一吸;(2)收脚抱球为一呼;(3)开胯上步为一吸;(4)弓步分掌为一呼。总而言之,动作不断呼吸也不断,动与息应,息与动联,如是而已,若必规定某一动作配合吸,某一动作配合呼,则必机械呆板,恐非太极拳行气之道也。自然呼吸,练拳就自然了,呼吸自然去配合动作,若专在配合上注意,反而配合不好,且往往练出病来。太极拳是气功,但讲的是顺气、养气、自然之气,不是讲的努气、憋气、滞气、不自然之气。这种与动作自然配合的呼吸方法是非常合乎生理要求的,这种自然呼吸而达到的气沉丹田的效果,能使太极拳的动作更加轻灵沉稳,松柔自然。

It is required that the breathing in *Taiji Quan* practice is supposed to be deep, smooth, and natural. There is no need to intentionally make breathing and movements cooperated. The way of respiration in *Taiji Quan* is mainly that, the air is lowered down to the pubic region to stir the internal air force stored there, responding to the continuous movements. The stirring of the internal air force in turn makes the breathing continuous, deep, and smooth. But we should not pay attention to this process; instead, we should let it circle all on its own. We make opening postures when exhaling and closing postures when inhaling. And most of the time, the transiting points of the opening and closing postures are exactly that of the exhalation and inhalation. Suppose the posture is changed from a closing one to an opening one, the exhalation consequently transits to inhalation, which then ends as the opening reaches its limit. For instance, when we part our feet in the "Beginning Pose" of the 24-Step *Taiji Quan*, we inhale as we lift the left heel to move the foot leftward, and exhale as we put the foot down on the ground. But there might be cases in which an opening is accompanied by an exhalation plus an inhalation (an opening begins with the exhalation and ends with the inhalation), or another exhalation is added to the process (an opening begins and ends with both exhalations with an inhalation in between). Likewise, a closing might not only be accompanied by an inhalation: an exhalation-or that plus another inhalation-might be added to the process. For example, the "Splitting the Horse's Mane" of the Simplified 24-Step *Taiji Quan*: (1) turn the body and move hands are in arc-lines (accompanied by an inhalation); (2) draw the foot back and make a ball-holding gesture (accompanied by an exhalation); (3) put the foot one-step forward (accompanied by an inhalation); (4) make the bow-shape step and separate the hands (accompanied by an exhalation). In short, both the movements and the breathing work continuously, responding to each other. If there were strict rules that certain movements be accompanied by inhalations and others by exhalations, the whole process would seem too rigid, which would probably not be the proper way of respiration for *Taiji Quan*. Natural breathing helps make the practice unrestrained, which leads to the spontaneous cooperation of respiration. Intentional attention to cooperation itself does not necessarily lead to cooperation; on the contrary, it often causes illnesses. *Taiji Quan* seeks to nurture the internal air force and train it to circle smoothly and naturally instead of nurturing and training the violent, blocked, unsmooth, and unnatural air force. This kind of natural respiration is in exact accordance with human physiology. It helps make the *Taiji Quan* movements more agile, steady, gentle, and natural.

学打太极拳

自然呼吸是肺部扩张和收缩,受肺活量的限制,呼吸时间的长短有一定的限制,不必有意识地去进行,能自动地有节奏地进行。太极拳的呼吸虽同样用"呼吸"两字,但性质内容不同于自然呼吸,太极拳的"呼"是"开","吸"是"合"。所谓开是开大,有发的意思,所谓合是缩小,有蓄的意思。开时周身气势都是开大膨胀,合时周身气势都是缩小含蓄,所以太极拳的"呼吸"是周身的"开"与"合"。由意来指挥,根据拳势需要,要开就开,要合就合,开中有合,合中有开,开之能再开,合之能再合,随心所欲,滔滔不绝,不受时间的限制,也不受自然呼吸的约束。平时练拳要自然呼吸,到一定阶段,慢慢地呼吸与动作会自然配合。

Natural respiration comes completely out of the lung's extension and shrinking. The depth of one's breaths is limited because of the restraint from vital capacity; therefore, natural respiration follows its own rhythm instead of being controlled intentionally. In *Taiji Quan*, the same words, "exhale" and "inhale," are used, but different properties are assigned to them. The "exhale" in *Taiji Quan* refers to "open," and the "inhale" refers to "close." "Open" means to extend or swell, possessing the sense of delivering; "close" means to shrink, owning the sense of storing. In opening, the whole body shows the manner of extending and swelling, while in closing, it shows the manner of shrinking and reserving. In this sense, the "exhalation" and "inhalation" in *Taiji Quan* are actually the "opening" and "closing" of the body, which, directed by the mind and in accordance with the moving course, work continuously, implying each other mutually, and completely unrestrained from time and natural respiration. As mentioned above, natural respiration should be adopted at the beginning, and gradually the breathing will cooperate with movements in a spontaneous way.

(二) 调解自然深呼吸法 Adjusted Deep Natural Respiration

所谓调解自然深呼吸,是在不破坏呼吸自然的原则下,有意逐渐加深自然顺势呼吸法。这种呼吸法必须在拳势熟练后才能采用,也可使动作与呼吸配合,但要特别强调呼吸的深长与动作的配合不应勉强,以免因结合不当引起胸闷不适。

This is to deepen intentionally and gradually natural respiration without interfering with its naturalness. It should be adopted after the mastery of body skills, and might be done in cooperation with the movement, but, as is emphasized, the cooperation cannot be compelled in order not to arouse discomfort in the chest.

这种呼吸法适用范围较广，便于太极拳的普及和提高。中老年人采用这种呼吸法时，应强调吸短呼长，吸轻呼重。延长呼气可使肺脏排出大量气体，从而也就能吸入较多的空气，提高肺的换气效率。可以避免表浅的呼吸所引起的胸闷、恶心、呼吸急促等现象的出现。此外，延长呼气还可以帮助改进肺组织的弹性，增强肺脏在减退期中的功能，对气管炎、肺气肿的防治可起一定的作用。

This kind of respiration has a comparatively wide applicability, and helps promote the *Taiji Quan* practice to a higher level. When middle-aged and old people use it, they are suggested to inhale in a short and light way and exhale in a lengthened and heavy way. Lengthening the exhalation is beneficial in many ways. It drains a greater amount of air out of the lung, which renders the possibility for the inhalation of more fresh air, thus enhancing the lung's efficiency of ventilation. It avoids the stuffy chest, nausea, and panting caused by shallow breathing. In addition, it enhances the functioning of a declining lung by improving its elasticity, acting in the avoidance or treatment of tracheitis and emphysema.

（三）逆式呼气法 Reversed Respiration

逆式呼吸法与平常呼吸法相反，即缓缓吸气时小腹逐渐内收，缓缓呼气时小腹部外突。平常呼吸法也称顺呼吸法，是吸气时腹部自然外突，呼气时腹部自然收缩。这种逆式呼气法如果运用得好，可使膈肌与腹肌的力量加强，加大腹压的变化，对改善腹腔血液循环可起一定的作用，易于做到"气沉丹田"。对有胃下垂、心脏下垂的人有较好的改善作用。

Normal breathing means that the belly swells in inhalation and shrinks in exhalation. In contradiction to the normal way, the reversed respiration demands that one should draw in the belly when inhaling slowly, and make it swell while exhaling. If wielded in a proper way, this type of breathing can strengthen the diaphragm and the abdominal muscles, and enhance the abdominal pressure, thus improving the blood circling in the abdominal cavity. It also makes it easy to lower the internal air force down to the pubic region. Finally, it benefits people who have gastroptosis or a drooping heart.

以上三种呼吸法既有共同点,又各有其特点,要根据自己个人的体质、病情和拳艺水平等具体情况灵活运用。无论采用哪种呼吸方法,都必须从实际出发,呼吸要保持从容不迫和舒适自然,都必须掌握循序渐进,只有这样才能有助于健康,才能逐步掌握好太极拳的呼吸方法。

The three kinds of breathing mentioned above share common characteristics, and at the same time maintain their own. Learners need to make choices according to concrete situations such as physical quality, illness, and attainments in *Taiji Quan*. No matter which one is adopted, the reality and the principle of gradual advancement should be taken into consideration, and the breathing needs to be unhurried and smooth. Thus, learners are able to build health and master the breathing skills of *Taiji Quan*.

八、太极拳的眼神——眼功

Eye Skills in *Taiji Quan*

练太极拳对眼神有个要求"眼随手动,手眼相随,目随势注",这一要求就告诉我们,在练太极拳时,要使眼神与手法、身法、步法协调一致,密切配合,才能做到"形神兼备"、"内外合一"。但我发现,有的人只注意动作程序的变化,不注意眼神的配合或配合不协调,显示不出太极拳的神韵。

A general requirement for eyes in *Taiji Quan* practice goes as "eyes move to follow the hands; eyes and hands are coordinated; eyes stare in accordance with the moving course." This is to say, the cooperation among eyes, hands, body movements, and steps makes it possible that "the form and spirit are both shown" and so "the internal and external are combined." However, I find that some learners pay attention merely on movements; they neglect the cooperation of eyes, or the cooperation they make is not highly coordinated, and therefore is not able to show the special charm of *Taiji Quan*.

造成这一现象的主要原因是对太极拳的眼神作用认识不足,"认为太极拳不像其他拳术那样快速有力,不用过多地注意眼神。"这一认识是错误的。我们说太极拳是中华武术的一个重要拳种,同样具有中华武术的主要特点。如练太极拳就是练精、气、神,而精、气、神除与动作配合外,主要靠眼神来表达。拳谚论:"眼为心之苗","神发与目"。在表现方法上,用尖锐之目光,视敌人之意向,伺隙蹈瑕,乘机而起,皆眼神之作用。在某种意义上可以说,与人搏斗之先在于"眼搏"——以目前注、将势审定,因"势"而化。与敌交手不可低头看地,打东看西,眼无目标,闭眼合目,钝视无睹。眼神——眼功,历来为拳家所重视,享有"眼观六路,耳听八方"之美誉。

This is due to an insufficient understanding of the functions of eyes in *Taiji Quan*. These learners may think, "*Taiji Quan* does not demand too much attention of the eyes, because it is not as fast and forceful as other kinds of *Kongfu* boxing." This is obviously a wrong idea. *Taiji Quan*, as one of the important Wushu styles, possesses the same major characteristics of Chinese *Kongfu*. *Taiji Quan* focuses on the nurturing of one's internal air force (qi), energy, and essence, which, besides the cooperation of movements, are mainly expressed by eyes, as is mentioned in the theories about *Taiji Quan*: "Eyes are the outpost of the heart (mind)," or "the spirit comes out of the eyes." For instance, one detects the opponent's intention with sharp eyes and finds chances to strike back; this is one of the functions of eyes. In a sense, one fights with his/her eyes first in an engagement-he/she stares at the opponent to judge the situation and make adjustments. In an engagement, one cannot attack or defend without looking at the opponent. The eye skills—eye flares—have always been a priority for *Kongfu* masters, as is mentioned in the criterion: "eyes attend to the six pathways, and ears heed the eight directions."

眼是接受对方动态的器官。它能"纳山川之大,及毫芒之细;悉云霄之高,尽泉水之深"。与人交手搏斗之前,要"观察阅览、顾盼窥视","观察"是观测,来判断

学打太极拳

对方的真"假"、刚柔急缓,"阅览"是纵贯全局,一览无遗。"顾盼窥视"是在观察阅览,审时度势的基础上,进一步观察对方所处的位置状态,目光所及,顾盼左右,窥视前后,捕捉战机,以求一逞。只有这样,才能"敌情预晓",对方使用的何招,用何战术,如何进攻,如何变化,是头先来还是脚先来,或高或低,或上或下,或左或右,或前或后,如何闪战,如何腾挪等,了如指掌,进而迅速做出判断,选择对策。只有这样,才能知己知彼,对克敌制胜起到先决作用。同时,还可视其眸子、测其心理,凡恐惧者,皆眼神恍惚;鲁莽者,瞪目而视;奸者,惯于眼视的斜、睨、瞟、眇——眼神的作用还远不止于此。

Eyes are the receptor of the opponent's actions. They can "take in things as huge as mountains and rivers, detect things as tiny as the hair or awn, reach heights as that of the sky, and attain depths as that of springs." Before engaging with the opponent, one needs to "observe, survey, and detect." To "observe" is to judge whether the opponent's movements are real or "false," or whether they are firm, fast, soft, or slow. To "survey" is to have a clear and general view of the whole situation. To "detect" is to further observe the opponent's position and state, and to look about for a chance of undefendable attack. In this way, one is able to have a clear idea about the opponent's tactics, attack and defense skills, and changes of movements, so that he/she is able to make quick adjustments and launch effective attacks. This is decisive in defeating the opponent. In addition, one can detect the opponent's psychology by looking into his/her eyes. Those who are afraid tend to look aimlessly; those who are rash tend to stare with eyes wide open; and those who are tricky tend to look askance, glance sideways, or stare with eyes half closed. These are only the mere functions of the eyes.

在与对手搏击时,还可以用眼睛的变化,来调动对方,如,视左击右,迷惑对方来分散对方的注意力。也可表示沮丧,令对方盲目乐观,麻痹轻燥,而我却以突然出击制胜。还可发出威光,使对方心理上受到刺激,令对方胆怯,同时及时发现空当,给以有力的打击。也可以凶狠之目光暗示对方,我要拼死一搏,使对方有所顾忌,起到领神作用,眼神歪视或斜视,表示战略上鄙视对方,使对方出现一种不服气或愤怒的情感,让对方出现自我干扰的心理活动……。反之,如果对方招法多变,真假虚实变化莫则,自己却目不暇接,扑朔迷离,被动挨打是在所难免的。

第三章 教学随笔

In engagements, one can also maneuver the opponent through changes in their eye expressions. For instance, one may distract the opponent by looking at one side while striking at the other side; or he may show depression to arouse carelessness in the opponent, and defeat him/her with a sudden attack. He can also stare with fearful flares to intimidate the opponent, and at the meantime find loopholes for an effective strike; or he may stare with fierce and savage flares to indicate the resolution of a life-and-death struggle. Besides, one may look sideways to show disdain for the opponent, so that the opposing part might be irritated and lose calmness. In contrast, if the opponent makes undetectable changes, it would be inevitable that one get smashed.

武谚论："先打眼，二打胆，三打手脚快与慢。"要想掌握搏击的精髓，登堂入室，先加强眼功的练习，练就一双犀利、明锐如电的眼睛。这就是要"心动形随，意发神传"，运用眼神来传神达意，以显示动作的完整和饱满的神采。

A popular saying in the realm of *Kongfu* goes, "firstly the eyes, secondly courage, and finally the agility of hands and feet." To get to the essence of attack and defense, one needs firstly train the eye skills-to train a pair of sharp, piercing eyes. This demands, "The will is followed by the body and revealed by the eye expression." Using eye expressions makes the movements complete and the spirit vigorous.

太极拳的眼神运用，主要有随视法和注视法两种。

The eye skills in *Taiji Quan* mainly include two types: following and gazing.

1. 随视法：是指目视方向，随手的运动或意念的方向而变化。也就是说眼神要追随动作中的主要手和运动方向或意念做相应的配合，无论过目暂见，前观后看，左顾右盼的眼法都应随动作或意念变化。注重眼随手转，手眼相随的协调配合。如 24 式太极拳的"左搂膝拗"步，当向右转动身体举臂时，眼应随手而动，而到左手搂，右手推时，眼神应比右手走得快些，眼领着手走，最后定点时眼眉略上挑，这样便显得有神采。其次眼随手而行，则腰自转动，即以腰为轴，以躯干带动

学打太极拳

四肢,并与眼神互相配合。如云手动作时,眼睛是注视着右手,不停地随着腰部转动,但对于左手的摆动,重心的左右移动,也没有放松不管,只是重点注意的是右手而已,等到左手转到上边时,注意力又转到左手上去。这样腰脊转动,带动两臂在空间划圆,两掌随着臂部运动,不断地内外翻转,眼神总是随着主要进攻手的动作运转,有眼随手转,步随身换之说法,两腿支撑整个身体左右移动和旋转,头部也随躯干自然扭转,同时两眼不断注视交换的上手,从而形成上下相随,节节贯穿,处处牵连,密切配合的全身运动。

1. **Following:** Eyes move in accordance with the hand or the direction pointed at by the will. That is to say, the eyes should follow the direction of the major moving hand, or cooperate with the mind. It emphasizes the coordination between the eyes and the hand. For instance, in the left form of the "Knee Brushing and Twisting Step," when the body is turned rightward and the hands are raised, the eyes should follow the moving of hands; at the time the left hand brushes and the right hand pushes forward, the eye flashes should move a little faster than the right hand in order to lead it, and at the end of this movement, the eyebrows rise slightly so that a brighter spirit is shown. Furthermore, if eyes move in accordance with hands, the waist turns spontaneously, i.e., the waist turns to lead the limbs in cooperation with eyes. For example, in the "Cloud-Waving Hands", the eyes are firstly set on the right hand, continuously moving with the turning of the waist; however, that does not mean the waving of the left hand and the transfer of weight are left unheeded: it is just that the temporary focus is on the right hand; attention will be turned to the left hand when it waves to the upper level. Thus, the waist and back are twisted to lead the arms wave in arc-shapes, and the hands, following the moving of arms, are twisted inward and outward continuously, while the eyes always move to follow the major attacking hand. *Taiji Quan* masters often say, "Eyes follow hands, and steps follow body turns." The body moves or turns leftward or rightward on the support of legs, with the head follows the body turns naturally, and at the same time, eyes are constantly set on the upper hand; thus, the whole body moves in a coordinated and closely connected way.

第三章　教学随笔

随视法要注意两点：(1)当手运动到面前或胸前时，眼可随手；(2)当手运动到比胸还低的位置时，就不要随势低头找手，要随着腰的转动，向前平视，否则就出现低头现象，随视时还要注意不要过于死盯住一个目标，这样会造成头晕目眩，避免呆视或斜视，要做到似看非看或视而不见。太极拳讲究绵绵不断，因而随视法处处皆用。

Two points should be emphasized here: (1) eyes follow the hand when it moves to the front of the face or chest; (2) when the hand moves to a position lower than the chest, do not try to follow it by lowering the head; instead, look horizontally at the front with the turn of the waist. Furthermore, do not always follow and stare at one target, it may cause dizziness; avoid blank or slanting staring. This state should be reached: seemingly, the eyes are set on one hand, but actually, they are not; the eye flashes go through the hand as if it is transparent. The "following" is used everywhere because of the emphasis on continuity in *Taiji Quan*.

2. **注视法**：是指定势时，眼平视前方或注视两手。主要用在一个动作或姿势完成时，眼睛要通过手或直接注视到远方。如："提手上势或手挥琵琶"之势，就是通过左手或右手目视前方，但注视法只是在短暂的瞬间完成的，因为太极拳在结构上的特点是前一个动作的结束，恰好是下一个动作的开始，要在似停非停之际，立刻接做下一个动作，保持前后动作的连贯性环环衔接，但这个瞬间是表达精气神的极好机会。

2. **Gazing:** Gazing means looking at the front or the hands in still poses. It is mainly used when a movement or posture is finished. The eyes flashes are fixed in the far front directly or through the hands. For instance, in "Playing the Lute," one gazes at the front through the left or right hand. But the "gazing" happens only in an instant, for in *Taiji Quan*, the end of one movement is exactly the beginning of another: a movement begins at the instant the preceding movement ends and stops, so that the continuity is maintained. However, this instant is still a precious chance to express one's spirit.

学打太极拳

九、太极拳的修炼方向
Starting Directions for Practicing Taiji Quan

从各种太极拳书中都可以看到"面向南起势","面向南"就是适应地磁方向,在寅时因太阳左升右落,地球自右向左转。物理学家埃尔萨曾指出,地球的转动可能在熔融的铁核心内造成一些从西向东旋转的慢涡流。这些年来实验证明,人体的经络具有明显的电磁物性,穴位是电极聚集点,存在着对磁性信号的敏感反应。那么,打太极拳强调"面向南"起势,实际上是顺看地球的地磁方向,促使地球与人体的生物磁相呼应而磁化,是一种对人体起着内外相映的天然磁疗。这样便可利用地球南北磁极进行治疗疾病和增长功力。因人体的气血与地磁息息相关。人体和地球的磁力线方向一致,会加速气血在人体内的循环。

In various books of *Taiji Quan* one sees the sentence: "Do the beginning pose by facing the south." To "face the south" means to accord with the direction of geomagnetism, for at 3 to 5 o'clock in the morning, the sun falls from the right (west) and rises from the left (east), and the earth turns from the right to the left (from the west to the east). Elsa, a physicist, once pointed out: the earth's turning might cause a slow east-west whirlpool inside its melted iron core. And it has been proved in recent years that the channels in the human body are obviously electromagnetic, and the acupoints, where the electrodes gather, are sensitive to magnetic signals. Therefore, to starting the exercise of *Taiji Quan* by facing the south is to accord with the direction of geomagnetism in order to make the geomagnetism respond to the biological magnetism of the human body, which is a kind of natural magnetic therapy. In this way, one is able to treat diseases and increase the internal air force by taking advantage of the earth's magnetic poles. The internal air and blood are closely connected to geomagnetism, and their circling will be accelerated if the human body is kept on the same direction with the magnetic force.

古人还依据身体疾病，来确定练拳的方向。如肝病面向东，心病面向南，肺病面向西，肾病面向北，风湿病患者，多因脾湿所致，所以练功切忌向北。宜向南方，南方属火，火生土，有助于脾的运化。

The forerunners had also decided the directions according to the types of illnesses. For instance, if the liver has problems, start the exercise by facing the east; if the heart has problems, face the south; if the lungs have problems, face the west; and if the kidneys have problems, face the north. For those who have rheumatism, they should avoid facing the north, because in most cases, rheumatism is caused by the wet spleen. It is appropriate for them to start the exercise by facing the south, for (according to the doctrine of the "five elements") the south belongs to the element of fire, and fire gives birth to earth, which is helpful for the spleen to work out its problems (In traditional Chinese medicine, the spleen belongs to the element of earth).

十、练太极拳的注意事项

Cautions

1. **练功十要：** 行功完后，要面常擦，目常揩，耳常弹，齿常叩，背常暖，胸常护，腹常摩，足常搓，津常咽，腰常揉。

The Ten Necessities: After the practice, do the following things regularly: wipe the face; rub the eyes; stir the ears; knock the teeth; warm the back; attend the chest; stroke the belly; rub the feet; swallow the saliva; massage the waist.

2. **练功十八伤：** 万事有度，行动时久视伤精，久听伤神，久卧伤气，久坐伤脉，久立伤骨，久行伤筋。七情上，暴怒伤肝，思虑伤脾，极忧伤心，过悲伤肺，多恐伤肾，多笑伤腰，多言伤液。其他方面：至饱伤胃，多睡伤津，多汗伤阳，多泪伤血，多餐伤髓。

学打太极拳

The Eighteen Harms: Everything has a limit, and doing things excessively may get you hurt. For movements, staring too long harms the essence; listening too long harms the spirit; laying too long harms the internal air force; sitting too long harms arteries and veins; standing too long harms bones; and walking too long harms tendons. As to the seven emotions, fury harms the liver; too much thinking harms the spleen; extreme worrying harms the heart; too much sorrow harms the lungs; excessive fear harms the kidneys; over-laughing harms the waist; and too much talking harms the saliva. For other aspects, eating too much harms the stomach; sleeping excessively harms the saliva; sweating excessively harms the positive essence in human bodies; weeping too much harms blood; and having too many meals in a day harms the marrow.

3. **练功十忌**：忌早起磕头、阴室纳凉、湿地久坐、冷着汗衣、热着晒衣、汗出扇风、灯烛照睡、子时房事、凉水着肌、热火灼肤。

The Ten Taboos: The following things should be avoided: to kowtow after getting up in the morning; to get cool in a shady room; to sit for a long time on wet ground; to wear clothes soaked with sweat in cool days; to wear dry and warm clothes in hot days; to get cool with a fan when sweating; to sleep with lights on; to have sexual intercourse at midnight; to cool the body with cold water; to burn the skin with fire.

附录
Appendix

1. **虚领顶劲**：即头顶正直，头顶的"百会穴"要向上微微顶起，好似一根绳将头顶悬挂起来一样，下额微收，颈部放松，舌舔上腭，时时保持精明轻妙的感觉，有头顶青天，脚踩大地的气概。

The neck is relaxed and the head upright: The head is kept upright with force exerted in mind up to the vertex as if it is hung up with a string. The chin is slightly withdrawn; the neck is relaxed; and the tongue sticks up to the maxilla. One should always have the feelings of lightness and alertness, and keep the lofty spirit as if standing steadily on the ground with the head pointed up against the sky.

2. **含胸拔背，即胸部向内涵虚**：舒松自然，使气下沉。所谓拔背，即是背部舒展并向上拔伸，只要做到"头顶悬则背自拔"。杨澄甫说："能含胸自然能拔背"。

Withdraw the chest and extend the back: Draw the chest in slightly to make it relaxed and comfortable, so that the air can lower down. The back is extended and pulled up. The back is pulled up spontaneously if the head is hung up. Yang Chengfu also said: "If the chest can be drawn in, the back, consequently, can be extended upright."

3. **松腰胯**：腰为全身之主宰，是上下身转动的关键。如腰能放松，则全身即能沉稳有力，又能转动灵活。定式时，腰和胯放松，则有利于沉气贯劲四稍，下盘

学打太极拳

也更加稳固。

Relax the waist and hips: The waist is the ruler of the whole body and the key point for the turning of the upper or lower body. When the waist is relaxed, the whole body becomes not only steady and forceful, but also agile in turning. In still poses, the relaxation of the waist and hips helps lower the internal air force and compel force to the ends of limbs; the lower body becomes steadier in this way.

4. 分虚实：练太极拳处处分虚实，虚实分清，则转动轻灵平稳，身法手法和步法的虚实变换，要求做到内外结合，上下相随，上下左右能分虚实，动作就能圆转自如。

Cut the void and solid forces clear: The void and solid forces are clear-cut everywhere in *Taiji Quan*. Once they are clear-cut, turnings become agile and steady. Complete coordination is required for the transitions between these two forces in the body, hand and foot movements. Thus, the movements can be natural and effortless.

5. 沉肩坠肘：沉肩也就是要肩部放松，向下沉塌，也叫塌肩。如两臂耸起，则意气上浮，妨碍内气的运行和血气的流畅。坠肘者，即是肘部有松坠下沉之意。所以练拳时，两臂不能挺直。要臂微屈，保持弧形，感觉两臂有一种内在的沉劲。

Keep the shoulders and elbows drooping: Shoulders should be relaxed and drooped downward; otherwise, the circling of the internal air force and blood would be hindered. Elbows maintain the sense of drooping, too. That is to say, the arms are not stretched straight; instead, they are slightly bent into arc-shapes and you may feel internal drooping forces in them.

6. 用意不用力：练拳时，要轻松自然，用意不用力，用意一，初学者用意指意念指挥动作的方向、角度、虚实等。用意二，学者在动作练熟后，用意念指挥每个招式的攻防含意。用意三，学者在名师指导下用意指挥每个招式的劲力。做到节节贯穿，不可有拙力。力由意生，日久方能发出真正内劲。

Use the mind (will) instead of force: a) beginners use the mind to determine the directions, angles, and void and solidity of movements; b) after the mastery of movements, learners use the mind to direct the attack and defense of each skill; c) learners use the will to control the forces of each skill. The force should go along a series of body parts until it reaches the end. There should be no maladroit use of force. Force is made and controlled by the mind, and the internal air force can be wielded after a long time of practice.

7. 上下相随：拳经所云："一动无有不动，一静无有不静。"每个动作都要以腰为轴带动全身。不可局部自动，或先手动后腰动，所以在练太极拳时，每一个动作都要求做到上下相随，协调完成，运动时须根于脚，发于腿，主宰于腰，行于手指。由脚而腿而腰至手，必须完成一气。腰脊领动，手足随动，眼神随之，上下连贯，浑然一气。

Coordination between the upper and lower body: It is mentioned in *Taiji Quan* theories: "If one part moves, others move, too; and if it stops, others stop, too." In each movement, the waist is taken as the axis to lead other body parts. No body parts are allowed to move by themselves; and it is forbidden that the hands move before the waist. Therefore, in the *Taiji Quan* practice, each movement demands the coordination and cooperation of the upper and lower body parts. The movement should be rooted in feet, delivered from legs, controlled by the waist, and launched by hands. The process needs to be done with utter continuity, in which the waist and the back take the lead, and the hands, feet and eyes follow, to make it a complete whole.

8. 内外结合：练太极拳要求上下相随，内外相合。行气用意为内，动作的虚实变化为外，二者形神兼备，不可分离。每个动作、姿势都要与内在的意紧密结合。

Combination of the internal and external: *Taiji Quan* requires the coordination of the upper and lower body, and the combination of the internal and external. The internal refers to the use of the mind (will) and the circling of force, while the external means the changes of movements. The two are tightly combined. Each movement or pose is closely connected to the mind or will.

9. 相连不断：太极拳整套动作演练起来如"行云流水，连绵不断"，如长江大河滔滔不绝。以心行气，以气运身，劲断意不断，意断劲相连，周而复始，连绵不断。

Continuity: The whole series of movements should be done with great continuity as water flows or clouds float. The mind guides the internal air force to circle around the body; both move in cycles continuously, and even if one of them is interrupted, the other one goes on so that the continuity is kept.

10. 动中求静：太极拳的动静是在活动的过程中相互交替的。所谓"动中有静，静中有动"，动作没有明显的分界。运动时必须保持均匀的速度，不可忽快忽慢，同时所有的动作、姿势一般要保持同样的高度。这样在动中也就求得静了。

Seeking stillness in moving: The process of *Taiji Quan* movements contains stillness and moving alternately, but there are no clear boundaries, as once said, "Moving contains stillness, and stillness contains moving." The movements must be done with even speed, and the poses are with the same height. In this way, stillness is obtained in moving.

11. 外三合：即手与足、肩与胯、肘与膝相合。

The three external harmonies: that between hands and feet, shoulders and hips, and elbows and knees.

12. 内三合：即心于意、意与气、气与力相合。

The three internal harmonies: that between the heart and the mind, the mind and the internal air, and the internal air and the force.

13. 太极十三式： 即掤、捋、挤、按、采、列、肘、靠、进、退、顾、盼、定也。

The thirteen basic skills of *Taiji Quan*: *bing*, stroking, squeezing, pressing, picking, breaking, elbowing, leaning, advancing, retreating, attending left, attending right, and stabilizing.

14. 气沉丹田： 即小腹肚脐下一个穴位。吸气时小腹收缩，呼气时小腹鼓荡。吸气时仿佛要将气吸到丹田处。

The internal air lowers down to the pubic region: The pubic region is an acupoint below the navel. Shrink the belly when inhaling, and swell it when exhaling. In inhalations, the air seems to be breathed in to the pubic region.

15. 轻灵沉稳： 轻就是用意不用力。灵就是圆转灵活。如拳论曰："一举动，周身俱要轻灵。"但初学者，应当先从轻字入手，不必急于求灵。也就是说，在初学者阶段要在"轻"字上下功夫，等轻字有了基础后再进一步要求圆转灵活。"轻"也是感觉灵敏功夫的入门阶梯。

"沉稳"就是指练拳时要精神沉着镇定，动作稳当踏实。"沉稳"是在全身放松的状态下练成的。即"用意不用力"。

Lightness, agility, and steadiness: "Lightness" means to use the mind (or will) instead of force. "Agility" refers to the flexible state. It is said in *Taiji Quan* theories: "Once moved, the whole body should be light and agile." Beginners, however, is supposed to start with the "lightness." In other words, one should focus on training the movements to be light at the beginning, and after this is mastered, he/she may go further to seek agility in the movements. "Lightness" is also the entrance to sensitivity.

"Steadiness" means the learner keeps calm, serene, and the movements are steady. It is attained in the state that the body is completely relaxed, i.e. the mind, instead of force, is used.

16. 腹式呼吸： 即缓缓深吸气时，脐下小腹逐渐内收，呼气时小腹部外突（放松），也叫做逆式呼吸法。如在做动作时合为吸开为呼。如野马分鬃收脚抱球为吸

学打太极拳

气,弓步分掌为呼气。搬拦捶上步拦掌为吸气,弓步冲拳为呼气。

Belly breathing: The part of the belly under the navel withdraws in the inhalation, and swells in the exhalation. This is also named the reversed respiration. In movements, the closing is combined with inhalation, and the opening with exhalation. For instance, in "Parting the Horses Mane," one inhales when drawing the foot back and making the ball-holding gesture, and exhales when making the bow-shape step and parting the hands. In "Turning to Carry, Block and Punch," one inhales as he steps forward and blocks, and exhales as he makes the bow-shape step and punches with the fist.

17. 眼到手到:即在练拳时,手法和眼神必须密切配合,目光一道击打部位,掌(拳)就要同时到。

When the eye flashes arrive, the hands arrive: This refers to the cooperation between eyes and hands. The moment the eyes are set on the attacking point, the hands (palm or fist) reach there.

18. 手到脚到:即在练拳时手法和步法必须配合,做到上下相随。如简化24式太极拳之搬拦捶,上步拦掌,要求上步和拦掌同时到达。不可先上手,后上脚,这样易被对方借力。

When the hands arrive, the feet arrive: This means cooperation and coordination should be attained between hands and feet. For example, in "Turning to Carry, Block, and Punch," the forward stepping and blocking must be done at the same time. Do not make the hand reach its position first and then step forward, because in that way, the opponent may take advantage of the blocking force.

19. 力顺劲达:力顺劲达是指习武练拳时,身体各部位的力量要协调一致,顺其自然,达于末梢。

Smooth and end-reaching force: The forces on the body parts need to be highly coordinated, transferring smoothly to all ends of the limbs.

20. 松腰坐胯：松腰坐胯即在做马步或其他动作时，腰部肌肉放松，两胯自然展开向下屈坠，就像坐板凳一样。如野马分鬃之弓步，白鹤亮翅之虚步分掌，弓步后腿不可跪膝、挺胯，后坐不可紧腰、突臀。"坐胯"要不失弹性。

The waist is relaxed and the hips are in the sitting posture: In the "bucking piling" or other movements, the muscles on the waist are relaxed, and the hips are lowered as sitting on a stool, for instance, in the bow-shape step in "Splitting the Horse's Mane," or the void step and hand parting in "The White Crane Spreading Its Wings." In the bow-shape step, the knee of the back leg cannot droop too much, and the hips cannot incline to either side. In the backward squatting (the void step), the waist should not be tightened and the buttocks cannot be projected out. The "sitting hips" should not lose their elasticity.

21. 收腹敛臀：收腹俗称"吸肚"就是把松畅鼓荡的腹部吸回去，这是个腹壁肌肉的主动收缩过程，收腹即会阴前舔。敛臀即收起臀部把臀部向前收一下，会阴前舔和敛臀同时进行且收放交替。含胸拔背和敛臀要贯穿与练拳实用的全过程。

The belly and buttocks are withdrawn: Withdrawing the belly means to make the swelling belly shrink in, which is a process where the muscles on the belly shrink actively. Withdrawing the buttocks means to move them forward slightly. These two actions happen at the same time, and the withdrawing and releasing are done alternately. The withdrawal of the chest and buttocks and the extension of the back are kept in the whole process of *Taiji Quan* practice.

22. 悬顶吊裆：悬顶、吊顶，即使头劲自然向上顶起，即同虚领顶劲。吊裆即控裆，裆胯不松塌，两腿不断用暗劲将裆部向上提顶，而外形不变。

Hang up the head and the crotch: Hanging up the head means the force in the head pushes up in a natural way (same as that in the "neck is relaxed and the head upright"). Hanging up the crotch means to control the crotch in order not to let it collapse. The legs constantly push the crotch up with undetectable force, and at the meantime help maintain its shape.

学打太极拳

23. 无及不过：在做动作时，如弓步之膝关节超出了脚尖，加大了弓步的程度为过，反之未与脚尖垂直未到弓步之位，即为无及。又如左搂膝拗步左手之搂掌超过了左胯偏胯为过。一句话：即在做动作练习时，不可做过了头的动作，也不可做不到位的动作。

No exceeding or falling short: For example, in the bow-shape step, if the knee of the bow-shaped leg goes beyond the tiptoe, the case of exceeding is formed; in contrast, if the knee does not reach the vertical line of the tiptoe, the case of falling short forms. Or, in the left form of "Knee Brushing and Twisting Step," if the left hand brushes across the left knee and goes beyond the left hip, the case of exceeding happens. In short, when doing the practice of movements, do not exceed or fall short of the required position.

24. 意到气到力到："意到"就是在特殊的环境和特定的思维方法并产生应激反应效果的意念训练的过程。"气到"就是通过系统而特殊的方法训练所产生的体感和反应。即通过意念训练逐步达到体内的能量储备，并使身体产生质的提高的过程。"力到"就是由身体的应激反应所产生的化学能转化为物理能的过程。

The readiness of the mind, the *qi*, and force: The readiness of the mind refers to the training of the will under special circumstances and with certain ways of thinking, which generates responses to certain stimuli. The readiness of the *qi* (the internal air force) refers to the senses and responses generated by a systematic, special training method. In other words, it is the process of storing internal energies and bringing about fundamental changes to the body through the training of the will. The readiness of force is the process of transforming the chemical energies generated by responses to stimuli into physical energies.

通过传统武术的特殊训练，挖掘人体的潜能，发挥其良能，使之在遇到危急情况时能产生超人的定力及观察能力，非凡的劲力和反应能力，使之实现内外兼修。

Through the special training of traditional Wushu, a person's physical potentials are awakened. When confronting dangerous situations, he/she is able

to keep extremely calm and observant, and call out extraordinary forces and responses. The external and internal are both nurtured in the special training.

25. **定如平准**：即立身中正不偏，能支撑八面，中正安舒，有虚灵顶劲之感。

   Stabilization: The body should not incline to any side, and it is steady, relaxed, and natural. The sense of "neck relaxed and head upright" is implied.

26. **活似车轮**：在练习拳势时，圆转以腰为轴。无处不随腰运动圆转，四肢自然活似车轮。

   As agile as a wheel: All turnings in *Taiji Quan* take the waist as the axis, around which the limbs move as agilely as the wheel.

27. **阶级神明**："阶级"意即逐步上升，像台阶梯子须一步一步地爬上去。"神明"意即似高明，随心所欲，形成条件反射，熟能生巧。

   Step to the state of complete mastery: "Step" here refers to the gradual advancing in the learning of *Taiji Quan*, as if climbing up a staircase. "Complete mastery" refers to the highest state in which one wields the *Taiji Quan* skills completely at will.

28. **由着熟而渐悟懂劲**：着熟即是打法，拳法。拳势。"懂劲"即着法练熟后即可悟出用劲的粘随、刚柔、虚实、轻重以及曲中求直，蓄而后发的道理。

   From grasping the skills (*Zhuo*) to gradually understanding the rules of force (*Jin*): "Grasping the skills" means to remember all those movements, postures, and positions. "Understanding the rules of force" means comprehending the rules of force wielding in sticking, following, firmness, softness, void, solidity, lightness, heaviness, seeking straightness in roundabout courses, and delivery after storage.

29. **曲中求直**：即圆中求直。如左右倒卷肱，左右搂膝拗步之推掌，卷臂均为划圆前推。

学打太极拳

Seeking straightness in roundabout courses: For example, in the hand pushing of "Reversed Brachium Twisting" and "Knee Brushing and Twisting Step," the arms are firstly twisted and waved in roundabout coursed before they are pushed forward.

30. 四两拨千斤：即用很小力战胜对方。做到无力打有力，手慢胜手快，以巧制敌。能使人实地心服，练拳能引进落空，虽千斤重也无所用也。

Turn around hundreds of tons of weight with the slightest force: This means to defeat the opponent with the slightest force. In this state, one manages to restrain strength and speed with softness and slowness. In other words, one manages to defeat, physically and spiritually, the opponent with skill. If one can draw the attacking force in to make it effortless, even if the opponent uses hundreds of tons of force, it would be useless.

31. 迈步如猫行：在练拳进退时，步法的形状好像猫走路一样，提脚、放脚，非常轻灵，在内劲方面像抽丝一样绵绵不断、贯穿不绝、若有若无。

Step as a cat does: The stepping of *Taiji Quan* is as a cat walks, which is extraordinarily light and agile. The upper body does not change at all when the foot is lifted and put down. As for the internal force, it is wielded as if reeling the silk thread off cocoons, continuous, never interrupted, and hard to detect.

32. 听劲：通常是耳之听也。在太极拳的"听劲"乃周身皮肤感觉之听。非通常用耳之听也。

Listening: Usually it refers to the ability of the ear. In *Taiji Quan*, however, it refers to the senses of the skin.

33. 太极——互相对立着的两个方面，即阴与阳，如图像之双鱼图形。

Taiji: the entity that contains two opposing sides (*Yin* and *Yang*), as the two fish-like patterns in the Taiji symbol.

34. 无极——统一体,指事物或过程和图像之圆形。

Wuji: the unity; the round shape of things, processes, or the symbol.

35. "双重之病": "双重"则必与对方相抵抗,对方用力,我也用力,发生顶劲。即未弄懂阴阳对立统一的辩证规律。

The "double force": Two forces confront each other, both pushing forward. The problem of "double force" occurs when the dialectic relation between *Yin* and *Yang* is not understood.

36. 不丢不顶: "不丢"即是人走我随;"不顶"即是人进我退。

No giving up or direct confrontation: "No giving up" means to follow when the opponent retreats; while "no direct confrontation" means to draw back when the opponent attacks.

37. 屈伸开合: 李亦畲在其《五字决》中写道:"合便是收开即是放。""气向下沉,由两肩收于脊骨,注于腰间,此气之由上而下,谓之开。"拳势不外蓄与发,故欲蓄劲待发,反映在内动上必然是吸气,这是合,意欲发劲出击,反映在内动上必然是呼气,这是开,在手足的外形上,开与合可以是伸进,也可以是屈退,胸部可能表现含,也可表现扩,需根据拳式的要求而定。

"吸为合为蓄,呼为开为发"是运动自然规律。一些拳技高超者,将意念中的开合随心所欲地用于各式各样的动作外形上,起到应有的作用,正是精通拳理的表现。

Bending, stretching, opening, and closing: Li Yishe wrote in his *The Five Character Knack*, "Closing is withdrawal, and opening is releasing;" "lower the air down by gathering it from the shoulders to the spine and pouring it to the waist; this downward moving of the air is called opening." The movements and postures are nothing but storing and delivering. Storing is reflected internally by inhalation—closing; and delivering is reflected internally by exhalation—opening. If reflected in hands and feet, opening and closing might be stretching or bending. The chest may withdraw or extend to represent the closing and opening. These are all dependent on the requirements of the skills.

It is a natural rule that "inhalation is closing, storing, and exhalation is opening, delivering." A true representation of the mastery of the *Taiji Quan* skills and rules is that some masters can assign at will the opening and closing in their mind to various body movements with effective results.

主要参考书目
Bibliography

陈鑫(2006)《陈氏太极拳图说》,山西科学技术出版社。
冯志强(1999)《陈氏太极拳入门》,人民体育出版社。
冯志强,李秉慈,孙剑云(2000)《太极拳全书》,学苑出版社。
顾留馨(1974)《怎样练习太极拳》,上海人民出版社。
顾留馨(2008)《太极拳术》,上海教育出版社。
李秉慈等(1990)《杨禹廷太极拳系列秘要集锦》,奥林匹克出版社。
李经梧(1993)《李经梧传陈、吴式太极拳集》,河北大学出版社。
唐豪,顾留馨(2001),《太极拳研究》,人民体育出版社。
汪永泉(1995)《杨氏太极拳述真》,人民体育出版社。
王建华(1996)《太极拳、太极拳剑学练500问》,北京体育大学出版社。
王培生(2003)《吴式太极拳诠真》,人民体育出版社。
王宗岳等著,沈寿点校(2000)《太极拳谱》,人民体育出版社。
吴孟侠,吴兆峰(1958)《太极拳九诀八十一式注解》,人民体育出版社。
吴图南(2006)《吴图南太极拳精髓》,人民体育出版社。
杨澄甫等(1984)《太极拳选编》,中国书店出版社。
杨振铎(2003)《杨氏太极拳、剑、刀》,山西科学技术出版社。
张耀忠(1989)《太极拳古典经论集注》,山西人民出版社。
周稔丰(1978)《太极拳常识》,人民体育出版社。
祝大彤(2008)《太极解秘十三篇》,人民体育出版社。

后记
Postscript

  我的太极恩师刘高明先生，河北任县人，生于1931年农历3月3日，卒于2003年3月，享年73岁。

  恩师自幼喜爱武术，1953年师承北京杨式太极拳第四代传人崔毅士（杨澄甫之高足）学太极拳，勤学苦练，深得杨派太极真传，自1960年起长期从事武术教练和裁判工作，后师从常振芳、李天骥、田秀臣学查拳、太极拳等。曾获新中国第一届全运会武术比赛太极拳第三名，1991年获国际传统武术比赛一等奖。1985年起在北京体育师范学院任教至退休。1974年起，多次接待外国学习团，教授太极拳，先后三次受聘去日本教授太极拳。日本前首相田中角荣夫妇、美国前总统尼克松先后在钓鱼台向刘高明先生学练太极拳。1990年香港森记出版社出版刘高明先生杨式太极拳录像带，在香港、新加坡、印度、马来西亚、英国等地发行。刘高明是杨式太极拳第五代传人之一，曾任北京市武协委员，北京杨式太极拳研究会会长，为弘扬中华武术，将传统武术推向世界做出了贡献。

  我自20世纪80年代末师从刘高明先生，有幸成为杨式太极拳第六代传人。师从刘高明先生还是经我的第一位恩师吴向光先生介绍的。

  那时没有双休日，只能下班后或星期天去找恩师学练，师傅说："星期天早上劳动人民文化宫一开门你就得到场，从东门进。"于是每到星期天早上我4点起床，5点准时骑自行车从西翠路沙沟出发，经长安街，到达劳动人民文化宫东门。有时早了，还有十几分钟才开门，我就在门外灯下做准备活动，门一开，花5分钱买一张门票进去，到河边练习基本功，可盼到老师来了，已是早晨7点半了，老师才开始教拳。整整三个月的时间。刘老师只教我学练了太极拳的前进、后退、平行步、下势独立、踢腿、内外摆腿、左右蹬脚等动作。每周如此。时

后记

过半年，我大着胆子向老师说："我每次6点准时进公园，把老师教的从头到尾练习数遍。"以为老师会表扬一下自己。可老师说："你进公园后干什么我都知道。"这时我才恍然大悟，原来老师要我从东门进，他却从南门进，在远处观望我在干什么，是在检验我是否真的来学拳。我又问："星期天怎么只有我一人，别人为什么不来？"老师说："我不是告诉过你，杨式太极拳我单独给你讲吗？"此时我才真正懂得了恩师的一片心。

是名师未必是明师，如教拳不得其法，虽教者谆谆，而学者藐藐，终难有大成。恩师既是名师，又是明师，带领我们大家练功，盘架子，耐心细致地讲述拳法、功法及功理，纠正动作，一丝不苟。在向老师学拳时，一招一式，手、眼、身、法、步，无不讲得"明白"。一套杨式太极拳，前前后后不知拨正了多少次，但每次讲的内容、层次都不一样，过后才说："杨式太极拳，看易实难，初学者很难规范地一次掌握住动作要领。"如劲路和呼吸等高层次的技术要求。对身法要求的涵胸拔背，提项吊裆、松肩垂肘、虚实分清及内外三合等要求更应循序渐进，持久练习才能掌握。恩师每次都要我去照镜子，来纠正身型、身法、步行、步法及动作、眼神，以提高训练效果。恩师又说："功夫一方面要练，一方面要想，要多动脑筋，深入细致地思考，只练不想是不行的，一个是它的运动方向，二是动作的规范，三是技术要领的要求，四是攻防的含意，五是眼神的随视。自己就是老师。"太极拳要领虽多，但主要是抓大体，练拳时，只要做到虚领顶劲，气沉丹田，以腰为中轴带动四肢百骸，缓慢不断地运行就行了，要松，要静，要稳。做到沉、整、缓、圆、轻、匀、续七个字。在盘架子时突快突慢形成断劲，还以为是刚柔相济，实则大错特错。每逢我练拳时，恩师总是在旁边不断提醒我。

恩师以德为本，无门派之争，处处谦虚谨慎，平时训诫弟子，不准谈论张长李短，不得挟技傲人。他能团结各门派和太极拳爱好者，是公认的德高望重的长者。

恩师教拳从不隐秘保密，讲到推手，他说："推手之劲道，不外乎两个字，即'顺随'，顺是避免双重，要走化不顶；随是因势制人，要紧贴不丢，能做到不顶不丢，是谓阴阳相济，便懂劲；能懂劲，则能千变万化，无穷无尽。太极拳的制人，没有一点儿成见和矫揉造作，而是敌人自己送上门来挨打的。"1993年，他的弟子田彦洲在国际太极拳推手比赛中获金奖。

在恩师的传授下，我与师兄、师姐在北京市太极拳比赛中纷纷荣获第一

学打太极拳

名,我也在全国太极拳比赛中获五连冠的好成绩。

恩师走了,带着拳学同仁永远的怀念走了,老人传承的学术将会长久地播扬下去。先哲已逝,风范永存。在恩师逝世五周年之际,笔者悲怀依依,"怆然为文",重提"做人乃生命第一要务"这一华夏文明的古老课题,谨愿炎黄子孙共同葆有高尚的人格,无论在自然灾害,在艰难困苦面前,在种种诱惑面前,都能雕琢灿烂的人生。